Jacques Derrida

Jacques Derrida: Key Concepts presents a broad overview and engagement with the full range of Derrida's work – from the early phenomenological thinking to his preoccupations with key themes, such as technology, psychoanalysis, friendship, Marxism, racism and sexism, to his ethico-political writings and his deconstruction of democracy. An international team of contributors provide both an examination of the key concepts central to Derrida's thinking and a broader study of how that thinking shifted over a lifetime. In doing so, this book offers the reader a clear, systematic and fresh examination of the astounding breadth of Derrida's philosophy.

Claire Colebrook is Edwin Erle Sparks Professor of English at Pennsylvania State University, USA. Her books include *Gilles Deleuze* (Routledge, 2002), *Irony in the Work of Philosophy* (2002), *Irony* (Routledge, 2004), and *William Blake and Digital Aesthetics* (2011). She is co-author (with Tom Cohen and J. Hillis Miller) of *Theory and the Disappearing Future* (Routledge, 2011).

Key Concepts

The *Key Concepts* series brings the work of the most influential philosophers and social theorists to a new generation of readers. Each volume is structured by the central ideas or concepts in a thinker's work, with each chapter in a volume explaining an individual concept and exploring its application.

Jacques Derrida: Key Concepts
Edited by Claire Colebrook

G. W. F. Hegel: Key Concepts
Edited by Michael Baur

Hannah Arendt: Key Concepts
Edited by Patrick Hayden

Jean-Paul Sartre: Key Concepts
Edited by Steven Churchill and Jack Reynolds

Pierre Bourdieu: Key Concepts, second edition
Edited by Michael Grenfell

Gilles Deleuze: Key Concepts, second edition
Edited by Charles J. Stivale

Jurgen Habermas: Key Concepts
Edited by Barbara Fultner

Immanuel Kant: Key Concepts
Edited by Will Dudley and Kristina Engelhard

Jacques Derrida

Key Concepts

**Edited by
Claire Colebrook**

Routledge
Taylor & Francis Group

LONDON AND NEW YORK

First published 2015
by Routledge
2 Park Square, Milton Park, Abingdon, Oxon OX14 4RN

and by Routledge
711 Third Avenue, New York, NY 10017

Routledge is an imprint of the Taylor & Francis Group, an informa business

British Library Cataloguing in Publication Data
A catalogue record for this book is available from the British Library

Library of Congress Cataloguing-in-Publication Data
A catalogue record for this book has been requested

ISBN: 978-1-844-65589-2 (hbk)
ISBN: 978-1-844-65590-8 (pbk)
ISBN: 978-1-315-74461-2 (ebk)

Typeset in Sabon
by Taylor & Francis Books

Printed and bound by CPI Group (UK) Ltd, Croydon, CR0 4YY

Contents

viii   *Contents*

Acknowledgement

In June 2014, while this book was in production, Niall Lucy died of cancer. In addition to being a great friend and colleague to many of us who contributed to this volume, Niall was also one of the most gifted writers working on Derrida, deconstruction and critical theory more generally. This book is dedicated to his memory.

Abbreviations

A	*Aporias*. Derrida 1993a.
AEL	*Adieu: To Emmanuel Levinas*. Derrida 1999.
AF	*The Archeology of the Frivolous: Reading Condillac*. Derrida 1980.
AL	*Acts of Literature*. Derrida 1992c.
BB	"But, beyond … (Open Letter to Anne McClintock and Rob Nixon." Derrida 1986c.
BS1	*The Beast & the Sovereign, Vol. I*. Derrida 2009.
BS2	*The Beast & the Sovereign, Vol. II*. Derrida 2011a.
C	*Circumfession, Jacques Derrida*. Derrida 1993c.
CF	*On Cosmopolitanism and Forgiveness*. Derrida 2001c.
D	*Dissemination*. Derrida 1981.
D2	"Dialogue entre Jacques Derrida, Philippe Lacoue-Labarthe et Jean-Luc Nancy." Derrida 2006.
DE	*Deconstruction Engaged: The Sydney Seminars*. Derrida 2001b.
EO	*The Ear of the Other: Otobiography, Transference, Translation*. Derrida 1988b.
ET	*Echographies of Television*. Derrida and Stiegler 2002.
LLF	*Learning to Live Finally: The Last Interview*. Derrida 2007b.
FL	"Force of Law: The 'Mystical Foundation of Authority'". Derrida 1992a.
GD	*The Gift of Death*. Derrida 2007a.
GT	*Given Time 1: Counterfeit Money*. 1992b.
I	"An Interview with Derrida." Derrida 1988c.
JD	*Jacques Derrida*. Derrida and Bennington. 1993.
LI	*Limited Inc*. Derrida 1988a.
LJ	"Letter to a Japanese Friend." Derrida 1986c.
LO	"Living On/Border Lines." Derrida 1979.
M	*Memoires for Paul de Man*. Derrida 1989.
MP	*Margins of Philosophy*. Derrida 1982.

N   *Negotiations: Interventions and Interviews, 1971–2001*. Derrida 2002e.

OC   *On Cosmopolitanism and Forgiveness*. Derrida 2002c.

OG   *Of Grammatology*. Derrida 1976.

OG2   *Edmund Husserl's "Origin of Geometry": An Introduction*. Derrida 1978b.

OH   *Of Hospitality*. Derrida and Dufourmantelle, 2000.

ON   *On the Name*. Derrida 1995.

OT   *On Touching*. Derrida 2005e.

P   *Points … Interviews 1974–1994*. Derrida 1994b.

PF   *The Politics of Friendship*. Derrida 1997.

PI   "Psyche: Invention of the Other." Derrida 2007c.

PM   *Paper Machine*. Derrida 2005c.

SM   *Specters of Marx: The State of the Debt, the Work of Mourning, and the New International*. Derrida 1994a.

SP   *Speech and Phenomena, and Other Essays on Husserl's Theory of Signs*. Derrida 1973.

PF   *Politics of Friendship*. Derrida 1997.

R   *Rogues*. Derrida 2005a.

RLW   "Racism's Last Word." Derrida 1985.

S   *Screenplay and Essays on the Film* Derrida 2005d.

SP   *Speech and Phenomena: And Other Essay's On Husserl's Theory of Signs*. Derrida 1973.

SQ   *Sovereignties in Question: The Poetics of Paul Celan*, Derrida 2005b.

TS   *A Taste for the Secret*. Derrida and Ferraris 2002.

VP   *Voice and Phenomenon*. Derrida 2011b.

WA   *Without Alibi*. Derrida 2002a.

WD   *Writing and Difference*. Derrida 1978a.

WM   *The Work of Mourning*. Derrida 2001a.

WP   Derrida, J. 2002. "Privilege: Justificatory Title and Opening Remarks." 2002d.

Contributors

Nicole Anderson is Associate Dean for the Faculty of Arts at Macquarie University, Sydney. She is the co-founder and Editor of the journal *Derrida Today* (Edinburgh University Press), and the Director of the bi-annual *Derrida Today* Conference. She is the author of *Derrida: Ethics Under Erasure* (Continuum, 2012); co-editor of *Cultural Theory in Everyday Practice* (Oxford University Press, 2008), and is currently writing a book for Routledge entitled *Culture* which explores the intersection between, and co-implications of, science and culture. She has published numerous articles on Derrida and deconstruction, continental philosophy, posthumanism, animals, ethics, biopolitics, cultural and film theory.

Robert Bernasconi is Edwin Erle Sparks Professor of Philosophy at Pennsylvania State University. He is the author of numerous articles on Hegel, Heidegger, Sartre, Fanon and Levinas, as well as Derrida. In addition to being the co-editor of *Derrida and Difference* and a number of collections on Levinas and on race, he is now the co-editor of the new journal *Critical Philosophy of Race*.

Robert Briggs teaches in the School of Media, Culture & Creative Arts at Curtin University. He is General Co-editor of Ctrl-Z: New Media Philosophy (www.ctrl-z.net.au), and his work has appeared in *Angelaki, CTheory, Social Semiotics, Textual Practice* and many other international journals of cultural theory.

Tom Cohen is Professor of Literary, Cultural and Media Studies at the University at Albany. He is the author of *Anti-Mimesis* (Cambridge 1994), *Ideology and Inscription* (1998), *Hitchcock's Cryptonymies* (Minnesota, 2005), and *Theory and the Disappearing Future* (2012, with Claire Colebrook and J. Hillis Miller). He has co-edited *Material Events* (Minnesota, 2001), and edited *Derrida and the Humanities*

(Cambridge, 2002) and *Telemorphosis: Theory in the Era of Climate Change, vol. 1*. His ongoing work concerns the mutation of mnemo-technologies, sense, epistemology and ethics in an era of ecocide. He is co-editor, with Claire Colebrook, of the Critical Climate Change series with Open Humanities Press.

Claire Colebrook is Edwin Erle Sparks Professor of English at Penn State University. She has published on literary theory, feminist theory, visual culture, poetry, and the philosophy of Gilles Deleuze. Her most recent books are *Essays on Extinction* (2 volumes), published by Open Humanities Press.

Penelope Deutscher specializes in twentieth-century and contemporary French philosophy and philosophy of gender. Her main publications include *Yielding Gender: Feminism, Deconstruction and the History of Philosophy* (Routledge, 1997); *A Politics of Impossible Difference: The Later Work of Luce Irigaray* (Cornell University Press, 2002), *How to Read Derrida* (Granta/Norton, 2006), and *The Philosophy of Simone de Beauvoir: Ambiguity, Conversion, Resistance* (Cambridge University Press, 2008).

Samir Haddad is Assistant Professor of Philosophy at Fordham University. He is the author of *Derrida and the Inheritance of Democracy* (Indiana University Press, 2013).

Kevin Hart is Edwin B. Kyle Professor of Christian Studies in the Department of Religious Studies at the University of Virginia. He has recently edited *The Essential Writings* of Jean-Luc Marion (Fordham University Press). His most recent scholarly book is *Kingdoms of God* (Indiana University Press), and a new edition of his selected poems is forthcoming from Notre Dame University Press.

Joanna Hodge is Professor of Philosophy, Manchester Metropolitan University. Her principal monographs are *Heidegger and Ethics* (Routledge, Taylor and Francis, 1995) and *Derrida on Time* (Routledge, 2007). She has been Chair of the Society for European Philosophy UK (2001–4) and President of the British Society for Phenomenology (2008–11).

Leonard Lawlor is Edwin Erle Sparks Professor of Philosophy at Penn State University. He is the author of seven books: *Early Twentieth Century Continental Philosophy* (Indiana University Press, 2011); *This Is Not Sufficient: An Essay on Animality in Derrida* (Columbia University Press, 2007); *The Implications of Immanence: Towards a*

New Concept of Life (Fordham, 2006); *Thinking Through French Philosophy: The Being of the Question* (Indiana, 2003); *The Challenge of Bergsonism: Phenomenology, Ontology, Ethics* (Continuum Books, 2003); *Derrida and Husserl: The Basic Problem of Phenomenology* (Indiana, 2002); and *Imagination and Chance: The Difference Between the Thought of Ricoeur and Derrida* (The SUNY Press, 1992). He is currently working on a new book called *Violence against Violence* (for Edinburgh University Press).

Maebh Long is Lecturer in Literature at the School of Language, Arts and Media at the University of the South Pacific. She is the author of *Assembling Flann O'Brien* (London: Bloomsbury, 2014), a monograph of theoretical engagements with Flann O'Brien/Myles na gCopaleen/ Brian O'Nolan. In addition to Irish and British Literature, Long's principle areas of engagement and publication are literary theory and philosophy, currently fragmentary forms in Derrida, Blanchot, and Schlegel. Her recent publications include articles on Derrida in *Parallax* and *Australian Humanities Review*, and on Flann O'Brien in *Double Dialogues, Flann O'Brien: Contesting Legacies* and *Flann O'Brien and Modernism*.

Niall Lucy was Professor of Critical Theory at Curtin University and co-editor (with Robert Briggs) of international online journal *Ctrl-Z: New Media Philosophy*. His books include *A Derrida Dictionary, Postmodern Literary Theory: An Introduction, Pomo Oz: Fear and Loathing Downunder* and (with John Kinsella) *The Ballad of Moondyne Joe*.

Anne C. McCarthy is Assistant Professor of English at Penn State University. Her research specializes in Romantic and Victorian literature, literary theory and aesthetics. She is currently at work on a book manuscript, "Suspension and the Sublime Aesthetics of Contingency," as well as an article-length study of manifestations of the sublime in contemporary popular culture. Her work has appeared in *Victorian Poetry, Romantic Circles – Praxis*, and, recently, *Studies in Romanticism*.

Timothy Morton is Rita Shea Guffey Chair in English at Rice University. He is the author of *Hyperobjects: Philosophy and Ecology after the End of the World* (Minnesota UP, 2013), *Realist Magic: Objects, Ontology, Causality* (Open Humanities Press, 2013), *The Ecological Thought* (Harvard UP, 2010), *Ecology without Nature* (Harvard UP, 2007), seven other books and ninety essays on philosophy, ecology, literature, food and music. He blogs regularly at http://www.ecologywithoutnature.blogspot.com.

Michael Naas is Professor of Philosophy at DePaul University. He works in the areas of Ancient Greek Philosophy and Contemporary French Philosophy. His recent books include *Miracle and Machine: Jacques Derrida and the Two Sources of Religion, Science, and the Media* (Fordham UP, 2012) and *The End of the World and Other Teachable Moments: Jacques Derrida's Final Seminar* (Fordham UP, 2014).

Jeffrey T. Nealon is Liberal Arts Research Professor of English and Philosophy at Penn State University. His latest books are *Foucault Beyond Foucault: Power and Its Intensifications since 1984* (2008) and *Post-Postmodernism: The Cultural Logic of Just-In-Time Capitalism* (2012).

Mauro Senatore is a CONICYT postdoctoral fellow at the Instituto de Humanidades in the Universidad Diego Portales, Santiago (Chile). He is the editor of the collective volume *Performatives after Deconstruction* (2013) and of a forthcoming issue of *The New Centennial Review* (2015) on Derrida and French Hegelianism. He is writing a book on dissemination in Derrida's early writings.

Alex Thomson is Senior Lecturer in English Literature at the University of Edinburgh. He is the author of *Deconstruction and Democracy* (Continuum, 2005) and *Adorno: A Guide for the Perplexed* (Continuum, 2006), as well as a range of essays on political theory, continental philosophy and Scottish literature.

1 Jacques Derrida: A biographical note

Mauro Senatore

Jacques Derrida was born on July 15, 1924, in El Biar, in the suburbs of Algiers, from a Jewish French family. His parents Haiim Aaron Prosper Charles and Georgette Sultana Esther Safar gave him the forename of Jackie. At this time, French Judaism in Algeria had undergone a progressive assimilation to the bourgeois Parisian life. Things changed from 1940, when, among other anti-Semitic measures, it was established that there would be a fixed number of Jewish children in primary and secondary education. Consequently, Jackie was excluded from the *lycée* he was attending in Ben Aknoun, nearby El Biar. He could go back to school only the following year. In 1947, he entered the Lycée Émile-Félix-Gautier, in the centre of Algiers. Later, he registered for the *hypokhâgne* class at the Lycée Bugeaud, a cycle of preparatory classes to take the exam for the École Normale Supérieure. He decided not take the exam in Algiers but, in 1949, moved to Paris where he gained a place at the Louis-le-Grand, the most prestigious of Parisian lycées.

In 1952, Jackie passed the exam for the École Normale Supérieure (ENS). There he had the first encounter with Louis Althusser who had been *caïman* in philosophy since 1948, namely, the teacher responsible for the preparatory classes for the *agrégation*. Over the summer spent in El Biar, he immersed himself in the reading of Husserl's *Ideas I* (translated and commented upon by Paul Ricoeur). In November, he began work on the problem of genesis in Husserl's philosophy as the subject of his *diplôme d'études supérieures*. Maurice de Gandillac, professor of philosophy at Sorbonne since 1946, was the supervisor of his work. Through his recommendation, Derrida visited Husserl's archives in Louvain, where he discovered the text of the *Origin of Geometry*, which had been published in German by Eugen Fink. Back in Paris, he wrote his dissertation, which seemed not to provoke reactions in de Gandillac. However, Jean Hyppolite, at the time director at ENS, invited Derrida to prepare the text for publication (which happened only about forty years later, in 1990).

Hyppolite also encouraged him to go on with the project of the translation of the *Origin*. Meanwhile, Derrida met Marguerite Aucouturier, his future wife, who was the elder sister of Michel, one of his best friends over the years of the Lycée and the École. In 1956, he was awarded a one-year bursary to pursue his research on Husserl at Harvard and left for the United States with Marguerite. A few days before returning to Europe, where he was expected to start military service, they got married in Cambridge. He spent his service in the small town of Koléa (nearby Algiers), mainly as a teacher in a school for the children of the soldiers.

Once back in Paris, in 1959, he took part in the Cerisy-la-Salle talk on "Genesis and Structure", in which he presented the paper "'Genesis and Structure' and Phenomenology" (published later in *Writing and Difference*). He was also offered by Jean Hyppolite to publish the translation of Husserl's *Origin* in the series *Epimethée* that the philosopher directed at the Presses Universitaires de France. On the occasion of the first public talk and the forthcoming publication, Derrida abandoned the forename "Jackie" for "Jacques". After teaching a *hypokhagné* class in Le Mans, in October 1960 he returned to Paris where he was appointed as a lecturer in general philosophy at the Sorbonne. Among other things, he taught a course on "The Present", that would later be developed into "*Ousia* and *Grammé: Note on a Note from* Being and Time" (first published in 1968). The appearance of Derrida's introduction to Edmund Husserl's *Origin of Geometry*, in 1962, did not pass unnoticed in French philosophical circles. Besides the appreciation of Hyppolite and Althusser, Georges Canguilhem and Michel Foucault congratulated Derrida, while Ricoeur invited him to present the text at his seminar for researchers at Sorbonne. Furthermore, the *Origin* was awarded the prestigious Cavaillès prize. In 1963–64, Derrida published "Cogito and History of Madness" (in *Revue de métaphysique et morale*; the text was read a few months earlier at the Collège philosophique, under the invitation of Jean Wahl), "Force and Signification", on Jean Rousset, and "Edmond Jabès and the Question of the Book" (in *Critique*), "Violence and Metaphysics. An Essay on the Thought of Emmanuel Levinas" (again in *Revue de métaphysique et morale*). These texts were included later in the volume *Writing and Difference* (1978).

In 1963 his first son Pierre was born. In the same year, he was appointed as a *maître de conference* at ENS. When he definitively left his position at the Sorbonne in 1964 he passed to ENS to collaborate with Althusser. In his first year as *caïman*, he gave a series of lectures on "Heidegger and the Question of Being and History" (published posthumously in 2013). In 1965, responding to Philippe Sollers' invitation, Derrida wrote an essay on Antonin Artaud "La Parole soufflé" for the review *Tel Quel*. In two issues across 1965 and 1966, *Critique* hosted the long essay "Writing before the Letter", which appeared as a review of recent works on writing (among them, *Gesture and Speech* by André Leroi-Gourhan) and which was to become the germ of *Of Grammatology*. In 1966, he presented "Freud and the Scene of Writing" at the Institut de psychanalyse in Paris and "Structure, Sign and Play in human Sciences" at the Baltimore conference on "The Language of Criticism and the Sciences of Man". Next year, when his second son, Jean, was born, Derrida published three of his early major works: the collection of essays, *Writing and Difference* (for Seuil, in the series "Tel Quel"), *Of Grammatology* (for Les Editions de Minuit, in a series related to *Critique*) and *Speech and Phenomena* (on the philosophy of Husserl, for Presses Universitaires de France).

In 1967, at the request of Paul de Man, whom he met at the Baltimore conference, Derrida gave a seminar in Paris for American students from Cornell and John Hopkins universities. De Man, who was teaching at Cornell, was interested in the reading of Rousseau that Derrida had developed in *Of Grammatology*. De Man wrote a first review of the work in the *Annales Jean-Jacques Rousseau*, followed by the longer article "Rhetoric of Blindness: Derrida Reader of Rousseau" published in *Poétique* in 1970.

In January 1968, Derrida presented "The Pit and the Pyramid: An Introduction to Hegel's Semiology" in the context of Hyppolite's seminar at the Collège de France and "Différance" to the Société Française de Philosophie at Sorbonne. Later, he was invited by Samuel Weber, a former student of Paul de Man, to give a lecture in a seminar on structuralist literary criticism organized at the Freie Universität in Berlin. On that occasion, Derrida met Peter Szondi, who was the founder of the Institute of Literary Theory and Comparative Literature and a close friend of Paul Celan, to whom Szondi introduced Derrida when he went to Paris. He was back in Berlin in 1969, where he met Rodolphe Gasché and Werner Hamacher. In 1968–9, he published "Plato's Pharmacy" in *Tel Quel* and "Dissemination", which was devoted to Sollers' novel *Numbers*, in *Critique*. The two texts, together with "The Double Session", that was read at the *Tel Quel* theoretical study group, were included later in *Dissemination*. In the same year, Derrida also taught for two months at John Hopkins University and in that period presented "The Ends of Man" at the New York conference on "Philosophy and Anthropology".

At the beginning of 1970, he was invited by Philippe Lacoue-Labarthe and Jean-Luc Nancy, to take part in a seminar on rhetoric in Strasbourg, in which he read *The White Mythology*. It was the starting point of future collaborations.

Besides *Dissemination* in 1972 Derrida published also *Margins of Philosophy* and *Positions*. The first volume consists of a series of independent essays, including the paper given in Strasbourg (translated as "White Mythology") and the one read in 1971 at the 15th congress of French speaking philosophical societies in Montréal, entitled "Signature, Event, Context" (which criticised the "speech act" theory of J.L. Austin). In 1972, in the context of the Cerisy conference on Artaud/Bataille, Derrida contributed to the session "Nietzsche Today", in which he read "The Questions of Style", later expanded into *Spurs* (published in 1978). It was also the year of the violent response to his early text "Cogito and History of Madness" that Foucault included in the two appendixes added to his *History of Madness*, on occasion of its republication.

In 1973 in France a special issue of the review *L'Arc* and a collective book edited by Jean Ristat were devoted to Derrida; in the same year the first translation of his work into English, *Speech and Phenomena* by David Allison, appeared in the United States. It was followed by Gayatri Spivak's translation of *Of Grammatology* (1976) and Alan Bass's translation of *Writing and Difference* (1978).

In 1974, Derrida published *Glas* with Galilée in the "Digraphes" series edited by Jean Ristat. The book, made of two columns, juxtaposed the reading of Hegel's philosophical discourse (emerging from Derrida's 1971–72 seminar on Hegel's family) alongside the rewriting of Jean Genet's literary text. In the same year, Derrida collaborated with the artist Valerio Adami in the production of silkscreens inspired by *Glas*.

After the success of Lacoue-Labarthe and Nancy's study on Lacan, *The Title of the Letter*, published with Galilée in 1973, Derrida proposed to Lacoue-Labarthe, Nancy and Sarah Kofman that they might co-edit a series at this small and elite publishing house. The group also planned a collective volume, *Mimesis*, for which Derrida suggested Bernard Pautrat, a former student and fellow of Derrida at the ENS, and Sylvaine Agacinski, philosopher and former attendant of Derrida's seminar at ENS. For this volume, Derrida wrote "Economimesis", a reading of Kant's *Critique of Judgment*. In 1974, Galilée began the publication of a new review, *Digraphe*, for which Derrida wrote another essay devoted to Kant's third Critique, entitled "Parergon" (reprinted with Flammarion in *The Truth in Painting*, in 1978).

At the beginning of 1975, Derrida directed himself against the reform of secondary education planned by the Minister René Haby. A major role in this fight was played by the movement GREPH (*Groupe de Recherches sur l'Enseignement Philosophique*), that he set up in collaboration with some teachers and fellows (including Agacinski, Kofman, Pautrat). Ultimately the Haby reform was never implemented. In the same year, through the mediation of Paul de Man, Derrida was appointed as a short-term visiting professor at Yale for three years. In the same year, he presented *Signeponge* to the Cerisy colloquium on Francis Ponge. In the meanwhile, the series "La philosophie en effet" and the project of *Mimesis* moved from Galilée to the publishing house of Henri Flammarion. Derrida wrote long prefaces for books published by Aubier-Flammarion such as *The Wolf Man's Magic Word* by Nicholas Abraham and Maria Torok and William Warburton's *Essay on Hieroglyphics*. The first text provoked a response from Jacques Lacan, who in his seminar attacked Abraham, Torok and Derrida himself (the first response from Lacan since Derrida's critique of Lacan's reading of Poe's "The Purloined Letter" entitled "The Factor of Truth" and published in *Poétique* in 1974). In 1977, he read a pseudo-improvised conversation with René Major about his previous work, at the seminar "Confrontations" organized by Major at the Institut de Psychanalyse. First appearing in the review *Confrontation* (with the title "Du tout"), the text would become the last part of *The Postcard*, that was published in 1980 and included a selection of his immense correspondence ("Envois") as well as the texts "To Speculate – on 'Freud'" (the third part of the seminar "Life Death" given at the ENS in 1974–75) and "The Purveyor of Truth". Derrida would finally tell the history of his relationship with Lacan in the paper presented at the 1990 conference "Lacan with Philosophers", entitled "For the Love of Lacan".

In 1980, the first symposium on Derrida's work, "The Ends of Man", run by Lacoue-Labarthe and Nancy, took place in Cerisy-la-Salle. Among the speakers were Luce Irigaray, Barbara Johnson, Jean-Francois Lyotard, Sarah Kofman, Rodolphe Gasché and Werner Hamacher.

In 1981, as a member of the Jan Hus Educational Foundation in France, an association founded in Oxford and committed to supporting Czechoslovakian universities, Derrida went to Prague for a seminar on Descartes. At the end of the journey, he was arrested at the airport by the Czechoslovakian police and charged with drug trafficking. The following day he was released following a vociferous response from the French media and government. In the same year, Derrida was involved in the creation of the *Collège International de Philosophie*, which, according to the project of the Minister of Research and Technology Jean-Pierre Chevènement, aimed to be a center of excellence able to promote innovative research and to set up relationships with similar institutions in the world.

In 1983, he was elected director of studies on "philosophical institutions" at the École des Hautes Etudes. A few days later, Paul de Man died. In homage to his friend, the following year, Derrida gave the three lectures "Mnemosyne", "The Art of *Mémoires*", and "Acts: The Meaning of a Word given", in Yale and in Irvine.

In 1986, he published with Galilée *Parages* (drawing together four texts on Maurice Blanchot, written and already published between 1975 and 1979) and *Shibboleth: for Paul Celan* (the text of a paper given in Seattle in 1984). He also accepted tenure for a part-time post of distinguished professor at the University of California Irvine, where, after the death of de Man, he was joined at Irvine by his friend J. Hillis Miller who moved from Yale. De Man and Miller (along with Geoffrey Hartman and Harold Bloom) had formed what came to be known as the 'Yale School' of deconstruction; this movement came to a virtual close with the subsequent "de Man affair" – the discovery of de Man's anti-Semitic wartime journalism, to which Derrida later responded. In the meanwhile, the Swiss architect Bernard Tschumi, who had won the 1982 competition of the Parc de la Villette, invited Derrida to contribute to his project through a collaboration with the American architect Peter Eisenman. The volume *Chora L Works*, published in 1997, described the stages of this collaboration that was abandoned after two years.

In 1987, Derrida closed the conference organised by the Collège under the title "Heidegger's Open Questions" with *De L'Esprit* which was published in the same year. Meanwhile, the appearance in France of Victor Farias' book *Heidegger and Nazism* renewed a long-running debate within the French tradition of Heidegger. A memorable stage of this debate took place in Heidelberg, at the beginning of 1988, when Derrida and Lacoue-Labarthe were invited to discuss the subject with Hans-Georg Gadamer. In 1987, Derrida also published with Galilée *Psyche: the Invention of the Other*, the title of which came from one of the texts included in the volume (first presented at Cornell in 1984).

A year later, on the occasion of the French publication of *Mémoires: pour Paul de Man* (1988), in a long footnote added to the original, Derrida replied to the attacks directed at deconstruction by the German philosopher Jürgen Habermas in his *The Philosophical Discourse of Modernity* (published in 1985 and translated into French in 1988). Appearing the same year was *Limited Inc*, the text of the earlier polemic with John R. Searle following the reading of Austin developed in "Signature, Event, Context." In the afterword of the text, "Towards an Ethics of Discussion", Derrida responded again to Habermas.

In 1989 he gave a long opening address, entitled "Force of Law", at the conference on "Deconstruction and the Possibility of Justice" organised at the Cardozo Law School in New York. In the same year he proposed to Geoffrey Bennington (a young British professor whom he first met during his visits in Oxford) to co-author a semi-biographical book on Derrida's own work that would be published in the series "Les contemporaines" for Editions Seuil. The result of the collaboration was the volume *Jacques Derrida* (published in 1991) consisting of Bennington's exposition of Derrida's thought and the latter's auto-biographical *Circumfession*. At the same time, Derrida wrote Mémoires d'aveugle, (or *Memoires of the Blind*) a reflection on drawing developed on the occasion of designing an exhibition for the Louvre. In 1991, he also published *L'autre cap* (*The Other Heading*, the text of a lecture given in Turin on "European Cultural Identity") and *Donner le temps, or Given Time* (based on a seminar given first at the ENS in 1977–78).

A second conference on Derrida, called *Le passage de frontières*, was organised at Cerisy in 1992. On that occasion Derrida presented the text "Aporias". In this year, he also agreed with Murray Krieger, head of the Institute of Critical Theory at Irvine, to entrust his personal archives to Irvine's Langson Library. Thomas Dutoit, one of Derrida's Irvine students, devoted himself to the work of classification and copying.

In 1993 he opened the Riverside conference on "Whither Marxism?" with the lecture "Specters of Marx", that was later expanded over the following months and published as a book. In the collective volume *Ghostly Demarcations* (published in 1999) Michael Sprinker drew together the reactions of some intellectuals to Derrida's text on Marx and his reply to them (entitled "Marx's and Sons").

In 1994 Derrida took part in a round table in Capri (Italy) around the word "religion" presenting "Faith and Knowledge: The two Sources of 'Religion' at the Limits of Reason alone." In the same year, he wrote *Archive Fever*, the closing address that he was due to deliver at the conference organised by Major and Elisabeth Roudinesco at the Freud Museum in London. He also published *Politiques de l'amitie* (*Politics of Friendship*), in which he expanded the first session of a seminar given in 1989–90.

The third *décade* on his work took place at Cerisy in 1997, under the title "The Autobiographic Animal". Derrida's lecture, "The Animal that therefore I am", went on for two days. Among other books, in this year he published *Adieu – to Emmanuel Levinas*, *Of Hospitality* (with Anne Dufourmantelle), and *Demeure: Fiction and Testimony* (on Blanchot).

In 1998 *Veils* came out of the collaboration with the writer and friend Hélène Cixous, who had first addressed him more than thirty years earlier to discuss his "Introduction" to Husserl's *Origin of Geometry*. *Veils* included a short text, first written by Cixous, "Knowing", and a longer text by Derrida, "A Silkworm of One's own". Furthermore, in the same year, Derrida gave the opening address "H.C. For Life, That Is to Say ..." at the Cerisy conference on Cixous. In turn, she devoted to Derrida the two books *Portrait of Derrida as a Young Jewish Saint* (2001) and *Insister of Jacques Derrida* (2006). In 1998, he was also invited to Frankfurt by Hamacher, where he delivered the lecture on the "University without Conditions".

Next year, the volume *Counterpath: Traveling with Jacques Derrida* offered a description of Derrida's traveling around the world for conferences and lectures through the letters sent to his former student and fellow Catherine Malabou. In this year, he also published *The Gift of Death*, based on a text first read at Royaumont in 1990.

In 2000, *On Touching: Jean-Luc Nancy*, a singular book in square format, with typographical variations, accompanied by the "works of reading" drawn by Simon Hantai, came out. It was preceded by a short version of the text that appeared in English in 1992, in a special issue of the review *Paragraph*. In the same year, Derrida gave an address to the Estates General of Psychoanalysis on "the impossible beyond of cruel sovereignty" (published in *States of Soul of Psychoanalysis*, 2000). He also published a book of dialogues with Roudinesco about contemporary ethico-political issues, entitled *For What Tomorrow*.

A few days after September 11th, Derrida was awarded the prestigious Adorno Prize, an interdisciplinary prize given previously to Pierre Boulez and Jean-Luc Godard, among others. On occasion of the award ceremony he gave the lecture *Fichus*. Immediately after, he left for New York to stand by his friends. There, he had an interview with Giovanna Borradori on terror and terrorism, which was included, together with an interview to Habermas, in her book *Philosophy in a Time of Terror* (published in 2003).

The fourth *décade* on Derrida, with a focus on the politics of friendship, was organised in Cerisy in 2002. He gave an opening address on "the democracy to come", which, a few months later, was published as *Rogues:Two Essays on Reason*. In the same year, Derrida signed an official agreement with the IMEC (Institut Mémoires de l'Édition Contemporaine, in Caen) according to which new items and the correspondence from France were entrusted to the French archives. Nowadays, the IMEC gathers almost all of Derrida's correspondence, the copies of the seminars taught until 1995 and the originals of those taught between 1995 and 2003.

In 2003 Maurice Blanchot died. On the occasion of his cremation, Derrida spoke to mourn his friend, as he had already done for other friends. A series of texts of this kind, written or spoken by Derrida, was collected in *The Work of Mourning* by Michael Naas and Pascale-Anne

Brault, who had already translated into English several longer works. Shortly after the death of Blanchot, Derrida was diagnosed with cancer of the pancreas. He delivered the lecture "Geneses, Genealogies, Genres and Genius" at the conference on Helene Cixous celebrating the gift of her archives to the Bibliotèque Nationale de France.

In 2004, he prepared with Marie-Louise Mallet (the organizer of the last Cerisy conferences on his work) and Ginette Michaud the special issue of the *Cahiers de l'Herne* devoted to his work. In August, *Le Monde* published an interview that he had released to Jean Birnbaum and carefully revised. The text of the interview, entitled "I am at War with Myself", was published posthumously as *Learning to Live Finally* (2005). Derrida died on 9 October 2004. Since his death, the two series of seminars on *The Beast and The Sovereign* (from 2001–2 and 2002–3) and on *Death Penalty* (from 1999–2000 and 2000–1) have been published and translated into English.

2 The Auto-Bio-Thanato-Heterographical

Maebh Long

In an interview held in 1983 Anne Berger said to Derrida: "I don't know if I'm addressing the man or the 'writer-thinker', I don't know what their relation is" (P: 132). In the deceptively simple question posed by one conducting an interview with a scholar – 'we had not decided whether we would talk about you or your texts, or about you and your texts at the same time' (P: 132) – we touch on the divisions between thinker and thought, life and work, biography and philosophy that have been a sustained feature of Derrida's texts. As Derrida repeatedly insisted:

> I do not believe in the conceptual value of a rigorous distinction between the private and the public. There can be the singular and the secret, but these resist the 'private' as much as they do the 'public'. In what I write one should be able to perceive that the boundary between the autobiographical and the political is subject to a certain strain.
>
> (N: 17–18)

The work produced by a philosopher is presumed to move towards universal truths, and as such is thought to be a public exercise transcending an empirical, personal identity or signature. The biographical details of the philosopher may impact on the language in which his or her work is transcribed, but the content is thought to be irreducible to the idiosyncrasies of the individual or the tongue. Biography is thus traditionally considered to be external to philosophy. As Derrida pithily exemplifies in the film *Derrida*, for Heidegger the response to the question 'What was Aristotle's life?', was "very simple. [...] "He was born, he thought and he died." All the rest is pure anecdote" (S: 61). Autobiography is thus usually avoided by classical philosophers, as they consider it an inappropriate exposure of the private in a public arena. It is, perhaps, in response to this perceived indecency that when asked what he'd like to see in a documentary about philosophy, Derrida replied "Their sex lives", asking, "Why do these philosophers present themselves asexually in their work? Why have they erased their private life from their work? Or never talked about anything personal?" (S: 105). Rejecting what he perceives to be a false opposition between the private individual and the public philosophy Derrida argues that "you must (and you must do it *well*) put philosophers' biographies back in the picture, and the commitments, particularly political commitments, that they sign in their own names, whether in relation to Heidegger, or equally to Hegel, Freud, Nietzsche, Sartre, or Blanchot, and so on" (PM: 145).

Nietzsche, Derrida writes in *A Taste for the Secret*, was a thinker who absolutely wrote his life into his work, as he practised a *"psychology of philosophers"*, understanding great philosophers to be the result of a "certain psychology", as "Philosophy is psychology and biography together, a movement of the living *psyche,* and thus of individual life and the strategy of this life, insofar as it assembles all the philosophemes and all the ruses of truth" (TS: 35). Derrida's texts operate at this intersection of the philosophical and the psychoanalytic, and his works often resonate with a confessional inclusion of aspects of his life which singularly respond to the text or theme under analysis. From the moment when, as a young Jewish boy in Vichy governed Algieria, he was removed from his school in keeping with anti-Semitic quotas, he argues that it was no longer possible "to distinguish the biographical from the intellectual, the non-intellectual from the intellectual biography, the conscious from the unconscious" (TS: 37). He thus incorporated the personal into his public work, provocatively describing himself in "Circumfession" as *"the only philosopher to my knowledge who, accepted – more or less – into the academic institution … will have dared describe his penis"* (C: 115).

However, in emphasising the intrusion of the personal into the intellectual it cannot be thought that the philosophical or theoretical is to be understood solely through the empirical events of a writer's life. Derrida's background and his relation to the French language, for example, may have been instrumental in his questioning of language and identity, but we cannot understand questions such as 'How can one write one's memoirs when one has no mother tongue? What language should they be in?'(M: 31) as no more than the inevitable product of a man who 'was-born-in-El-Biar-on-the-outskirts-of-Algiers-in-a-petit-bourgeois-family-of-assimilated-Jews' (S: 59). A text is not a code to be deciphered through the events of the author's life, and often 'the one who reads a text by a philosopher, for instance a tiny paragraph, and interprets in a rigorous, inventive and powerfully deciphering fashion is more of a real biographer than the one who knows the whole story of the individual's life' (S: 59). All texts contain a narration of the self, and all reading is an engagement with a biography. In rejecting the opposition of the "classical, 'novelised' narrative of the 'life of the great philosophers'" to a "systematic, or even a structural, philosophical reading" (P: 220), Derrida rejects both the concept of a universal system independent of the personal and idiomatic, *and* the notion of "psychobiographies" which "claim that by following empirical procedures of the psychologistic – at times even psychoanalystic – historicist, or sociologistic type, one can give an account of the genesis of the philosophical system" (EO: 5). Texts are neither philosophical systems external to the life of the author, nor cryptograms which fall open once the 'stable origin' of the encryption – the author's life – explains their manufacture.

Instead of positioning ourselves on either side of the binary we must explore the '*dynamis* of that borderline between the "work" and the "life", the system and the subject of the system' (EO: 15), and examine the nature of the subject and of singularity when 'the *autos* disturbs self-relation' (TS: 41). The philosophical question of the 'Subject' is intertwined with the singular subject's signature, and the concept of Being is also the question of 'who:' a question that does not end in the realisation of a central identity, but which questions the concept of a self who knows how to say 'I'.

> Call it biographical, autobiographical or existential, the form of the question *who* is what matters to me, be it in, say, its Kierkegaardian, Nietzschean, or Heideggerian form. *Who? Who asks the question who? Where? How? When? Who arrives?* [...] It is clear that the *who* withdraws from or provokes the displacement of the categories in which biography, autobiography, and memoirs are thought.
>
> (TS: 17)

How then can we write an autobiography when we do not know how to say 'I'? How can we write a biography when we do not know what 'who' designates? How can we sign a text? Derrida's texts explore the complicity between a writing of the self and a writing of the other, a writing of the life of a subject and a writing of death, a writing of contaminated autobiography, biography, thanatography, and heterography.

Beginning, then, with death, Derrida writes that the phrase '"I live" is guaranteed by a nominal contract that falls due only upon the death of the one who says "I live" in the present' (EO: 10–11). To be human is to die; one's name is always the name of a person who will be dead, and one's signature is always the mark of the eventually deceased. After death "Only the name can inherit, and this is why the name, to be distinguished from the bearer, is always and a priori a dead man's name, a name of death" (EO: 7). To write, to sign, is to relate to absence and one's own demise – as Maurice Blanchot puts it, "to write is to accept that one has to die without making death present and without making oneself present to it" (Blanchot 1995: 66). The presentation of the self is a writing of the death of the self, a *thanatography*:

> To write one's autobiography, in order either to confess or to engage in self-analysis, or in order to expose oneself, like a work of art, to the gaze of all, is perhaps to seek to survive, but through a perpetual suicide – a death which is total inasmuch as fragmentary. To write (of) oneself is to cease to be, in order to confide in a guest – the other, the reader.
>
> (Blanchot 1995, 64)

Writing on the self is a drive to survive by way of a constant suicide, a killing of the self to enshrine it. An act of writing makes one a writer, but when the act of writing ceases the text remains, at the expense of the death of he or she who wrote. When that text is read, the new interpretation brought by the reader animates the text and the author, but in so doing changes them, killing them in the rebirth. In "Circumfession" Derrida offers the phrase 'I want to kill myself' as a phrase incessantly returned to throughout his life and work. Yet, 'I want to kill myself,' he writes, "speaks less the desire to put an end to my life than a sort of compulsion to overtake each second, like one car overtaking another, doubling it rather, overprinting it with the negative of a photograph already taken with a 'delay' mechanism" (C: 39). The compulsion to die is also a compulsion to live, to follow each dead breath with a new breath, each dead instant with a new instant. Hence "I posthume as I breathe;" each breath signals the end of a previous breath, a living and a dying (C: 26).

In the case of autobiography one writes in order to preserve oneself, but kills oneself in that act, and is killed once again when one re-reads what has been written. Furthermore, in gathering the events of a life together the attempt is made to present a stable, unified, self-present self, but by gathering the self, the self is changed. The self that gathers is wholly different to the selves that are gathered:

> There is not a constituted subject that engages itself at a given moment in writing for some reason or another. It is *given* by writing, by the other: *born* as we were bizarrely saying a moment ago, born by being given, delivered, offered, and betrayed all at once.
>
> (P: 347)

The self which presents itself to itself, or the self that writes and the self that is written about, are not the same (and are different from the self who reads or views). There is a blind spot as one reflects, an invisible trait that cannot be captured as one looks at oneself looking. The self-portrait, like the autobiography, inhabits every text, but is never fully present, always a ruin and in ruins. Thus the self, preserved, is a different self, and the autobiography comprises heterography, and thanatography, as the written self is always other and dead. In addition, in the drive to preserve a memory or two the memories themselves are changed, as the mode of preservation changes the memories: written events are not the same as the events experienced. Preserving and gathering become suicide, but an autoimmune suicide: what dies is not the self as such, but the very idea of a whole, self-present, pure self. The strong, self-present, undivided *autos* presumed by the autobiographical genre is a fiction.

For Derrida Nietzsche was a writer whose philosophy was a gathering of the self, making an "immense bio-graphical paraph out of all that [he] had written on life or death" (EO: 7). But while Nietzsche made repeated use of his own name, Derrida argues that Nietzsche's signature was highly mediated by the structure of the Eternal Return and the concept of a future signature. Quoting from *Ecce Homo*, Derrida explains that Nietzsche felt that his "real" identity was wholly different from the one his contemporaries associated with his name. Nietzsche's identity stems from what he knows he will become, what he is in the future. It is only when he dies, when the sum total of his life is measured, that he can be said to have lived. As such he takes his authority from his future self, from a line of credit given to him by himself and that will be authorised by the countersignature of the future reader. He thus tells his life to himself; his autobiography is biography as he is his text's addressee. But "since the 'I' of this *récit* only constitutes itself through the credit of eternal return, he does not exist" at the point of writing (EO: 13). Thus,

> Nietzsche's signature does not take place when he writes. He says clearly that it will take place posthumously, pursuant to the infinite line of credit he has opened for himself, when the other comes to sign with him, to join him in alliance and, in order to do so, to hear and understand him. [...] The ear of the other says me to me and constitutes the *autos* of my autobiography.
>
> (EO: 51)

Nietzsche "*writes himself to the other* who is infinitely far away and who is supposed to send his signature back to him" (EO: 89). His signature only takes place in the act of reception; as such he has no relation to himself, he has no identity, until he, his life, his work, is re-signed by the other. It is in the act of reception by the reader that his identity is realised. While Derrida is specifically speaking about Nietzsche, this is also structurally true beyond Nietzsche:

> It is rather paradoxical to think of an autobiography whose signature is entrusted to the other, one who comes along so late and is so unknown. But it is not Nietzsche's originality that has put us in this situation. Every text answers to this structure. It is the structure of textuality in general. A text is signed only much later by the other.
>
> (EO: 51)

Even the most overtly autobiographical text, adhering to all the conventions of the autobiographical genre, awaits a reader, awaits one who will counter-sign the text and the future contexts in which the text will operate. All autobiographies are troubled by the "autos" and become posthumous works, suicidal biographies signed by the other.

In 'Paper or Me, You Know' Derrida writes that each breath marks a longing for an 'absolute memory', describing his "sigh[ing] after the keeping of everything" as his "very respiration" (PM: 65). Every exhalation is a longing to preserve, to retain and remember everything that happened. An autobiographical, confessional text traditionally requires the bringing together of all the threads that explain, expose, present and re-present the self. But in presenting the self we not only have to involve the threads of many others, we also have to assemble threads of events that never took place: 'Still today there remains in me an obsessive desire to save in uninterrupted inscription, in the form of a memory, what happens – or *fails to happen*' (AL: 34). This "adolescent dream of keeping a trace of all the voices which were traversing me – or were *almost doing* so" (AL: 35) meant that all that occurred and did not occur should be retained, as

> what *happens* – in other words, the unique event whose trace one would like to keep alive – is also the very desire that what does not happen should happen, and is thus a 'story' in which the event already crosses within itself the archive of the 'real' and the archive of 'fiction'. Already we'd have trouble not spotting but separating out historical narrative, literary fiction, and philosophical reflexion
>
> (AL: 35)

The writing of a (soon-to-be) dead author recounts 'dead' events, events that never took place, that are not and were not. The autobiography is thanatography, and the recounting of real events is also a work of fiction.

While the writing of the self is a writing of death and of the other, each writing on an other is also an exploration of the self. As Derrida writes regarding Paul de Man:

> where de Man says of Baudelaire that he says of Guys what in truth he says of himself, how can one avoid reading in this passage something Paul de Man is having said by these two others about himself, for himself, in his name, through the effects of an irony of the signature?
>
> (M: 62–63)

Under the irony of the signature every text is an autobiographical text, a text on the self and a text on the other. The self becomes mediated through what Derrida refers to as transferential figures, and "The most private autobiography comes to terms with great transferential figures who are *themselves* and themselves *plus* someone else (for example, Plato, Socrates, and a few others in *The Post Card*, Genet, Hegel, Saint Augustine, and many others in *Glas* and *Circumfession*, and so forth)" (P: 353). Every text is an anacoluthic autobiography/heterography – an ironic, interrupted exegesis of the corpus of the other that is an ironic, interrupted exegesis of the corpus of the self. The story of the self does not recount the life of a single, unified self present to itself, but a self split by alterity, signed, in a moment of allography, by the other. Thus, under the irony of the signature, the overwriting of the self by the other is also an underwriting that ironically both secures and disturbs the self. The truth of the life of the self becomes the (perjured) confession of a death given over to the other. In signing itself the self must wait for the countersignature of the other, for the other to read, repeat and step in a different direction. The countersignature of the other comes "to *lead it* [the text] *off* elsewhere, so running the risk of *betraying* it" (AL: 69). Thus the (ironic) countersignature of the other, the change from auto-biography to heterography, is an autoimmune act: "you have to give yourself over singularly to singularity, but singularity then does have to share itself out and so compromise itself, *promise to compromise itself*" (AL: 69). A promise is a co-promising which is both a compromise *and* compromising. Each text, and each autobiography, is *ironic and auto-immune*, an auto-interpretation or self-critique that both turns every text into a writing of the self, and in that process undoes the self. The irony of the signature is a paraph of the autoimmune, the ironic signing that erases itself as it signs. It signs the ironic contamination of the self and the other, as each text is undersigned by the self, a signature that is already a signing of alterity.

In presenting the self through the other we must not forget that one of the transferential figures through which Derrida presented himself was "Derrida." We see a later Derrida re-signing his texts, gently steering them in different directions, asserting – inserting – the political within texts previously read as apolitical, the ethical in texts thought of as engaging themselves elsewhere. He, as other, re-writes his texts through the authority those texts gave him, presenting a later Derrida through the earlier, turning earlier interests into later ones, rewriting his works, guiding interpretations, marking off a legacy and a future for his texts and his name. Hence, as Catherine David said in a 1983 interview; "To read you, one has to have read Derrida," (P: 117). Similarly, Derrida's readings of Nietzsche and Hegel become, as Eugenio Donato pointed out, a performance of "Derrida rereading *Of Grammatology* today" (EO: 55).

As we move towards a conclusion, we might ask what form a "Derridean" (auto)biographical text would take, and might find an idea in *Jacques Derrida. Jacques Derrida* comprises "Circumfession", by Derrida, and "Derridabase", by Geoffrey Bennington, and presents a text in which the eponymous hero is the life and the work of a multiple, fragmented, shifting figure. Together these separate and conjoined texts form a work which is complete and incomplete, as "Derridabase," which describes "the general system" of Derrida's thought, is undermined and undercut by "Circumfession", which, running along the bottom third of the page, demonstrates and performs the impossibility of describing, and therefore closing, Derrida's system (C: 1). "Derridabase" consists of Derrida as read by Bennington, who attempted systematically to detail and delimit the logical categories of Derrida's thought without quotation or biographical detail. The systemisation of deconstruction will, however, make it predictable, and therefore rob it of a future, and so Derrida responded to Bennington's death sentence with "Circumfession", a text which revealed this systematisation or programmability to be doomed to failure. Derrida destabilises his *Thought* with his *thoughts*, with autobiographical fragments of his life, a proliferation of signatures, phrases masquerading as transcendental signifiers, ambiguously directed apostrophes, doubles and doubled discourses. Responding to Bennington's – and, through him, all other previous and future – attempts to systematise him, Derrida goes to war against this self/other, and presents, not a thetic undoing, nor a propositional engagement, not a descriptive analysis of inaccuracies or exclusions, but a confessional testimony of exceptional singularity – an "interrupted autobiothanatoheterographical opus" (C: 213).

As writer of the "absolute theologic program" and holder of god-like absolute knowledge (*savoir absolu* (S.A.)), the figure called G. – Geoffrey Bennington, but also alluding to Derrida's mother Georgette – must be confessed to, not in order to *present* knowledge, but to *produce* it. Derrida confesses, and thus changes his life, produces a different truth, bears witness to what did not occur, and recounts memories of "fictive" events. As Derrida writes in *Demeure*, it is here "that the possibility of fiction *and* lie, simulacrum *and* literature, that of the right to literature insinuates itself, at the very origin of truthful testimony, autobiography in good faith, sincere confession, as their essential compossibility" (D: 42). "Circumfession" writes to exist, writes to produce an unpredictable text and self, and so live, and yet is caught by the double bind of writing – writing is always of death. In "Circumfession" the self is questioned through multiple figures, and identity and events become troubled. Thus Derrida's mother is both the woman who cried each time he left – "she who wept as much as Monica [St. Augustine's mother] at each of my departures, from the first", and she who never cried – "the one who literally could not weep for him" (C: 177; 51) Derrida is both "drunk with uninterrupted enjoyment", knowing no one "who has been happier than I, and luckier, euphoric," and yet is also "the counter-example of myself [...] constantly sad, deprived, destitute, disappointed, impatient, jealous, desperate, negative and neurotic" (JD: 268). Derrida is the double of his dead brother: Derrida was conceived, he felt, to replace him, and was thereby "excluded *and* favourite" (JD: 279). He is also the double of his sister, whose initials are also J.D., and the double of Augustine and Rousseau (he stole grapes and figs, and compares his mother to Monica, Augustine's mother). The *autos* is also *heteros* and Derrida is ventriloquised by voices that are his and other. But all the descriptions of Derrida's life, all the secrets revealed and the ghosts allowed to speak do not offer a single "gift with which to sew up the chain of all my texts" (JD: 136).The fifty-nine long sentences which comprise "Circumfession" present multiple, fragmentary and contradictory stories of the self, proffering a mode of writing on the borders of literature and philosophy, truth and fiction, work and life, self and other such that *Circumfession* is "*Everybody's Autobiography*" in which, for each "everybody," "it only happens to me" (JD: 311; 305).

3 Supplement

Robert Bernasconi

In *Of Grammatology* Derrida took up the term *supplément* from his reading of both Jean-Jacques Rousseau and Claude Lévi-Strauss and used it to formulate what he called "the logic of supplementarity" (G: 144–45). Derrida returned to Lévi-Strauss's use of the word "supplement" in "Structure, Sign and Play" (WD: 289) and in *Given Time* (GT: 66–77), but I will focus here on Derrida's reading of this word in Rousseau's *Confessions, Discourse on the Origin and Foundation of Inequality among Men,* and *Essay on the Origin of Languages* because his reading of Rousseau has proved so powerful and because the logic of supplementarity is better illustrated than generalised.

As Derrida observed, Rousseau in these works employed binary oppositions: nature versus society, passion versus need, south versus north, and, most significantly for Derrida in the late 1960s, speech versus writing. In the course of declaring these oppositions Rousseau can be found writing the ambiguous term *supplément* and its cognates into his narratives. The supplement is an addition from the outside, but it can also be understood as supplying what is missing and in this way is already inscribed within that to which it is added. In this way the word, "supplement" seems to account for "the strange unity" of two gestures: "on the side of experience, a recourse to literature as appropriation of presence, that is to say, ... of Nature; on the side of theory, an indictment against the negativity of the letter, in which must be read the degeneracy of culture and the disruption of the community" (G: 144).

To the extent that Derrida presents the supplement as the unity of two gestures it is not yet fully radicalised. One can find in other authors' formulations that suggest a notion of supplementarity to the extent that what stands first and what follows it can vary according to one's perspective. One might say that the so-called Cartesian circle where the order of reasons is different from the order of being has that same structure. Or one might point to Georges Canguilhem's formulation, articulated at the same time as that Derrida was writing *Of Grammatology*, the historical ante-riority of the future abnormal, while logically second, is existentially prior (Canguilhem 1991: 243). But Derrida's claim goes beyond the idea that these two meanings of the supplement can be seen to function together in Rousseau's texts and elsewhere in spite of their apparent opposition.

When Derrida announced that "the logic of supplementarity," rather than the logic of non-contradiction, can be said to regulate or organise Rousseau's texts, he was introducing a new way of reading texts that con-stituted a major departure from what had gone before. At this time other philosophers still insisted on reading the canonical texts of philosophy according to the imperative that contradiction cannot be tolerated, with the consequence that there was a hermeneutical imperative to do whatever one could to reunite seemingly inconsistent claims. Derrida responded to this imperative by showing how the supplement allows Rousseau – and us – to say the contrary without contradiction (G: 179; Bernasconi 1992: 143–44).

Identifying these twin gestures within Rousseau's texts gave rise to what came to be called "double reading." The practice of double reading as it relates to the supplement can best be illustrated by following the two tracks that Derrida identifies in Rousseau's texts. To begin with, Rous-seau's *Essay on the Origin of Languages* argues that the origin of (spoken) language is in the South. Writing comes second and has its origin in the North. But Derrida observes that in the course of giving this description Rousseau refers to gestures joined to speech (Rousseau 1992: 31). Derrida comments: "Gesture, is here an adjunct to speech, but this adjunct is not a supplementing by artifice, it is a recourse to a more natural, more expressive, more immediate sign" (G: 235) as when one can simply point at an object and there is no need to speak (Rousseau 1998: 292). Speech, far from being the original, is "a substitute for gesture" (G: 235). How-ever, insofar as gesture can be seen as a form of writing, then the apparent priority of speech over writing is put into question. Writing as an addition (which is originally conceived as a simple exterior to speech, substituting itself for it), comes to be seen as anterior to speech and in a way integral to it. In other words, that something can be added to what is initially thought of as in and of itself complete, and is presented as an origin, reveals that the lack in sense precedes the origin and contaminates it.

The priority of speech is what Rousseau declares, corresponding to what he wants or desires which, according to Derrida, is full presence: but, as we have seen, Rousseau's narrative tells a different story. The declarations conflict with the descriptions. Derrida shows, however, that their interrelation is regulated, thereby establishing that the two readings are not independent and ultimately cannot be separated. They belong together "in one divided but coherent meaning" (G: 132). They constitute "structural poles rather than natural and fixed points of reference" (G: 216). In this way the second reading can be said to "supplement" the first, as writing supplements speech. And it is "undecidable" which meaning dominates the text.

There is another dimension to this reading. As we saw, for Rousseau, speech, and thus the South, initially represents presence, before it emerges that sometimes gesture performs this function better (G: 237). This ties Derrida's reading of Rousseau to Heidegger's account of Western metaphysics in terms of the priority of presence. The deconstruction of Rousseau thus belongs to the deconstruction of Western metaphysics. Rousseau's text, on Derrida's reading, both exhibits Western metaphysics and at the same time undercuts it. Or, better, the text deconstructs itself. Just as Rousseau wants to mark a full presence but finds that it has never existed, so Derrida finds that there never was such a thing as Western metaphysics as such (Bernasconi 1989: 246).

Derrida does not explore in the same detail how the same logic of supplementarity governs Rousseau's *Discourse on the Origin and Foundation of Inequality among Men* but it is not hard to reconstruct it on the basis of what Derrida says about the *Essay on the Origin of Languages*. In the *Essay* Rousseau sets out to explain the break with nature – nature's departure from itself – solely on the basis of "natural causes" (Rousseau 1998: 289). It is the same in the Second Discourse, when it comes to explaining how one could leave the state of nature. The basis for the movement beyond nature into society must already in some way be implanted within nature, thereby complicating the notion of nature, which is no longer to be seen as the full presence of an origin but as a lack that could in a different idiom be located beyond being as presence. This is why Rousseau can say that the state of nature no longer exists, perhaps never existed, and probably never will exist (Rousseau 1991: 13). Nevertheless this lack controls all discourse about the society, which is produced to supplement what is lacking there. In Rousseau's essays on both the origin of inequality and the origin of languages, the powerful notion of origin takes on another character such that, as Derrida puts it elsewhere, "the movement of supplementarity" is "the movement of play, permitted by the lack or absence of a center or origin" (WD: 289).

Just as in Rousseau that which is beyond nature and which thereby makes up for what is lacking in nature is implanted within nature, so that nature is not the full presence that was sought, so albeit in a slightly different fashion, what is beyond being in Plato necessarily governs that absent origin by which it is supposed to be ordered. Derrida wrote in "Plato's Pharmacy": "The absolute invisibility of the origin of the visible, of the good-sun-father-capital, the unattainment of presence or beingness in any form, the whole surplus Plato calls *epekeina tes ousias* (beyond beingness or presence), gives rise to a structure of replacements (*suppléances*) such that all presences will be supplements substituted for the absent origin, and all differences, within the system of presence, will be the irreducible effect of what remains *epekeina tes ousias*" (D: 167). This shows just how far Derrida is from the straightforward exploration of the ambiguity of the word *pharmakon* as both remedy and poison that is sometimes attributed to him. He located the logic of supplementarity in still other texts and contexts. So, for example, around the same time that he published *Of Grammatology* he wrote *Speech and Phenomena* in which he described the relation of indication and expression in Husserl's *Logical Investigations*: "If indication is not added onto expression which is not added onto sense, we can nevertheless speak in regard to them, about an originary 'supplement': their *additon* comes to *make up for* a deficiency, it comes to compensate for a primordial non-self-presence" (SP: 74). All the details of Derrida's argument cannot be rehearsed here, but it culminates in the now familiar claim that indication dictates expression on the grounds that writing cannot be added to speech "because, as soon as speech awakens, writing has doubled it by animating it" (SP: 83).

One of Derrida's clearest explications of the logic of supplementarity is in his reading of Condillac's *Essay on the Origin of Human Knowledge* in *The Archeology of the Frivolous* from 1973. He finds in Condillac's discussion of the attempt to create a language for a science of economics, that there is a need to supplement our speaking and writing (Condillac 1795: iii). With reference to Condillac's discussion of how the defect of language might be addressed by a certain kind of supplementing that refers to an anteriority with reference to which there is something lacking. Derrida argues that there is need for a second sense of the supplement: "But what is necessary – what is lacking – also presents itself as a surplus, an overabundance of value, a frivolous futility that would have to be subtracted, although it makes all commerce possible" (AF: 101). In other words, as the present comes to present itself the necessity of what is lacking is produced as a certain frivolity. Or, as he explained in "Freud and the Scene of Writing," the supplement is "added as a plenitude to a plenitude" and for this reason he could insist that it equally compensates for a lack" (WD: 212). It is in keeping with this insight that Derrida insisted both that no ontology could think the operation of the supplement (G: 314) and, at the same time, the time of the closure of philosophy, that the logic of supplementarity imposes itself on us in our reading of the texts from the history of Western metaphysics.

4 Suspension

Anne C. McCarthy

State of Suspension

" ... the state of suspension in which it's over—*and* over again, and you'll never have done with that suspension itself ... " (LO: 63). Take this utterance, for the moment, as something bracketed, cited in the fullest Derridean sense of the term, surrounded on both sides by ellipses (that is, by suspension points or *points de suspension*), lifted from a text that begins, as Derrida's often do, by suspending the question it sets out to address, pausing to hold it up, to hold us up, in a moment of contemplation. "over—*and* over again": the pause initiates the possibility of the endless repetition of endings; "you'll never have done with that suspension itself"—suspension resists the demand for closure, for transparency. All it can reveal to the gaze of authority is its own essential equivocation, its own being-otherwise.

What would it mean to suspend suspension, to pause the pause, to interrupt interruption and thereby hold it up, examine it? Fixation and contemplation, punishment and mitigation, an inactivity actively maintained: the paradoxical, aberrant quality of suspension reveals itself at every turn. Attempts to define it often draw upon a kind of internal catachresis that keeps it from fully coinciding with itself, manifesting in contradictory phrases: passive activity, active passivity. Fading into the background, it calls attention to the attenuated presence of what it suspends. Thus the suspension of a privilege makes us realise what we have lost, the suspension of judgement may be taken as an indicator of the soundness of that judgement, and the request that an audience suspend its disbelief causes that audience to anticipate the unbelievable.

Though we customarily speak of uncertainty as a lack or privation, suspension enables uncertainty to appear as something other than a negative form of knowing. It provides a way of avoiding typical responses to that uncertainty, such as dismissing what is not known as being unimportant, reacting with hostility to that which seems to threaten the claims of epistemology, or, for that matter, falling into the paralysis of a recursive scepticism. To think suspension as suspension means thinking it beyond privation, as constitutive of what it suspends. We might think of suspension as that which holds (holds together, holds back), but does so loosely, allowing for movement and the coming of the unexpected. Yet suspension is also constitutive, providing the condition of possibility for what is suspended. Here, the operations of suspension resemble that of *différance*, opening intervals and breathing spaces in the structure of signification. Like the work of mourning, or the impossibly possible ethics of Derrida's late work, one enters into suspension without end: "you'll never have done with that suspension itself."

Within Derrida's thought, suspension is both spatial and temporal, pervasive and elusive. It operates under a number of different signs, and in a number of different languages that either resist or yield to translation in ways that are not easily gathered together: *epochē*, *arrêt*, *syncope*, bracketing, iteration, deferral, *Aufhebung*, and *différance*. But suspension is less often linked to Derrida's name than many of these other terms. Translation from French into English blurs the lines further: suspension is a cognate in the two languages, but only approximately so— less, perhaps, at the level of idiom. The concept of the "suspension of reference," an ostensibly deconstructive phrase most often used to describe the ambivalence of literary language, owes its development more to Paul de Man (1919–83) and J. Hillis Miller (1928–), who write in English, than to Derrida. However, the fact that suspension is not so fully identified with a Derridean signature makes it, paradoxically, a useful frame for reading his works. Remaining at least somewhat unconditioned by the over-determination of a deconstructionist discourse that has, in many ways, become all too familiar to contemporary critical theory, suspension points to those dimensions of Derrida's thought that retain "an essential *unfinishedness* that cannot be reduced to an incompleteness or an inadequacy" (LO: 85). We'll never have done with this suspension.

Signification

Forever unable to saturate a context, what reading will ever master the "on" of living on? For we have not exhausted its ambiguity: each of the meanings we have listed above can be divided further (e.g., living on can mean a reprieve or an afterlife, "life after life" or life after death, more life or more than life, and better; the state of suspension in which it's over—*and* over again, and you'll never have done with that suspension itself), and the triumph *of* life can also triumph *over* life and reverse the procession of the genitive.

(LO: 63–64)

"Living On," Derrida's essay on Percy Bysshe Shelley's poem, "The Triumph of Life", begins with self-reflexive meditation on its own title, questioning the terms under which the French *survivre* becomes the English "living on" and underlining the ways that linguistic representation eludes mastery. A second, shorter essay, "Border Lines," runs across the bottom of the page and muses more directly upon the difficulties of translation that so often preoccupy Derrida's work. The dual structure of the page itself already poses the dilemma of suspension, of an undecidable reading practice—a text that is not singular, but also not simply two texts. One embarks upon the process of reading with no small amount of hesitation, perhaps even a pang of indecision that registers the necessity of deciding.

The longer passage in "Living On" shows that the state of suspension with which we began arises between parentheses, one in a list of potential meanings that serves to displace the meaning of "living on." Suspension undoes finality, turning cessation ("it's over") into repetition ("*and* over again"). In so doing, suspension gives rise to signification. In a well-known (and often cited) passage from "Signature Event Context," Derrida writes, "Every sign, linguistic or nonlinguistic, spoken or written … in a small or large unit, can be *cited*, put between quotation marks; in so doing it can break with every given context, engendering an infinity of new contexts in a manner which is absolutely illimitable" (LI: 12). Signification is, in Derrida's view, founded and secured by the very thing that seems to threaten it. Iterability, the ability of any mark to suspend reference, to mean otherwise, to be readable as a mark beyond the context of its inscription, becomes, in Derrida's account, the condition of possibility of language. Moreover, it enables us to perceive a self-difference that potentially goes even deeper than language or signification, a fundamental discontinuity within the structure of reality itself.

The suspension of suspension is not reducible to stability. Rather, it sets off a series of other interruptions, displacements, spacings. It thus belongs to the realm of the "always already" in Derrida's thought—to that category of deviation revealed to be part of a more originary structure: "The break intervenes from the moment that there is a mark, at once [*aussi sec*]. And it is not negative, but rather the positive condition of the emergence of the mark" (LI: 53). The conceptual resources of suspension, opening to the experience of what Elisabeth Weber (2007: 325) characterises as a "decisively critical moment, a decisively critical space," enable a thinking of absence that is not, or not only, a negative form of presence. In terms of Derridean theories of signification, it is a constitutive discontinuity, making signification possible only on the condition that it could, potentially, signify something else. If there is no such thing as fully present meaning or complete communication in Derrida's view of language, then much of what passes in everyday usage as understanding is really a form of what Samuel Taylor Coleridge described as "that willing suspension of disbelief for the moment, which constitutes poetic faith" (Coleridge 1983: 2.6). Such faith does not ignore the evidence of difficulties or even the impossibility of communicating; rather, it holds those concerns in abeyance, so that something else can take place.

Call it, perhaps, a plenitude without presence, marked by an ellipsis (*points de suspension*) which signifies omission and pause, but also an opening or waiting for response. An ellipsis at the beginning of a text indicates an obscured origin, something that we won't ever quite get back to, a visual dislocation of beginnings by the "already in progress." A terminal ellipsis performs a closure that is not exactly an ending and which risks being read as indecision or, worse, a perverse refusal to come to a conclusion. In the foreword to *Points ...* , a collection of interviews with Derrida published in French as *Points de suspension*, Peggy Kamuf notes that the ellipsis in the English title was intended to evoke "punctual interventions suspended from, for example, the other's discourse and often interrupted by an interlocutor" (Kamuf 1994: viii). From this perspective, an ellipsis—at the beginning, the end, or even within the text itself—might be coded as a gesture of inclusion, an invitation for the response of the reader, who may then add her signature.

But suspension, especially for Derrida, must also always register the operations of a kind of essential contingency, the possibility of always becoming otherwise—the reversal of the genitive, or the disruptive force of translation. Running across the bottom of the pages of "Living On," the paratext of "Border Lines" anticipates the unanticipatable effects of its own translation, suspension, sublimation (*Aufhebung*): "This translation, like any other, leaves something out, an untranslated remnant. It arrests movement. Illegitimately: for 'literature' and in general 'parasitism,' the suspension of the 'normal' context of everyday conversation or of 'civilian' usage of the language, in short everything that makes it possible to move from 'death sentence' to 'suspension of death' in the French expression *arrêt de mort*, can always come about ... in 'everyday' usage of the language, in language and in discourse" (LO: 94–95). Contingency is what makes signification a matter of ethics rather than epistemology, what enables the ethical, as Gayatri Spivak has argued, to interrupt or suspend the epistemological.

Literature

"Experience of Being, nothing less, nothing more, on the edge of metaphysics, literature perhaps stands on the edge of everything, almost beyond everything, including itself" (AL: 47). Like Miller and de Man, Derrida turns to the language of suspension when he speaks of literature: "There is no literature," he tells Derek Attridge, "without a *suspended* relation to meaning and reference" (AL: 48). But for Derrida, suspension of reference as such is only the beginning, an initiatory moment where one may begin to register contingency and the possibility of being-otherwise. Suspension informs the experience of literature, even as it denies it an essence. "Poetry and literature," Derrida argues,

> provide or facilitate "phenomenological" access to what makes of a thesis a *thesis as such*. Before having a philosophical content, before being or bearing such and such a "thesis," literary experience, writing or reading, is a "philosophical" experience which is neutralized or neutralizing insofar as it allows one to think the thesis; it is a nonthetic experience of the thesis, of belief, of position, of naivety.
>
> (AL: 46)

Derrida describes literature as an experience of suspension in ways that are strikingly similar to Coleridge's "willing suspension of disbelief"—itself an early phenomenological articulation of literary experience. Where Coleridge speaks of a "human interest and a semblance of truth" that may be accessed even (and especially) through a literature of the supernatural, Derrida argues that literature does not so much obviate the question of belief as it allows us to experiment with it, trying out different positionalities (including a position of naiveté) in order to understand something of positioning itself.

The suspended experience of literature (including both the suspension of disbelief and its morally and pedagogically-charged cousin, narrative suspense), is an act of both holding back and giving over. It operates, as Derrida writes, "without annulling either meaning or reference" (AL: 47). Literature holds us up, slows us down, exposes a general structure of equivocation that is no longer simply the paralysis of indecision. Jonathan Culler argues that "Derrida is practically unique in connecting the political significance of literature to the status we designate with the term 'fiction': to its suspending or bracketing of reference, including reference to the empirical author" (Culler 2008: 7). Here, suspension provides the hinge between the literary and the political, again opening a critical space not reducible to transparency and gaining its force from an ability to interrupt, irrevocably, the movement of referential thought. Derrida's suspension does not look to an end or a *telos*; its *telos* is suspension itself—the *epochē* (the Greek word for suspension, as well as phenomenology's bracketing) and the aporia.

There's an unavoidably aberrant dimension to the act of suspension—and not just in the literary language of referential aberration. The suspension of disbelief has often been criticised as a form of special pleading for authorial inadequacy or worse. Suspension is always the exception to the rule, a gesture directed against law itself. It is both a punishment—one may be suspended from school or from one's position as the result of a serious infraction—and the mitigation of punishment (as in a suspended sentence or the suspension of death—*arrêt de mort*—that occupies much of Derrida's attention in "Living On"). Yet the possibility of an unjust suspension of the rules is also, irreducibly, the possibility of justice itself, a theme to which Derrida returns again and again. No justice without aporia, without suspension. "[J]ustice," Derrida writes, "would be the experience of what we are unable to experience" (FL: 244)—an experience accessible only through the mental movement of willing suspension. He opposes this justice to a concept of law, the "element of calculation"; the suspensive power of justice is what takes us beyond calculation, into the critical space able to open to the future.

Weber writes, "Such a radical suspension happens in the moment of undecidability in which any decision, in spite of the declared autonomy of the decider, is 'founded,' and thereby, in fact, forever unfounded" (Weber 2007: 326). It is another moment of giving over, of passing beyond rules, beyond any claims about groundedness, beyond the epistemological—even while, at the same time, aporia demands a willingness to be held up, to hold ourselves up, to allow for the experience of frustration, a suspension with which we will never have done. Derrida, it seems, would have us remain forever paralysed at this contradictory crossroads, having to commit ourselves unequivocally to two mutually-exclusive paths. The call to justice—and here we could also add terms like gift, forgiveness, the ethical—is a call never to have done, to a perpetual suspension that cuts across even seemingly successful instances, those times when justice is served and all sides seem to understand each other within an apparently shared idiom.

Impossibility

"It must plunge, but lucidly, into the night of the unintelligible" (CF: 49). How does one live in a state of perpetual suspension, holding back and giving over, prior to and separate from decision and calculation? Derrida himself claims that "deconstruction loses nothing from admitting that it is impossible" (PI: 15), but it is nonetheless difficult to remain always on the edge of the abyss, to embrace the discomfort of the aporia. On the one hand, the demand for decision, beyond calculation, beyond the horizon of the possible; on the other, the impossibility of deciding, inflexible and equally demanding. Only a posture of suspension—holding back, giving over—can meet this contradictory situation of "infinite speculation" (PI: 15). Suspension is not, for Derrida, the *exclusion* of anything, not repression or forgetting, but a way of bracketing, keeping contingency present, including it, even though it no longer serves the same inhibiting function.

Suspension, then, names a practice of awareness, emerging from the non-space of the aporia, that Derrida develops throughout his writings in a variety of registers. To adopt these practices means that we must assent to a certain experience of "never-having-done," and also means that we must continue to take contingency and instability seriously, not allowing these concepts to become domesticated through frequent use. In closing, it is useful to recall a crucial distinction that Derrida makes in "Psyche: Invention of the Other":

> The invention of the other is not opposed to that of the same, its difference beckons toward another coming about, toward this other invention of which we dream, the invention of the entirely other, the one that allows the coming of a still unanticipatable alterity, and for which no horizon of expectation as yet seems ready, in place, available. Yet it is necessary to prepare for it; to allow the coming of the entirely other, passivity, a certain kind of resigned passivity for which everything comes down to the same, is not suitable. Letting the other come is not inertia ready for anything whatever.
>
> (PI: 39)

Preparation without expectation is a difficult charge, and to meet it requires something like a Coleridgean "poetic faith," a suspension that is not paralysis but an actively-maintained openness to a plenitude that continually evades presence.

We will never have done with that suspension itself, with the need for postures and practices of awareness. This is the case whether we speak in Derridean terms of the coming of the other or, in the discourse of contemporary post-Derridean philosophy of the radical, absolute contingency which underpins what the speculative realist philosopher Quentin Meillassoux has dubbed the *"great outdoors*, the *absolute* outside of critical thinkers ... which was given as indifferent to its own givenness" (Meillassoux: 2008:7). At the most basic level, Derrida asks us to meet the world without preconceived notions of what we will find there. Such a meeting itself is always already impossible, partial—for Derrida and for us. While Meillassoux's "great outdoors" has been heralded by some (though not by Meillassoux himself) as a turning away from deconstruction, Derrida's suspensions already point the way to an aesthetics of contingency, even if he retains a concept of finitude that has been challenged in this recent philosophical discussion. Suspension, indeed, constitutes the core of Derrida's strange realism and his ability to continue to speak to the future. To reject his call to suspended awareness amounts to a refusal of reality, even as that reality evades the constructions we put upon it.

Over—*and* over again.

5 Religion

Kevin Hart

In his early writings Jacques Derrida is not especially interested in religion (Baring 2011). His primary critical object is what he calls the "metaphysics of presence," which, as he points out, has structured Christianity in part though not in whole. The expression "metaphysics of presence" is not to be found in Martin Heidegger but the concept surely is (Heidegger 2010: 173). Heidegger argues that western metaphysics is constituted in a highly determined way, and when naming that way he borrows a word from Immanuel Kant: "onto-theology" (Kant 2001: 349). For Kant, onto-theology is a way of trying to apprehend God by way of being: as the *highest* being, the *original* being, and the *being* of all being. And Kant argues that onto-theology is ultimately a failure: we can have no theoretical knowledge of God. Yet the deity can be known practically: we can please God by adhering to the categorical imperative, "Act only according to that maxim whereby you can at the same time will that it should become a universal law." That imperative falls squarely within the realm of reason, not revelation, and everything else associated with religion – works of grace, miracles, mysteries, and means of grace – merely border upon religion considered within the limits of reason alone. I look over Heidegger's shoulder to Kant because some of the ideas of the sage of Königsberg will become important for the older Derrida. In particular, he will contest the categorical imperative and reformulate the project of religion considered within the limits of reason alone.

For the young Derrida, though, it is Heidegger rather than Kant who is the principal philosopher to be reckoned with. Onto-theology, for Heidegger, is the consequence of an ambiguity in the very idea of metaphysics as conceived by Aristotle: the study of being as being. On the one hand, this formula denotes the study of being in general, *on hē on*, and is therefore known as ontology. On the other hand, it indicates the study of the highest being, the *theion*, which is known as theology. Since the highest being accounts for being in general, and since we cannot know the highest being unless we account for the essence of being in general, Heidegger argued that metaphysics is constituted as "onto-theology." The ambiguity in Aristotle's definition of "metaphysics" is not merely an accident, Heidegger said: it has given rise to the history of metaphysics from Plato to Nietzsche. Yet there is a slip in Heidegger's word "onto-theology" that *is* accidental. *Theion* names the highest being, yet when he writes "onto-theology" he uses the Greek word for "god," *theos*. If metaphysics in the Christian era were onto-theology – a synthesis of ontology and theology – it would involve a relation between being in general and God regarded as the highest being. But that is not what Heidegger had in mind. He maintained that onto-theology arises in Greek philosophy, long before the advent of Christ. The expression "onto-theiology" denotes what he described: the relation of the essence of being in general and the highest being.

Heidegger maintained that the God of metaphysics was not the God that people could worship, and in later life suggested that were he to write a theology the word "being" would not figure in it. God encounters human beings in the sphere of being, he said, but we have no right to identify being and God. The God of the philosophers is indeed dead, and since the Enlightenment we have had to live in a disenchanted world; and so he talks (with Hölderlin in mind) of the flight of the gods. Some theologians will point out that Heidegger inherits a notion of being that comes from Duns Scotus: neither divine nor created being but a neutral, indeterminate being that was held to be the appropriate object of metaphysics. For these theologians, onto-theology begins with Scotus, reaches its most subtle form in Descartes, and remains a problem not only for Heidegger but also in his writings. Derrida offers no view of this revision of onto-theology. Like Heidegger, he holds that metaphysics, considered as onto-theology, has a vast historical scope and a tenacious strength. Unlike Heidegger, he does not talk of enduring the absence of God or the gods, or waiting for the poets to alert us to new traces of the divine.

So Derrida's primary and constant interest is in the "metaphysics of presence." The expression gathers together several levels of "presence." There is the *ontic* register (an object's presence in time), the *ontological* (the determination of being as presence), and the *epistemological* (a subject's presence to another subject and to itself). This is the only metaphysics there is, Derrida tells us, although it cannot be circumscribed. So one finds it in philosophy, as one would expect, but also in linguistics and literature, economics and art criticism, political science and theology: in short, everywhere. The power of this metaphysics can be contested from within each of these areas by attending closely to those places where a text differs from itself, yielding glimpses of alternate ways of viewing reality than those afforded by the tradition that has dominated the west in one way or another. Derrida dubs this movement of textual self-differing *la différance*, and points out that it is not another, deeper name for being. It is the condition of possibility for anything to signify and, at the same time, the condition of impossibility for anything to have a self-identical meaning. *La différance* never appears *as such*: it is a trace, and has always already withdrawn when we notice its effects in a text.

The metaphysics of presence has always been linked to one or more varieties of deconstruction, Derrida tells us, and this insight leads to two issues in his thought that concern Christian theology. The first is, as he points out in *Of Grammatology* (1967), that Christianity becomes metaphysical only when it bases itself on the founding notions of Greek philosophy: *ousia* (substance), *nous* (reason), *logos* (thought), *telos* (goal), and so on (G: 13). Christianity has a complex history of appropriating Greek conceptuality; it begins in the New Testament, and is heavily marked in the writings of many Church Fathers and the medieval schoolmen. It should be noted that Judaism, with its profound commitment to commentary on Torah, has been drawn far less into the history of metaphysics. That said, one should not infer that Derrida is offering an oblique Jewish apologetics. Although he was born a Sephardic Jew, his intellectual culture has been European and Christian. In general, we might say that the position he develops allows for the possibility of a non-metaphysical theology (in the extended sense of "metaphysical" that he promotes) in Christianity, although it is not something that he has explored in any detail.

Of course, there is no reason why a Jew who, as he says in "Circumfession", can "quite rightly pass for an atheist," would be interested in contributing to Christian theology (C: 155). Yet Derrida has reason to doubt that a non-metaphysical theology, though possible in theory, could be developed along the lines that have often been envisaged for it. His reservations come into focus when we consider the second consequence of his general position. If *la différance* is beyond being and unable to be captured by our concepts, it resembles the God of apophatic theology. To get clear about this, we need to distinguish kataphatic and apophatic theologies. In Christianity, a kataphatic theology reveals the Father in the Son through the Spirit. There is a descent of the Word that allows us to speak of it affirmatively. Apophatic theologies are intertwined with kataphatic theologies: they reflect on how the predicates ascribed to God in kataphatic theologies ("good," "light," "beauty," "love," and so forth) cannot properly be ascribed to the eternal and infinite deity. They ascend to God by way of denying the adequacy of speech. Because God transcends the world, God also transcends our language about the world; and if we are to ascend to the deity we can do so only by an apophatic way, by suspending, contesting or denying the predicates that are revealed in kataphatic theologies. When talking of *la différance* Derrida often mimics the syntax of apophatic theologies ("neither this nor that"), but it does not follow from this practice that it is divine. God is transcendent, while *la différance* is quasi-transcendental: a condition of both possibility and impossibility. Besides, even the most apophatic of apophatic theologies, Derrida suspects, covertly construes God as full presence, and therefore gets entangled in the metaphysics of presence. Apophatic theology would therefore seem to be an unlikely guide to developing a non-metaphysical theology.

Is Derrida correct to implicate the metaphysics of presence in negative theologies? Yes and no. That there are moments of metaphysics in the *Divine Names* and *Mystical Theology* of the Pseudo-Dionysius, for instance, is not to be disputed. But that the Pseudo-Dionysius affirms a deity whose hyper-essentiality is a blazing moment of self-presence is not supported by his writings. The God evoked in the *Corpus Areopagiticum* is neither present nor absent, neither being nor non-being, neither one nor many, and is entirely free to determine itself. More generally, we should be skeptical about any claim that Christianity belongs in a simple or straightforward way to the history of metaphysics. There have been movements of deconstruction at work in Christianity from its earliest times, and it might be argued that the very word "deconstruction" has a partial heritage in Luther's word *destructio* in the *Heidelberg Disputation* (1518) which is formed as a response to St Paul's words "I will destroy the wisdom of the wise" (1 Cor. 1:19), itself a quotation of Isaiah 29:14. Luther's criticisms of the Catholic "theology of glory" influenced Heidegger when thinking about his word *Destruktion* ("destructure"), which, along with *Abbau* ("unbuild"), is one of the immediate forebears of the word *déconstruction*.

Derrida is far too careful a reader to suggest that Christianity falls easily or wholly into the metaphysics of presence. Even so, it needs to be kept in mind that he frames Christianity with respect to its philosophical, not theological, horizons. His early writings are guided by Husserl's highly philosophical notion of God as an "ultimate consciousness" that guarantees the actuality of any given moment in the temporal flow (Husserl 1991: 394; OG2: 146–48). To be sure, no sharp line divides philosophy and theology: even those theologians who explicitly distance themselves from philosophy can be oriented by undisclosed metaphysical assumptions. Yet we need to be aware that Derrida does not have an exact and exacting knowledge of Christian theology. One consequence is that, when he considers religion, he will tend to overlook examples and counter-examples that are well known to historians of theology. Another consequence is that he will rely on theological distinctions of an earlier period that have since come under criticism within the guild. The most pressing of these is that historical fact and existential faith belong to utterly different orders. This position, principally associated with Søren Kierkegaard and Rudolf Bultmann, has never won widespread acceptance among Catholic theologians, and has been fiercely contested within Protestantism by Wolfhart Pannenberg, among others. Derrida could surely defend his views, but his lack of close knowledge about contemporary debate over faith and history or faith and reason means that some theologians have taken less time to read and consider his work than they might have done.

If Derrida has reservations about apophatic theology indicating a non-metaphysical theology, he is more sanguine about the chances of a deconstructive theology. The aim of such a movement would be, he said in 1985, "to liberate theology from what has been grafted on to it, to free it from its metaphysico-philosophical super ego, so as to uncover an authenticity of the 'gospel,' of the evangelical message" (Creech et al. 1985: 12). We are not to imagine deconstruction coming from an imagined outside to tamper with theology; rather, it would already be at work within theology, calling (as he says) "Aristotelianism or Thomism" into question, criticizing "a whole theological institution which supposedly has covered over, dissimulated an authentic Christian message" (Creech *et al*. 1985: 12). Reading these words, we can see that a certain deconstruction, as Derrida understands it, is already theological, and that its theology arises out of the Reformation. Yet it is easy enough to see how a deconstructive theology of another stripe could call into question Protestant assumptions about a return to a pure origin and an unmediated relation with God. There is no *one* deconstruction, Derrida says; it might be added that there is no *one* deconstructive theology, either, and certainly no *one* theology that takes deconstruction as one of its conversation partners.

Derrida's engagement with negative theologies is mostly confined to the mid 1980s and early 1990s. "How to Avoid Speaking," a close reading of apophatic theology in the Pseudo-Dionysius, Meister Eckhart and Martin Heidegger, first appeared in *Psyché: Inventions de l'autre* (1987) while *Sauf le nom*, his engagement with Angelus Silesius, was published in 1993. Other texts of the same period treat the theme, most notably *Khôra* (1993), and it must be said that Derrida never loses interest in the ruses of apophaticism. One or more "apophatic theology" is always at issue when talking of *la différance*, and the scare quotes are never to be removed, for they remind us that *la différance* is unsayable because it is quasi-transcendental and not because it is transcendent in the religious sense of the word. From the early 1990s, however, another emphasis can be detected in Derrida's interest in religion. Now it is not a matter of showing that deconstruction is not a disguised apophatic theology, or that apophatic theology relies on presence. Instead, it is a question of "religion today," of how we are to rethink faith and the holy, evil and the messianic, prayer and sacrifice. Derrida's later thoughts on religion can be organised around the expression "religion without religion."

Religion without religion? The phrasing recalls Augustine's in his *The Literal Meaning of Genesis*. There he evokes God as "Measure without measure," as "Number without number" and as "Weight without weight" (Augustine 1982: 1, 108). In all three instances, the preposition "without" signals divine transcendence. Equally, the phrasing recalls Blanchot's: "death without death," "being *without* being" and "relation without relation" (Blanchot 1995: 340; Blanchot 1993: 47, 73; Derrida 1986: 90–91). Blanchot has recourse to this syntax precisely in order to decline the very transcendence that Augustine wishes to affirm. The relation without relation, for instance, is a way of being in the world other than that of dialectical transformation of the other person (Hegel) or immediate fusion with the Other (the mystics). Blanchot comes upon the idea when critically reflecting on Emmanuel Levinas's *Totality and Infinity* (1961). There Levinas rethinks ethics along the lines of an asymmetry between myself and the other person. There never has been a time when I have not been called to help another person, Levinas says. The other calls to me as though from on high, and this asymmetric relation can never be reversed without also erasing ethics.

The expression "religion without religion" comes up when Derrida notices that Jan Patocka's thought coheres, in various ways and to different extents, with that of several other philosophers he admires: Paul Ricœur and Jean-Luc Marion, Kant and Hegel, Kierkegaard and Heidegger. Levinas is also named, and (with appropriate reservations) we could add Derrida himself to the list. This powerful tradition, cued into a much longer sequence of western philosophy, proposes, he says, "a nondogmatic doublet of dogma, a philosophical and metaphysical doublet, in any case a *thinking* that 'repeats' the possibility of religion without religion" (GD: 49). We can approach this claim by way of any of the philosophers Derrida names, and no two would take us to exactly the same place. Jean-Luc Marion, a devout Catholic, will lead us where we can find phenomenological justification for the possibility of revelation, while Kant proposes to see if Christianity can be brought within the limits of bare reason. For the sake of concision, let us follow Heidegger whose distinction between *Offenbarung* and *Offenbarkeit*, revelation and revealability, is one that Derrida has adapted to his own ends. The Heidegger who does not accept the Christian revelation nonetheless keeps open the possibility of a new revelation of the divine, the traces of which will be registered by the poets. This hope in the spiritual receptiveness of poets is alien to Derrida, and yet the distinction is of use to him: it indicates an aporia that can be found in all periods but that has perhaps been especially significant since the Enlightenment. Revelation and revealability do not arrange themselves by way of a strict distinction, as Heidegger thought. Not at all: each answers to a general structure of iterability, a repetition that begins in and leads to difference and deferral. Let's take a moment to explore this thought.

Is it revelation or revealability that leads us to the transcendental ground of religion? In other words, does revelation make manifest the conditions of possibility for revelation after the fact? Or is it that the conditions comprising revealability must precede any revelation merely for us to know that it *is* a revelation? An aporia must be negotiated, Derrida tells us; we must undergo the experience of being pulled in two directions without any possibility of those forces ever being resolved. Why not? Because they are incommensurable: revealability can be calculated but revelation cannot. Theologically, this negotiation would mean that we would think revelation and revealability together, giving rise "to a structure of experience in which the two poles of the alternative cease to oppose one another to form another node, another 'logic,' another 'chronology,' another history, another relation to the order of orders" (PF: 26). It would have been interesting to see how Derrida would have explored this new relation. His interest, however, has been in *Offenbarkeit* more than in *Offenbarung*, since that enables one to talk of faith without dogma, of a general structure of messianicity without relying, in a confessional sense, on a historical messianism, whether Christian, Jewish or Islamic.

Derrida concedes the possibility that the general structure of messianicity cannot be detected without one or more historical messianisms. His implication seems to be, however, that in principle revealed messianisms can be transformed into an archive that opens the future and keeps it open. Consider Judaism. Derrida is drawn to "what constitutes Jewishness *beyond all Judaism*" (AFFI: 74). Jewishness is interminable while Judaism is terminable. So runs Yosef Hayim Yerushalmi's distinction in *Freud's Moses* (1991), and Derrida finds it of considerable help when specifying messianicity. Yerushalmi maintains that Jewishness is an affirmation of a radical future, a hopeful waiting for what can come only from the future as such: justice. Only the Jew has this hope, Yerushalmi insists: it is an absolutely unique trait of being Jewish, one that survives the loss of belief in God and the rejection of the corporeal election of Israel. It is the absolute character of this trait that Derrida disputes. On his analysis, the singularity of "being Jewish" is divided in advance, for there can be no unique mark without the possibility of its being repeated. Yerushalmi does not affirm *Offenbarung* yet he does endorse without reservation the absolute uniqueness of being Jewish, and in considering his understanding of interminable Jewishness Derrida points to the priority of *Offenbarkeit*: in this case, the possibility of a singular people.

Unlike Yerushalmi, Derrida argues for a messianicity that radically exceeds Jewishness as well as Judaism. At issue here is a claim that needs to be inspected: there is a faith that is prior to the determinate faiths of all positive religions. All human interaction presumes that a certain faith – let us call it "credence" in order to distinguish it from all specific acts of faith – has been extended. In order for me to talk with you, I ask you to trust me to tell the truth. Even if you intend to lie to me, you ask me, in and through the act of addressing me, to have faith in you. What Derrida calls messianicity comes down to be a general structure of the promise, one that inhabits the speech of each and every person, regardless of whether he or she believes in a particular Messiah. It is this archi-promise, structurally informing all our talk, that opens the future, Derrida argues. The "yes" of the archi-promise must be confirmed, however; it must always be followed by another "yes" or the promise will remain empty. Openness towards the future is not an endless, passive waiting for justice to come. Our responsibilities already press hard upon us. Only in acting now, in affirming the archi-promise with a "yes," can we bring about justice. But justice itself will never come. There will never be a time when freedom and justice are embodied fully in a constitution or a society. When people speak in such terms, freedom and justice have already congealed into law. In such a society there may be a tomorrow and a next week and a next year, but there is no future. The future consists of there being always more justice to come, not because we converge only slowly upon utopia but because material circumstances are always changing.

Derrida greatly admires a passage in *The Writing of the Disaster* (1980) where Blanchot tells the story of the Messiah, the most just of all the just, sitting among beggars and lepers at the gates of Rome. "When will you come?" he is asked by someone who recognises him. The question indicates that there is a disjunction between the Messiah's presence and his coming. Messianic time cannot be calculated in terms of a past present, the present day, and a future present. Not at all: it is the time when justice occurs, a wholly other register of temporality. Justice does not happen, it occurs. To grasp why this is so we must distinguish between law and justice. An act might be passed in the Legislature and become law: on a particular day, over a given political space, new liberties or obligations are declared that concern you and I. The law happens. No matter what the law says, however, I cannot set a bound on my responsibility to you. Quite simply, I can have no theoretical knowledge of my obligations. Contracts, programs and rules, along with other judgments of a theoretical kind, can point out the sort of responsibilities I might have, but the extent of those responsibilities cannot be determined, and I cannot have foreknowledge of situations to come that might call for further acts on my part. No matter how much I work to help you – teaching you, caring for you, fighting for your rights, and so on – I cannot say at a given time that I have behaved justly to you. Justice does not occur in any time that has or will be present to my consciousness. It occurs, if it does, in the archi-promise that is prior to each and every specific promise and in the radical future from which justice comes.

I said at the beginning that the young Derrida looked over Heidegger's shoulder to Kant but that his relationship with Kant is worked out only when he is much older. It was Kant's view that we can have no theoretical knowledge of God: none of the traditional proofs for the existence of the deity works at all. Yet we can have practical knowledge of God. We can please God if we follow the categorical imperative. This moral law is irreducibly Christian, Derrida argues; it is complicit with an evangelisation that seeks to exclude all religious differences. Now Derrida does not wish to affirm anything that licenses cultural violence in the way that the moral law does. However, in advocating a messianicity without messianism he is urging a general structure that impinges on all people. Messianicity, he tells us, constitutes "*a universalizable culture of singularities*" (Derrida 1998: 19). Unlike the Kantian categorical imperative, messianicity can be universalised without bringing all people under the one law, without erasing each person's singularity. Where Kant commends a program in which it is possible to please God without relying on dogma, Derrida affirms that which exceeds all programs and answers to the impossible. Kant proposes an experiment: to think religion *within* the limits of bare reason. Derrida attends to an experience: religion *at the* limits of reason alone, namely messianicity without messianism. The parallel is not exact, for Derrida says nothing about pleasing God. And this requires comment.

Derrida is the first to point out that "religion without religion" is not a new movement in philosophy. It can be found, in different ways, in

Heidegger and Kierkegaard, in Hegel and Kant. Doubtless one could continue going backwards and finding other examples. Averroës (Ibn Rushd), for one, maintained in the twelfth century of the Common Era that there is one truth that can be approached in various ways, including revealed theology and philosophy. That the teachings of the Qu'ran are true is not disputed, but their deep truth is to be found by the philosopher who extracts it from the shell of allegorical representation. Philosophy thus becomes the judge of theology. This juridical relationship is found everywhere one finds "religion without religion," and nowhere more clearly than in Kant. Now Derrida wishes to revise Kant's *Religion within the Limits of Reason Alone*, and in particular wishes to preserve and extend the democratic impulse he discerns there. Religion is to be freed from dogma, from the ecclesiastical hierarchy, and grounded in the universal, namely the moral law. We pass from revealed faith to reflective faith, from theology to philosophy; and in doing so we keep fanaticism at bay. Leaping forward from the late eighteenth to the late twentieth century we find Derrida repeating the gesture. Messianicity without messianism passes from revealed faiths to reflective faith; and in doing so it removes us from contemporary fanaticisms and the growing danger of violence. In fact, Derrida goes further than Kant, past the opposition of dogmatic and reflective faith, and certainly past the polarity of *Offenbarung* and *Offenbarkeit*, to the barrenness of *khôra*, which in this context I read as a nickname for *la différance*.

Religion without religion would be a radical openness to the future, an endless calling for justice. It would figure faith as the credence we extend to the other person, and the holy as the singularity of the other person. This is indeed religion without *religion*, without priests and liturgies, without dogmas and superstitions. Notice, though, that it is not religion without *hierarchy*: philosophy remains the judge of theology. Far more seriously, it might also be argued that it is also a religion without *God*, that it reworks a classical ideal of philosophical virtue. The point needs to clarified before being accepted or rejected. In "Faith and Knowledge" Derrida takes on board Kant's view that *"in order to conduct oneself in a moral manner, one must act as though God did not exist or no longer concerned himself with our salvation"* (ibid. 11). Yet in general he also takes seriously Augustine's question in the *Confessions*, "What then do I love when I love my God?" (Augustine 1991: X. vii.11; C: 122). Augustine answers in terms of the spiritual senses. Since he quite rightly can "pass for an atheist," Derrida would have to translate the question, he says, and while he does not supply a direct answer we might say that it would be justice.

6 Ecology

Timothy Morton

The owls are not what they seem.

Twin Peaks

There is a deep similarity between thinking ecology and thinking what Derrida called "the structurality of structure" in "Structure, Sign and Play in the Discourse of the Human Sciences," the extraordinary lecture at Johns Hopkins that marked the arrival of deconstruction in the USA (WD: 352). Like structuralism, thinking ecology is about thinking relationships. Yet as we think these relationships, strange and paradoxical things begin to happen. We discover that what ecology names is an open-ended "structure" without centre or edge. And we discover that this weird open-ended, sprawling gathering of beings is peculiarly scalable. That is to say, at every scale, everywhere we look in the sets of relationships that define ecology, we find paradoxical, open-ended, centreless, edgeless phenomena. This applies to the difference between a human and the chimpanzee who shares 98% of the human's DNA. It applies to the difference between a human and a hominid. It applies to the difference between one ecosystem and another. It applies to the difference between the inside and the outside of the biosphere—where does it reside, in point of fact? At the edge of the atmosphere? At the edge of Earth's magnetic shield, vital for shielding life-forms from cosmic rays? Or at the Sun, vital for life as such? And so on.

Determining the inside from the outside in a definitive way involves violence—it is in fact the "originary violence" of metaphysics, the violence that is metaphysics, argues Derrida (WD: 151–52). Is there an alternative?

We find that edges between things are neither thin nor rigid—nor are they nonexistent. There is a difference between a duck and a duck-billed platypus. Yet the boundary between things is full of all kinds of differences that proliferate as DNA mutates, as thinking continues, and as life-forms interact. Thinking the structurality of structure means that thinking is in a loop, which is far from being a neat circle (if circles are indeed neat). Being in a strange loop is very much what it means to think in an ecological way: think of feedback loops, but also think of how there we were, running our steam engines then our cars, when it crept up on us that all the while we had been generating enough carbon compounds to envelop us all in an entirely new era of geological time, the Anthropocene (I shall discuss this more fully in a moment). Being in a loop also is very much what it means to be an ecological being such as a tree or a strand of DNA. Where do I stop and start? Where does an environment begin?

Like structuralism, ecology seems to promise a fantasy of a total explanation for everything. It seems to proffer that everything is inter-connected in a holistic web of life. Yet the more one thinks about inter-relationships between grasses, microbes, nitrogen and tailpipes, the less neat and holistic the "web" becomes, until it resembles something like what post-structuralism used to call textuality. Holism collapses. This is because for holism, the whole is greater than the sum of its parts, and is to some extent "more real" than them. But this does not hold. A single weather event such as a storm is not less real than the climate of which it is a manifestation. It is caused by the climate, but distinct from it. In the very same way, a sentence in a poem is not reducible to the poem as a whole; there is an uneasy, lopsided relation between them. I might be able to change the sentence and end up with something like the "same" poem—or not. There is no prefabricated model, and there is no obvious boundary line that demarcates where the poem, upon losing words and lines of itself, stops being the poem in question.

Thinking ecology means thinking about how life-forms engage with non-life. Yet life-forms are also made of nonlife. It seems obvious that carbon dioxide molecules are not alive—but is DNA alive? Where does the boundary reside between life and non-life? Consider the humble (or not so humble) virus. A virus is a string of RNA or DNA that cannot live on its own, but instead inhabits another cell, taking over its functions and thus propagating itself. A virus is very much like a long sentence of the sort called a Henkin Sentence in logic: "There is a version of me in this system" (Hofstadter: 541–42).[1] While the nucleus of the cell is busy finding this version of the sentence in its archive, the cell becomes a virus factory. If you think a virus is alive, then a computer virus—also a string of code that contains things like Henkin sentences—is also alive.

One way to resolve the paradox is to insist that there is no life, or sentience. Those things, so the argument goes, are just illusions or epi-phenomena: good enough for the likes of us (humans), but not that real.

What is not tolerated is the feeling of ambiguity and anxiety concerning what counts as real. But what if this ambiguity were hard-wired into what is real, as a condition of its possibility?

Consider a single strand of DNA. On the one hand, it is a physical thing, like a line drawn by a pencil. On the other hand, it is a semiotic thing, like a line that means the letter /l/. Yet the boundary between where its physical aspects stop and where its semiotic aspects begin is neither thin nor rigid—which is also the case with our letter. One of Derrida's legacies was to open up a wide, fluid boundary between things like letters and things like marks and things like lines, populated by all sorts of strange entities (D: 54, 104, 205, 208, 222, 253). It is not so easy to draw a dotted line between the physical and the semiotic. Such lines are nowhere to be found on the surfaces of frogs, poems, clouds and permafrost. Yet since Plato, as Heidegger and Derrida both explored, Western philosophy has been in the business of trying to find these dotted lines. On the other hand, there is indeed a difference between the physical and the semiotic. We have a paradox. The question is whether the paradox can be reduced or eliminated, or whether it would be better to tolerate it. In other words, perhaps philosophy should get out of the dotted line business and into the allergy medicine business, where the ambiguous, shifting differences between things that constitute their identity can be allowed to exist, namely to play out in all their somewhat disconcerting ways.

We care for some life-forms in a special way because we deem them to be sentient. Yet where does the boundary reside between sentience and non-sentience? Biology is beginning to show, for instance, that plants are sentient in all kinds of ways: they protect themselves from danger, they communicate, they warn. Turing's Test for artificial intelligence is performative. You read the writing that slides out from the closed door of the room in which the supposed person (or algorithm) resides. If you are convinced that you are reading sentences by a person, then you might as well be (Turing 1990: 46). This sets the bar quite low for what constitutes personhood: it is some kind of good-enough performance by which I convince you that I may not be an android. Personhood is thus predicated on being paranoid that you or I might be a robot. This is precisely Descartes' problem—perhaps I am simply the puppet of an all-powerful demon. Before he brings in God as a *deus ex machina* to calm down these jitters, the default, zero degree condition of being a person is suspecting that you might not be one.

When we think these necessarily ecological thoughts, we discover a spectral realm in which all kinds of strange, uncanny entities flit about, hard to distinguish from one another in a thin or rigid way: vampires, ghosts, fingers, pieces of brain, phantom limbs, flowers, tropes, self-concepts, earlobes, appendices, swim bladders, minds, eyes, meadows, tardigrades, viruses. I mention meadows because these seemingly "natural," innocent and pleasant things exemplify the wonderful trouble with ecological thought. Meadows have characteristics that seemingly lie outside of logic, if we think logic means that you are not allowed to contradict yourself. For instance, I remove a blade of grass—do I still have a meadow? Why yes. I can go on removing blades until there are none left and the logic will still hold that the meadow is still there. So I decide that there are no such things as meadows—they are too vague; we might as well cover over the now grassless patch of dirt with some concrete, since there never was a meadow in the first place. This kind of logic is in league with the happy nihilism of "progress," a strange loop in itself whereby we have arrived at the Anthropocene with its global warming and mass extinction. If we want to care for ecological beings, we might need to revise the idea that in order to be logical you must be non-contradictory.

Derrida forces us to see that beings we might want to care for—biosphere, meadow, tree frog—lie outside the law of non-contradiction.

Ecological entities just refuse to fit into a normative box called *Nature*. Nature only works when some things are natural and some things aren't. In other words, Nature (I capitalise it to heighten our sense of the artificiality of the construct) can't mean absolutely everything, without ceasing to function as Nature. But ecology just is about everything, and how everything is interconnected: trees, telephone poles, foxes, toxic waste, cancer cells. There is no way to demarcate what concerns ecology in advance. Up until the later eighteenth century, it was possible to make such demarcations with a straight face. But Hume blew up pre-packaged concepts of cause and effect, and Kant gave us the reason why they should be blown up; demarcations are even less plausible in the age of Derrida two hundred years later. The concept of Nature was born during the Romantic period, at the very moment at which normative distinctions between natural and unnatural (hence normal and pathological, and so on) became untenable. It is almost as if at the very moment of the inception of modernity (which is another term for the age in which Derrida wrote), a fantasy appears of a thing, a place, a horizon outside (human) culture and history and artifice.

Yet this concept is already contaminated with what it tries to fend off. There are so many ways to show this—here is just one. Let me try to convince you that I am a Nature lover, or a Nature writer, or Natural in some other sense. I have to use many sentences. The more sentences I use, the less convincing I sound. I have to keep telling you, over and over again, to stop reading this and go out and smell the air, be in Nature. Yet what I end up with are pages and pages of Nature writing, possibly dictated to my wife, who is sitting conveniently beside me in this tent as I commune with Nature. (I here name the conditions of production of Edward Abbey's inaptly titled *Desert Solitaire*.)

This is by no means to assert that there are only (human) discursive products, and no chimpanzees or coral. Such an assertion would also be a way to close the anxious gap between what exists and how it appears, the gap opened up two hundred years ago at the inception of the modern period, which is also the inception of what is now called the Anthropocene, a geological period in which humans unconsciously affected Earth systems in a decisive way, marked by layers of carbon in Earth's crust. Deconstruction is not a form of idealism that solves the problem of the gap between what is and how it appears by losing the penguins and fir trees and replacing them with penguin discourses or ideas, or history or *Geist*, or for that matter modes of production or class struggle. Deconstruction, as opposed to all attempts to smooth over or abolish the gap, leaps right into the gap and decides to remain there for as long as possible.

I can't know in advance whether a thing is conscious, or sentient, or alive. As I explore this thought, more and more entities begin to slip into what has been called, in robotics design, the Uncanny Valley. The Uncanny Valley is a region of design in which a robot designed to appear human appears instead like a zombie, a disturbing *Doppelganger*. Robots such as R2D2 don't have this problem: they are unlike humans enough not to appear uncanny. The uncanny is the strangely familiar and familiarly strange. Since I can't tell whether you are a robot or not in advance, the baseline of my encounter with you is a necessarily uncanny one, in which you seem to be like me, but in a shifting and uncertain way—and this also applies to myself, since I am also one of these strange beings whom I encounter, for instance when I look in a mirror or talk about myself in essays about ecology. This wavy line of thinking continues until we find that the valley is not a valley at all, but rather a gigantic plain on which all beings are assembled. There is no regular, Natural place in sight, and no completely, obviously artificial place in sight.

Evidently the uncanny applies to the notion of ecology as such, because the term *ecology* involves the Greek *oikos* (home). The German for *uncanny* is *unheimlich*, which suggests a feeling of being at home and not at home at the very same time. The default condition of being at home is a feeling of strangeness, precisely because it is so familiar. There is something weird about one's child or a long-term partner, precisely because one keeps on waking up near them. The concept of Nature tries to iron out the necessary uncanniness that ecology glimpses. The concept of Nature is in this sense the diametrical opposite of ecology. That is why I continue to argue that we need ecology without Nature.

Ecological beings at whatever scale are uncanny; that is, they are what they are, yet not exactly what they are, whichever way you look. They exemplify what Derrida calls the *arrivant*, an arrival—he is thinking of the future—that cannot be predicted in advance, yet is not just anything at all, or nothing. Welcoming this *arrivant* is the ultimate gesture of hospitality. My term for the *arrivant* is *strange stranger*. A badger, a flock of starlings, a bee swarm or an antelope are all strange strangers— they are strange even to themselves and their strangeness is irreducible such that the more we know (about) them, the more strange they become (Derrida 2000: 3–18; Morton 2010: 14–15, 17–19, 38–50).

I shall close by summarising the recent argument of Nicholas Royle, in his deconstructive book *Veering*. The term *environment* contains the word *veer*, as does the term *perversion* (Royle 2012: 2–3 and *passim*). The environment is not a neat, spherical thing that envelops me per- fectly, such that I know exactly where I am and what I am at every moment. It is not cozy. The environment is what *veers around*, disturb- ingly changing course, moving, flowing. The question arises of whether veering is avoiding something, or heading for something. Or indeed whether veering means pushing something, or allowing it to be pulled— when a ship veers, it is following the directives issued by the currents, yet at the same time, it appears to have some sort of direction, some kind of intention.

The same happens when we read. Derrida's most notorious concept, that of *différance*, is a very elegant term for what happens (M: 1–28). The meaning of a sentence is always just off beyond the end of it, and the same goes for words and the squiggles we read as letters. We are pulled along by the sentences—or we keep making a decision to con- tinue along. Reading is a kind of veering. Reading is en*viro*nmental. At whatever scale I look—novel, chapter, sentence, word—I find veerings in the manner I have just described. There is a weird push–pull going on between me and things that are not me, such as sentences and chapters. In the same way, there is a weird push–push going on between me and the ignition of my car, between me and my gut's microbiome, between me and the polar bears. Ecology is the name of the thinking that reveals more and more of these push–pull scenarios, these veerings. Or allowings-to-drift. There may be infinite gradations of pushing and pulling between the not-quite-existent poles of total dominance and total submission.

One way to read the epigraph (Lynch, 1990) is that it means that there is categorically nothing at all. This kind of nothing is what Paul Tillich calls *oukontic*, which sometimes I like to think of as "not even nothing" (Tillich 1951: 188). Absolutely nothing is real—which is a metaphysical statement, albeit of a certain nihilistic kind. "Nothing is real" becomes like "There is a God" or "Everything is really just atoms."

Another way to read the sentence is that nothing is as it seems. This kind of nothing is what Tillich calls *meontic*, a nothingness that Heidegger sometimes calls nihilation—nothing-ing (*ibid.*). This kind of assertion is not metaphysical, because it points out that there are all kinds of rippling, shimmering gaps between being and appearing—and within being and within appearing. There are trees, and tree appearances—and uncertain, wavering gaps and folds between trees and tree appearances. It is not that really, truly, there are no trees at all, or no such thing as trees.

To inhabit a world permeated by this nothingness is to be ecological. It is also to see things like trees as tricksters who are and are not as they seem. It is mistake to think that indigenous people are immersed in a lifeworld without anxiety—that you could be in such an anxiety-free zone is a modern fantasy par excellence. Trees might be people, or not. They might be waving at us, or not. They might be sentient, or not. In this sense, what is translated as "nature" in the fragment of Heraclitus— *Nature loves to hide*—is not the Nature I was just discussing, the normative policeman of pathologies and perversions versus straightness and healthiness. Trying to get rid of the hidden aspect for once and all is what is called violence. Science does not reduce the strangeness of things. The world as described by ecology is a peculiar charnel ground between realms, where spirits and spectres tarry with owls, trees and bewildered detectives looking for the structurality of structure. Ecological awareness means being able to tolerate this "things are not as they seem" to the greatest extent possible. Even to appreciate it, or admire it. To tolerate what Western philosophy has often called "evil."

Note

1 The viral sentence (known as a Henkin sentence) sounds amazingly like Lacan's "il y a de l'un."

7 deconstruction and Ethics: An (ir)Responsibility

Nicole Anderson

"deconstruction *and* Ethics"; the conjunction here might raise a couple of questions for readers unfamiliar with Derrida's work. Does the "and" convey an essential connection between the two words on either side, and thus perhaps suggest that deconstruction is ethical or can be read ethically? Or, does the "and" convey an antithesis between the two words, suggesting that deconstruction is in opposition to ethics, and is therefore unethical or nihilistic? Predominantly, in the historical reception of the ethical in Derrida's work scholars have argued that either deconstruction is ethical (or can be read ethically), or it is unethical or nihilistic. But as we will see, Derrida's work is not so black and white. To suggest that Derrida's work is either ethical or unethical (in the metaphysical sense) is to miss the point of deconstruction. To oppose the ethical to the unethical would be to perpetuate what Derrida deconstructs: the binary oppositions by which metaphysics is characterised. This chapter will briefly outline this historical reception before arguing that deconstruction entails a paradoxical move; one that enables a simultaneous challenge to, without rejection of, the binary choice-making and decision-taking that has been characteristic of metaphysical ethics. The chapter will conclude with an explanation of the positive nature of this paradox in and through Derrida's discussion of responsibility and irresponsibility. To ease us into an understanding of this paradoxical move let us begin with a discussion of the role ethics plays as a metaphysical concept.

1. Ethics: a metaphysical concept

Ethics is an abstract noun and therefore is not generally spelt with a capital 'E', as it is in the title of this chapter. However, the capital in this instance attempts to convey visually the important role that nouns play in the construction of Western metaphysics, as well as the prominence of metaphysical ethics in Western culture. Since Plato and Aristotle, metaphysics has been taken up in many forms and defined or critiqued in various ways according to the multiple philosophical topics that it encompasses: from immortality, God (theology); Being (ontology); reality (cosmology); beings (philosophical anthropology); morality and truth (ethics), and so on. Attempts have been made to define metaphysics. Aristotle called it the 'science' of "primary principles and causes" (Aristotle 1998: 982b, 9). Immanuel Kant conceived of metaphysics as a rational investigation of the principle of reason (Kant 1934: 28), while Martin Heidegger claimed that metaphysics is an "inquiry beyond or over beings, which aims to recover them as such and as a whole for our grasp" (Heidegger 1993: 106). More recent philosophers and defenders of metaphysics argue that it concerns itself with "*the fundamental structure of reality as a whole*" (Lowe 2002: 2–3). Not to ignore their specificities, underpinning these varying definitions is a common account of metaphysics as that which grounds the questions of God, Being, reality, morality, ethics, truth, and so on, in absolute and fundamental principles.

Nouns (as well as binary oppositions) are one means by which to construct the fundamental grounds or principles, and this construction works in the following way: because nouns are things, places, people, abstract ideas, animals and objects, they are generally locatable in space and time. Being locatable, in turn, means that our perceptions of space and time are formulated on the teleology of "cause and effect," meaning that time is not only perceived and experienced to move in linear fashion: past, present, future, but also enables a sense of self, and of others and objects, ideas, things, places (i.e. nouns) as unified and stable *across* time and space (universality). This experience of unity and stability is what Derrida calls the "presence of the present." To define it another way, the 'presence of the present' is the located-ness; 'now'-ness; or the 'presence' of some 'thing' in the present moment of time and thought. Given that nouns, which characterise metaphysics, encapsulate the 'presence of the present', and given that ethics is a noun, then ethics is a metaphysical principle through and through.

However, there is more than one form of metaphysical ethics, indeed there are varying accounts: from Contract, Christian, Deontological, Utilitarianism to Feminist ethics, but what they all have in common, or what makes them all metaphysical, is that they all focus on regulating behaviour by prescribing a set of universal principles (Diprose 1994: 18). To be able to have a common focus relies on the common assumption "that individuals are present as self-transparent, isolated, rational minds and that embodied differences between individuals are inconsequential" (Diprose 1994: 18), and "that the individual comes prior to relations with others" (Diprose 1994: 102). To be ethical, then, requires that the subject be present to itself, that is, not only self-conscious, but as a consequence also rational, and thus autonomous. Derrida's work challenges these assumptions.

Even though the ethical has been a concern of Derrida's from his earliest works, such as *Of Grammatology* and "Violence and Metaphysics," he has not explicitly discussed "ethics" (as a metaphysical concept) in any sustained form. Rather he has taken a different approach by implicitly raising the problem of metaphysical ethics in and through his deconstructive treatment of concepts such as "responsibility", "justice" and "law," and "hospitality", in books and essays such as the *Gift of Death*, *Of Hospitality*, *Adieu: To Emmanuel Levinas*, *Politics of Friendship*, "Violence and Metaphysics", and "Force of Law". Through these deconstructive "treatments" Derrida is able to avoid offering an ethical principle or model to live by, or to regulate behaviour. He does not provide us with an ethical treatise or philosophy, because to do so would be to perpetuate what ethics is, and what deconstruction is not: a metaphysical concept.

This is not to say that either deconstruction *is* ethical, or that deconstruction opposes itself, and can be opposed, to ethics, and is therefore unethical or nihilistic. It is neither ethical nor unethical because deconstruction is not, as Derrida argues, a "method, critique, analysis, act or operation" (LJ: 4). To oppose the ethical to the unethical would be to perpetuate the binary opposition on which metaphysics has been founded. This is why deconstruction in this chapter is spelt with a lower-case 'd': so as to attempt to avoid turning deconstruction into a proper noun with all the attendant problems this would entail. In other words, deconstruction is not a 'thing'; it is not a noun, which would characterise it as having an essential nature.

Deconstruction therefore is hard to define because there is not just 'one' deconstruction, unchanging and metaphysical: instead as Derrida tells us there are only "deconstructions in the plural" (Derrida in Papadakis 1989: 73), that is, deconstruction is "irreducibly plural" (FL: 56), because it 'is different from one context to another' and "takes the singularity of every context into account" (Derrida in Papadakis 1989: 73). For Derrida, then, "[d]econstruction takes place, it is an event that does not await the deliberation, consciousness, or organisation of a subject, or even of modernity. *It deconstructs it-self. It can be deconstructed*" (LJ: 4). For Derrida, this means:

> The movements of deconstruction do not destroy structures from the outside. They are not possible and effective, nor can they take accurate aim, except by inhabiting those structures. Inhabiting them *in a certain way*, because one always inhabits, and all the more

when one does not suspect it. Operating necessarily from the inside, borrowing all the strategic and economic resources of subversion from the old structure, borrowing structurally, that is to say without being able to isolate their elements and atoms, the enterprise of deconstruction always in a certain way falls prey to its own work.

(OG: 24)

Given Derrida's description here, the implications of deconstruction for, and on, ethics, is revealing. If deconstruction as an "irreducible plurality" *inhabits* structures (metaphysical, philosophical, etc.), then those structures are constantly in the process of deconstructing themselves, and thus consequently their structure is constructed by something "other": by a non-structure (which is not the opposite to structure as in de-struction, but can be defined as an alterity, heteronomy, or otherness). That is, metaphysics is not a pure presence referring to a pure foundation or origin, but contains or is traced through with something else: an alterity and "otherness" that disrupts presence and metaphysical foundations and determinations. Deconstruction reveals that structures are enabled by, or come into being because of, non-structures (alterity, otherness, heteronomy).

Likewise, ethics is constructed by the non-ethical, and thus contains an otherness that interrupts its presence. Thus, ethics deconstructs itself. In other words, as Derrida explains, there is a 'non-ethical opening of ethics' (OG: 140), meaning that ethics is ethics only because there is the non-ethical. Again, like non-structure, the non-ethical does not mean the opposite to ethics, rather the non-ethical can be characterised as an otherness that is incalculable, unanticipated and irreducible (by this I do not mean the 'other' is completely unknown, if it was it would not be recognisable) (Anderson 2012). But this also means that even though the non-ethical is not the opposite of the ethical, it does contain the possibility of bringing a violence and destruction that can be done to me or you, precisely because we cannot anticipate or calculate the other and what it may bring to us or how it may respond (AEL: 111–12; Bennington 2000: 43).

2. Critiques of deconstruction

It is because Derrida formulates ethics as constructed in and through non-ethics, that many critics of deconstruction have argued that the relation between deconstruction *and* ethics is a negative one. The general critique goes like this: because deconstruction reveals ethics to be contingent on something 'other' than metaphysical foundations, truths, and categorical imperatives, then truth and meaning become contingent and contextualised to the point that moral action, meaning and interpretation become so indeterminate that what results is the denial and hence destruction of authority, institutions, structures or meaning for its own sake (nihilism). Critics, then, argue that deconstruction is not morally or ethically productive and positive, and is therefore nihilistic and indeterminate. Furthermore, critics have argued that because deconstruction is irreducibly plural, it ends up aestheticising and contextualising language and action through dissolution of the ethical and rational force of meaning and communication. Although recent scholars have critiqued Derrida for similar reasons, two famous and influential examples of this critique in a sustained form is found in Jürgen Habermas' *The Philosophical Discourse of Modernity* (1987),[1] and in John Searle's paper "Reiterating the Differences" (1977), the latter is a response to Derrida's paper "Signature Event Context" (1977), to which Derrida, in turn, responds in book length form in *Limited Inc* (1997).

3. An ethical turn

If deconstruction isn't a "method, critique, analysis, act or operation" (LJ: 4), and therefore does not and cannot offer an ethical theory, precisely because it *inhabits* metaphysical structures from within so that structure itself is revealed to be constructed in and through non-structure, then how exactly is ethics deconstructed? That is, how does deconstruction interrupt the tradition of ethics if deconstruction isn't a metaphysical structure? Given this, is it possible to read deconstruction as ethical? In response to the critique of deconstruction as nihilistic and unethical, in the late 1980s and through the 1990s a number of scholars came to the defence of Derrida's deconstruction, arguing that deconstruction could be read as ethical. This period marked what has been termed an "ethical turn" in the Anglo-American reception of Derrida's work (this 'ethical turn', however, is not marked in the work of Derrida, where, as mentioned earlier, the ethical has been a concern of Derrida's since his very first books).

Arguably, what characterised this 'ethical turn' were scholars predominantly drawing on Derrida's engagement with, and therefore reading Derrida almost exclusively through, Emmanuel Levinas's ethics. To summarise Levinas' ethical position briefly: Levinas defines his ethics as a 'calling into question of my spontaneity by the presence of the Other … The strangeness of the Other, his irreducibility to the I, to my thoughts and my possessions, is precisely accomplished as a calling into question of my spontaneity, as ethics' (Levinas 1996: 43). For Levinas, this ethics precedes and displaces the traditional understanding of metaphysical ethics. In other words, as Derrida articulates it, Levinas wants to rectify the Greeks' disregard of the other precisely by seeking the other in 'the ethical relationship', which as "a nonviolent relationship ... to the Other, ... [is] capable of opening the space of transcendence and of liberating metaphysics" (WD: 83). That is, Levinas calls upon ethics (defined as the moment when the other puts the same, the ego, into question) to liberate us from Greek metaphysics (WD: 83), which continues to permeate philosophy and culture to the present day. However, for Derrida, Levinas cannot possibly succeed in achieving the nonviolent "opening toward the beyond of philosophical discourse" while he continues to use the language of metaphysics (WD: 110). The only way Levinas can do this is by using what he rejects: the philosophical language inherited from the Greek *logos*.

As a consequence of his engagement with Levinas, many scholars defending Derrida against the attack of nihilism understood Derrida's notion of the "other" (as difference) through Levinas' ethics of the other. From this, two predominant views ensued: on the one hand, there were those scholars, such as Simon Critchley (1992, rpt 1999) and Drucilla Cornell (1992), that not only made an attempt to reduce Derrida's deconstruction to Levinas' ethics, but in the process also assimilated Derrida's notion of the other to Levinas' 'nonviolent relationship to ... the Other' (WD: 83). On the other hand, there were a number of scholars (for instance, Geoffrey Bennington and Robert Bernasconi, among others), who recognised the importance of Levinas and his ethics for Derrida's thinking, while at the same time, also acknowledging Derrida's radicalisation of Levinas's ethics of the other. One of the differences between Levinas and Derrida that becomes apparent in and through the latter's radicalisation, is that for Derrida ethics is always already violent, and thus the other, as mentioned earlier, potentially brings the worst: violence and destruction to me or you (WD: 111–12).

Derrida, then, is not entirely assimilable to Levinas' ethical position, as some scholars argue.[2] A greater sense of his difference from Levinas can be found in Derrida's discussion of responsibility in the *Gift of Death*, which we will turn to shortly. It is in and through this discussion that we may begin to understand that despite the challenge deconstruction poses for metaphysical ethics, deconstruction does not set itself up as an alternative ethical system or theory, in fact, "there is ... no philosophy and no philosophy of philosophy that could be called deconstruction and that would deduce from itself a 'moral component'". And yet, Derrida claims that

> this does not mean that deconstructive experience is not a responsibility, even an ethico-political responsibility, or does not exercise or deploy any responsibility in itself. By questioning philosophy about

its treatment of ethics, politics, the concept of responsibility, deconstruction orders itself I will not say on a still *higher* concept
of responsibility ... but on an exigency, which I believe is more
inflexible [intraitable], of response and responsibility. Without this
exigency, in my view no ethico-political question has any chance of
being opened up or awakened today.

(ON: 364)

It is because deconstruction is able to pose questions to ethics, politics,
responsibility, and so on, that not only does deconstruction "deploy"
responsibility "in itself", but it is possible to derive from deconstruction a
new understanding of ethical acts, as the following section will now elucidate.

4. (Ir)responsibility

As mentioned in the opening paragraph of this chapter, deconstruction
entails a paradoxical move; one that enables a simultaneous challenge to,
without rejection of, the binary choice-making and decision-taking characteristic of metaphysical ethics and responsibility. This paradox is most
evident in Derrida's book the *Gift of Death*. In this book Derrida argues
that morality and ethics are paradoxically constituted by the "irresponsible". However, this general ethical paradox is elucidated in and
through the individual paradox with which Abraham, in the biblical
story, is confronted: God commands Abraham to sacrifice on Mount
Moriah, as a burnt offering, his son Isaac (Genesis 22: 1–19). Abraham is
faced with a harrowing choice or decision: he has either to fulfil his
responsibility towards the *singular*, in this case God, or to obey the
general ethical laws of his society, and fulfil his responsibility towards all
others (Isaac, Sarah, his friends, family and community). And by singular
or singularity Derrida is referring not just to God, but to that which is
irreducible, unrepeatable, heterogeneous and idiosyncratic (another
person or event, for instance). Abraham decides to keep his responsibility
to God (the absolute singular and unique other) and sacrifice Isaac, but
in the process he inevitably betrays and disobeys the universal general
laws/ethical principles of his society and culture, that is, his duty to all
others known (family) and unknown (larger community).

Through this biblical story Derrida is able to demonstrate that in
acting irresponsibly, in the traditional sense, towards all others (the laws
and ethics of his society) Abraham is being responsible towards God,
towards the singular. Derrida calls this responsibility towards the singular other or event, "absolute responsibility" (as opposed to a general
or metaphysical notion of responsibility). Derrida further describes

"absolute responsibility" as that which is extraordinary, as something that remains "inconceivable" and "unthinkable', precisely because it involves the other in its "uniqueness, absolute singularity, hence non-substitution, nonrepetition, silence and secrecy" (GD: 61), while general responsibility (or the universality of ethics and the law) is so precisely because it requires substitution, repetition, and thus applicability and commensurability to all others.

Given this, absolute responsibility "is not a responsibility, at least it is not general responsibility or responsibility in general," "it must therefore be irresponsible in order to be absolutely responsible" (GD: 61). In other words, to be responsible to an/the other, one has to be irresponsible to *all others* (ethics). Importantly what this further suggests is that the irresponsible is not in opposition or antithesis to ethics and responsibility (just as non-structures and the non-ethical are not in opposition to metaphysical structures and ethics, respectively). Rather, ethics and responsibility are constituted by irresponsibility. Derrida captures these paradoxes of responsibility in a famous passage from the *Gift of Death*:

> There are also others, an infinite number of them, the innumerable generality of others to whom I should be bound by the same responsibility, a general and universal responsibility (what Kierke-gaard calls the ethical order). I cannot respond to the call, the request, the obligation, or even the love of another without sacrificing the other other, the other others. *Every other (one) is every (bit) other [tout autre est tout autre]*, every one else is completely or wholly other. ... As soon as I enter into a relation with the other, with the gaze, look, request, love, command, or call of the other, I know that I can respond only by sacrificing ethics, that is, by sacrificing whatever obliges me to also respond, in the same way, in the same instant, to all the others.
>
> (GD: 68)

For Derrida, then, the paradox is that there are two equal, because absolutely imperative, duties: one to the *singularity* of any 'one' or other, and one to the duty of being responsible to "every Other" (the *general*, and thus the law). The fact that Derrida argues that there are two equal and imperative duties suggests that deconstruction is not about rejecting universal or metaphysical ethics. Rather what Derrida demonstrates is that the two equal and imperative duties to which we are required to respond, produce a tension: a paradox and aporia not resolved by a simple decision or choice between the two, but rather an aporia that exposes the undecidability within, and the inherent violence of, every choice or decision. This undecidability constitutes responsibility as exigency. In other words, it is this aporia that Derrida calls "ethics as 'irresponsibilization'", because it is "an insoluble and paradoxical contradiction between responsibility in general and absolute responsibility" (GD: 61).

5. Conclusion

It is through this notion of "irresponsibilization" that deconstruction reveals the potential violence of every ethical decision. In the paradoxical contradiction between 'responsibility in general and absolute responsibility' – that is, in the two equal, because absolutely imperative, duties – we have to decide, and in deciding (no matter how uncertain, ambiguous or undecidable that decision is) we either do violence to all others, or to a singular other, or to both at the same time. For Derrida we are all situated in an "economy of violence", and that means that there is never a non-violent ethics or responsibility, as Levinas would want (WD: 313, n.21). It is here that Derrida is profoundly unassimilable to Levinas's ethics. And yet it is in and through his engagement with Levinas' notion of ethics defined as a "calling into question" of me *by the other*, that enables Derrida to deconstruct, via his notions of "absolute responsibility" and "irresponsibilization", a metaphysical ethics that prioritises the subject over the other. This is not to say that Derrida or deconstruction rejects metaphysical ethics, and it does not mean that decision and response cannot be made or require no thought at all. Rather, decision and response cannot be ultimately calculated in advance and thus prefabricated (and thus prescriptive, universal and applicable over time and across all contexts). Having to decide, then, means having to account, or to be absolutely responsible, for *how* and to *whom* we respond, in a way that a prescriptive ethics does not enable.

It is in this way that deconstruction is absolutely affirmative in that it not only opens the way for the other – as an irreducible difference to come – but consequently allows for a more nuanced ethical, or rather "absolutely responsible" *relationship* with difference, with the other, itself. In Derrida's words, deconstruction is "the *yes* of the other, no less than the *yes* to the other" (AEL: 35).

Notes

1 While the urgency of combining political and philosophical forces against the 'West's' war with Iraq in 2002 led to a rapprochement between Derrida and Habermas (see Habermas and Derrida 2003), it does not occlude the real and

significant philosophical differences between them, nor the criticism's Habermas made of Derrida in the 1980s.

2 The discussion and debate around the Derrida-Levinas connection continues into the twenty-first century with writings on the issue by Anderson (2012), Dooley (2001), Grebowicz (2005), Hägglund (2008), Plant (2003), to name only a handful. While more general writings on the ethical has continued by prominent scholars such as Geoffrey Bennington (2000), Hent de Vries (2001), John Llewellyn (2002), J. Hillis Miller (2009) and Michael Naas (2008).

8   Teletechnology

Robert Briggs

In one sense, there is a very straightforward answer to the question of what Derrida means by "teletechnology". For the term most often functions in Derrida's work as a name or shorthand for the entire apparatus – the set of technologies, industries, professions, practices and conventions – of what we more routinely call "the media": the press, television, cinema, radio, the Internet as well as related mobile, networked and digital channels or industries of public communications. What Derrida hopes to achieve by referring to that field or apparatus by way of the term "teletechnology" is, however, another matter altogether. Perhaps unlike many other Derridean concepts, that is, the significance of Derrida's work on "teletechnology" comes less from its status as a concept (or even as a "non-concept") than from the kinds of questions – aesthetic, ethical, political – that are raised by the *fact* of teletechnology, and by the apparent prevalence *today* of the media and of information and communication technologies more generally. So, whereas the terms "arche-writing", "différance", "pharmakon", "parergon", "spectrality", "supplementarity", and so on, appear to name quasi-transcendental structures or themes, or at least seem to have their most immediate implications for the ideal objects and topics of philosophy, Derrida's work on teletechnology focuses its attention on a more historically bound, banally empirical set of institutions and practices – institutions and practices, moreover, that have already been widely theorised (hence claimed) by a number of "non-philosophical" disciplines, such as mass communications, sociology, political science, and popular culture studies.

That is not to say that there is no philosophical significance to Derrida's take on teletechnology. Indeed, one of the effects of Derrida's use of that term in place of the more familiar term "media" is precisely to displace our ordinary, intuitive or pre-reflective understandings of media technologies and practices. Whenever we refer to or talk about the media in a given situation, we presuppose as given certain understandings of what the media are, of what they are for, of how they work, of where they've come from, of how to interact with them, and so on. One of the tasks of philosophy (at least since Hegel, if not since Plato) is precisely to bring presuppositions to light, to show the ways in which what we might call ordinary thinking operates within a horizon of intelligibility which enables us to think, reject, affirm, critique, fear, love or simply experience a particular aspect of the world precisely by leaving *unthought* much of the background to such experience. For Derrida, moreover, the history of philosophy is likewise dependent on such presuppositions: much of his work has focused on what he calls the metaphysical tradition's privileging of "presence", and his various reflections on teletechnology can be understood as perfectly consistent with that focus. At the same time, the turn to the media reflects Derrida's desire to attend to the question of "today", of orienting or opening contemporary existence to a future that is something other than the continuation of the present. And "to think one's time", as he puts it in *Echographies of Television*, his most sustained reflection on teletechnology, means registering the ways in which time itself, the time of speaking and of thinking, and first and foremost the very experience of (this) time, is produced, organised, or *mediated*:

> Today, more than ever before, to think one's time, especially when one takes the risk of speaking publicly about it, is to register, in order to bring into play, the fact that the time of this very speaking is artificially produced. It is an *artifact*. In its very happening, the time of this public gesture is calculated, constrained, "formatted", "initialized" by a media apparatus (let's use these words so that we can move quickly). This would deserve near infinite analysis. Who today would think his time and who, above all, would speak about it, I'd like to know, without first paying some attention to a public space and therefore to a political present which is constantly transformed, in its structure and its content, by the teletechnology of what is so confusedly called information or communication?
>
> (ET: 3)

Derrida's discussion of the media in terms of teletechnology thus serves a double purpose: on the one hand it links reflection on media technologies to a broader concept and history of technology generally, while on the other hand it orients deconstruction in this case not so much towards the philosophical or logocentric production of presence (in the form of ideal objects) as towards the technical and industrial construction of presence *today* in the form of mediatised "actuality" or "liveness".

In order to make sense of the second of these moves, then, it perhaps helps first to situate Derrida's reflections on teletechnology in relation to his earlier work on writing and the critique of presence. Briefly, "presence" is Derrida's shorthand for a range of philosophical concepts that attempt to define being – to identify its "is-ness", by way of such terms as essence, nature, substance, identity, ideality, spirit or consciousness (Allison 1973: xxxii-iii). Such attempts, on Derrida's reading, seem always to privilege the values of autonomy, immediacy, fullness, purity, continuity, priority, originality, universality or transcendentality, while negating or subordinating the values of difference, alterity, exteriority, materiality, secondarity, absence, contingency, relationality, mediation, and so on. Derrida's interest in writing, particularly in earlier works such as *Of Grammatology*, lies in the way that writing seems routinely to be imagined in terms of its fundamental difference from speech. As the means of communication that appears most intrinsic to human being, that is, speech has always been taken as the proper medium of thought, hence of truth and reason, because speech appears coextensive with thought, meaning and intentionality as such (in the sense that one is able to *hear oneself think*). By contrast, writing, on this view, is merely an external system of graphic signs for representing a language or communication that precedes it (i.e. speech). Writing is thus a derivative and inessential *technology* of communication that – by virtue both of its exteriority to thought and of the in-principle capacity of a written text to convey meaning over distance and time – is prone to miscommunication and misunderstanding. Such belatedness and fallibility consequently doom writing to the role of merely *re*-presenting and relaying, via technological means, the forms of truth and meaning that enjoy their full presentation only through the medium of speech. Against this view of writing as imperfect copy of speech's full presence, however, Derrida argues that the core traits of "the classical concept of writing" – absence, iterability, spacing, exteriority – are "valid not only for all orders of 'signs' and for all languages in general but moreover, beyond semio-linguistic communication, for the entire field of what philosophy would call experience, even the experience of being: the above mentioned presence" (LI:9). To the extent that writing "means" belatedness, absence, delay, representation or derivation, hence dependence, difference, and so on, Derrida's depiction of all communication and of all experience in general as an experience of writing thus functions as a critique of all the forms of presence (self-sufficiency, originality, ideality, and so on) that metaphysics has always presupposed or privileged as fundamental, as the very origin of existence.

By the same token, this affirmation of writing is also an affirmation of technology, of the structural "necessity of the prosthetic as technological and rhetorical supplementarity" to thought and existence (DE: 22). Classically, writing's status as technology is founded first on its externality and artificiality – on the fact that, unlike the faculty of speech, writing is a prosthesis rather than an organ morphogenetic to the body: "technics in the service of language", as Derrida puts it in *Of Grammatology* (GD: 8). Second, writing is technological by virtue of its capacity for potentially limitless reproduction, such that any written text or fragment may be read in the absence of its author – again, unlike speech, whose existence and enunciation are supposedly tied to the presence of a speaker. Derrida's insistence on writing as the condition of "presence" (hence also as the impossibility of presence) thus positions technology in general not as external to or in opposition to the human body or to authentic human being, but rather as the very ground or "medium" of experience. In this way, Derrida's take on writing amounts to an affirmative relation to technology that stands against the "position of reactionary resistance to technology" (DE: 78), such as that underpinning Romantic, New Ageist or Puritanical rejections of modern technologies, and even the view of modern technology adopted by Martin Heidegger (or perhaps by a certain reading of Heidegger) in his *Question Concerning Technology* (Heidegger 1977).

Following this trajectory, Derrida's work on teletechnology can be read as an elaboration or development on this theme of the always-already prosthetic and technological nature of being. As he remarks in *Echographies*, when asked by his interviewer Bernard Stiegler about the "specificity" of teletechnology in the general structure or history of writing: "this specificity, whatever it may be, does not all of a sudden substitute the prosthesis, teletechnology, etc., for the immediate or natural speech" (ET: 38). By the same token, the new apparatuses of teletechnology do not consign writing to the past, as though new forms of digital and multimedia mark an order of technology that radically diverges from the structure or principles of writing. Accordingly, any apparently critical remarks Derrida might go on to make about teletechnology should not be read as launched in the name of some more authentic form of experience, communication or community. Teletechnologies "have always been there", Derrida insists; "they are always there, even when we wrote by hand, even during so-called live conversation" (ET: 38). And it is in this insistence that we can begin to identify the non-synonymity of "teletechnology" with "media". For the conventional sense of the latter term positions communications media as technologies that, logically speaking, are external to and separate from the event that is *subsequently* "mediated". On this view, media are channels for relaying some prior image or thought or event, whose fullness or identity will become compromised or impoverished by the editing of the event, by the capture of only certain perspectives (the point of view of the camera), by the presentation of the event by way of only so many dimensions (two-dimensional image) or senses (sight and sound, but not smell, touch, etc.). The point of critical focus suggested by this conventional account thus sharpens on the inevitable failure of the media text adequately to represent the actual event. And so news journalism, for instance, is thought to provide an inevitably biased or distorted picture of what is really happening, on account of the limits of the camera, the need to arrange the elements of the story, the need to edit to length, if not also the determined partisanship of the journalist and the news organisation he or she represents. On Derrida's account, though, while teletechnologies undoubtedly filter, select, reorganise, paraphrase, hence *interpret* events in all these ways, they do not thereby compromise the fullness or presence of "the event itself". They do not simply "distort" the event precisely because the event itself is *already* riven by spacing, absence, iterability, relationality, and so on – by the *necessity*, that is, of filtration, selection, reorganisation and paraphrase. Events are *defined* by their essential incompleteness, by the need to be supplemented by another event, such as the event of interpretation, which itself is defined by insufficiency, substitutability and relationality, and so is unable to complete the event it seeks to interpret. Indeed, to the extent that a given event is, in principle, able to be "captured" and "transmitted" and thereby interpreted by media technologies, the fact that it just so happens *not* to be thus captured and transmitted already amounts to a teletechnological selection or interpretation. Events are not full of meaning in and of themselves, in other words, but always require teletechnological supplementation, regardless of whether there happens to be a news crew on stand-by.

Or to put the point another way: why are some events televised and others not? Why are some events broadcast live, with a duration that matches that of the "event itself" (say, a Presidential or Prime Ministerial address), whereas others are delayed and edited (news reports), or even extended (slow-motion replay)? Further still, how is it that the existence of teletechnologies may enable the very occurrence of events (as in the scheduling of a photo opportunity or the holding of a televised debate during a political campaign) – events that would be inconceivable in the absence of the media? These questions speak to the fact that events do not happen simply in advance of or independently from the advent of their representation or mediation by way of media technologies. Rather, the eventness of the event, its status as (media) event, is a *product* of the filtration, selection, organisation and interpretation that characterise the work not just of "the media" but of teletechnology in general.

It is the produced-ness of events that most regularly attracts Derrida's interest in his discussion of teletechnology. And it is this produced-ness – its structure, its limits, its possibilities – that Derrida is referring to when he reflects on the artificial, or rather *artifactual*, nature of "one's time", of the present. Derrida coins the term "artifactuality" in order to underscore the ways in which "actuality" is "not given but actively produced, sifted, invested, and performatively interpreted by numerous apparatuses which are *factitious* or *artificial*, hierarchizing and selective, always in the service of forces and interests to which 'subjects' and agents ... are never sensitive enough" (ET: 3). But while the term "actuality" may to English ears recall in this context simply a genre or type of media production (TV news, documentary footage), the French term that it translates accommodates a number of discrete notions: the abstract concept of "topicality" or "relevance", the more concrete sense of what is "actually happening" or "in effect", the thought of "current events" or "current affairs", as well as the idea of "the news" in the sense of media reports on what is happening (see Translator's note in ET: 164, note 2). And so "actuality", before it refers to media representation, encompasses a broader arena or discourse of public life and political reality. By the same token, the concept of artifactuality (as with teletechnology) refuses or complicates the apparent ontological distinction between the "reality" that we experience or perceive and the "media" that we read or watch, particularly as that distinction is reproduced in the notion of "representation". The notions of teletechnology and artifactuality point, therefore, not simply towards what in media and cultural studies is called a "politics of representation" but rather (or moreover) towards an analysis of the construction and transformation of the very field of perception and experience.

Teletechnologies, in other words, *make* time. And they *make* space. Or, further: to the extent that teletechnology is not simply a kind of object, a set of particular technologies, but rather that which constitutes and delimits the field of perception and experience, teletechnologies are the very *processes* of making time and making space.

These phrases – "making time" and "making space" – are suggestive of at least three different ways of thinking about teletechnology's relations to time and space. In the first instance (and as already highlighted), teletechnologies constitute the time and space of events as "mediated" by news media. They produce the scheduling, duration and sequencing of (reported) events – concentrating and re-ordering the time of an event through editing; extending its duration through repetition and slow-motion techniques; shifting its time through pre-recording, archiving and delayed broadcast or publication; and intensifying the "nowness" of an event, its "presence", through its audio-visual recording and reproduction as "live" event. Similarly, teletechnologies produce the space of events not only by reporting the apparent dimensions and locations of such events, but also by distributing (reported) events in space – constructing the communicative space of the public sphere as well a sense of the territory and borders of nation-states, in relation to which current events gain political significance. Beyond this production of the time and space of "reported" events, moreover, teletechnologies modulate our very experience of time and space *as such*. When it is possible to communicate "instantaneously" with another person half-way around the globe, how "distant", how far removed is that other person, as compared to an era, not too long past, in which the only accessible or affordable means of communication was surface mail? Or again, what happens to one's experience of the *passing* of time, of its ephemerality or contingency, when audio-visual recording and archiving allow us to "re-live" an experience again and again (as in the recording and replaying of a home movie)? As Derrida puts it, "as soon as we know, 'believe we know', or quite simply *believe* that the alleged live or direct event is possible, and that voices and images can be transmitted from one side of the globe to the other, the field of perception and of experience is profoundly transformed" (ET: 40).

Alongside these very active senses of the phrases making time and making space, moreover, one can hear in them a third meaning: the idea of "accommodating" or "making room" – as in making time or space *for* events. Again, the media select, filter and interpret events as they "represent" events; they make room for (certain) events in the sense of letting them "in", giving them some attention. But the media make time or room for events largely on their own terms, according to their own commercial interests, operational imperatives and technical constraints. Following this third sense of making time, the critical question becomes less one of the media's inevitable failure to represent the world adequately than one of the varying *temporalities* of the media. At stake, in particular, is the structural incompatibility of certain aspects of "the world" *vis-a-vis* media time: the incapacity of such aspects to adjust or accommodate themselves to the communicative imperatives or protocols that define the media as they exist and operate today. As Derrida remarks,

> the least acceptable thing on television, on the radio, or in the newspapers today is for intellectuals to take their time or to waste other people's time there. Perhaps this is what must be changed in actuality: its rhythm. Media professionals aren't supposed to waste any time. Neither theirs nor ours. Which they are nonetheless often

sure to do. They know the cost, if not the value, of time. Before denouncing, as is constantly done, the silence of the intellectuals, why not give some thought to this new mediatic situation? And to the effects of a difference in rhythm? It can reduce certain intellectuals to silence (those who require a bit more time for the necessary analyses, and who refuse to adapt the complexity of things to the conditions imposed on their discussion); it can shut them up or drown out their voices with the sound of others – at least in places where certain rhythms and certain forms of speech are dominant. This other time, media time, gives rise above all to another distribution, to other spaces, rhythms, relays, forms of speaking out and public intervention.

(ET: 6–7)

These rhythms of media time and these distributions of media space – the making of time and space *for* particular events – are, of course, part and parcel of the making of the time and space *of* events. It is the rhythm of television, its demand for digestible soundbites and unqualified assertions, that helps *produce* the communicative "awkwardness" or "incompetence" of the professional academic who is called upon to impart his or her insights to the so-called general public. Moreover, what is this "general public" itself other than an artifact of mass communication technologies (such as radio and television) that are capable of reaching very large numbers of people, more or less *regardless* of specific differences in age, class, education, location, socio-economic status, ethnicity, political affiliation, interests and so on between the individuals who make up that audience? In what sense, in other words, is there a consistent and coherent "general public" already in existence and waiting to be spoken to, prior to the advent of mass media address?

Or again: what happens to the actuality of the "Occupy Wall Street" movement, say, when the many diverse events that could be collected under that name are made to concentrate into a very limited number of carefully filtered and artfully framed incidents of "unprovoked" violence or "unjustified" force on the part of protestors, while the more routine operations of political activism receive minimal air time or page space? What space is there in a nightly news bulletin or a daily newspaper for detailed reporting and commentary on the otherwise *uneventful* occurrence of peaceful demonstration? And in the absence of such space, what scope is there for such demonstrations or activism to attain the status of significant *public* event? By the same token, how is it possible that, as I write, people physically located in London or Melbourne or Tokyo are also "occupying" Wall Street? If the protests that have occurred in those geographically dispersed locations are nevertheless able to be recognised as part of the same event, this is because new media and new forms of communication have played their role in transforming the space of geopolitics. Where once the sphere of a citizenry's political influence seemed limited to the arena of *national* politics, the development of digital and networked technologies of communication (such as the Internet and mobile telephony) has enabled the formation of new political "alliances" on an international scale. Accordingly, where once global politics was shaped by the actions of leaders of nation-states, intergovernmental bodies and multi-national corporations, who at best only indirectly "represent" ordinary citizens on this global stage, these new forms of teletechnology have helped shape the possibility of what Derrida, as far back as 1994, referred to as a "New International" that extends to "the *worldwide* economic and social field, beyond the sovereignty of States" (SM:84).

For Derrida, the emergence of this "New International", which he sees as embodying "a link of affinity, suffering, and hope" among those who "ally themselves" in the "critique of the state of international law, the concepts of State and nation, and so forth" (SM:85–86), testifies to the profound mutation to political space enacted through and by the ongoing expansion of teletechnology. As he argues in *Echographies*, "what the accelerated development of teletechnologies, of cyberspace, of the new topology of 'the virtual' is producing is a practical *deconstruction* of the traditional and dominant concepts of the state and citizen (and thus of 'the political') as they are linked to the actuality of a territory" (ET: 36). Contemporary forms of teletechnology, in other words, allow for or constitute new conduits for international politics, for forms of political alliance "without coordination, without party, without country, without national community ... without co-citizenship, without common belonging to a class" (SM: 85). To the extent, moreover, that Derrida appears to sympathise with the formation of such alliances against or beyond the "official" conduits of geopolitical power, it is clear that, from the point of view of deconstruction, the different rhythms of teletechnology and the associated transformations to media time and to public space should not be assumed to be "bad". Indeed, Derrida insists he is "not an enemy of the media", because, whatever else they may be, "the media are also a democratic power, a key instrument of democratisation" (DE: 46). If Derrida seeks to achieve any specific critical effect with his notion of "teletechnology", then, it is always in relation to those aspects of the media that seem anathematic to democracy and justice – such as the fact of what Derrida calls "the hegemonic, homogenizing, homohegemonic power" (ET:47) of the media: the monologic of the media's productions, the invariability of the *type* of events they produce, and the power of media rhythms to demand conformity to such types. In the face of such power, Derrida argues, there is a need "to introduce heterogeneity within this more and more hegemonic structure, so that there is not one main media, something like CNN, governing the flow of information all over the word" (DE: 45).

To the extent that deconstruction is also engaged in the artifactual production of events – through its interventions within institutions, its re-readings of philosophical texts and traditions, its injunctions to follow a certain spirit of Marxism (SM: 86–94) and to develop a critical culture of the media (DE: 43–48) – deconstruction likewise takes shape in relation to teletechnological mechanisms and processes. As a form of thinking or writing that works to introduce heterogeneity within the homohegemonic structure of "the" media by countering and changing the *rhythms* of actuality, deconstruction remains, however, and *must* remain, incompatible with the media. It must do so, even if critical thought may sometimes develop within the media, or must seek, in any case, to "cooperate with the people in the media who are ready to do critical work" (DE:46). In that sense, the critical move that deconstruction proposes is not opposition to contemporary teletechnology, but rather intervention and transformation. As Derrida remarks, "perhaps it is necessary to fight, today, *not against* teletechnologies, television, radio, e-mail or the Internet but, on the contrary, so that the development of these media will make more room for the norms that a number of citizens would be well within their rights to propose, affirm, and lay claim to" (ET: 33). To the extent, moreover, that this injunction to "fight" does not appear to apply to deconstruction uniquely, then perhaps what Derrida ultimately hopes to achieve through his development of the concept of "teletechnology" is recognition and affirmation of the need for every person, every "citizen", to become a media and cultural critic so far as they are able.

9   Friendship

Samir Haddad

The concept of friendship appears in Derrida's work at the end of the 1980s, operating as an entry point into his analyses of democracy and the political. Broadly speaking, Derrida examines the ways in which theories of friendship relate to theories of political belonging across the Western philosophical tradition, and critically interrogates the manner in which both appeal to ideas of brotherhood. Such appeals, Derrida suggests, operate to reinforce the exclusion of women, and thus dramatically reduce the emancipatory potential of these theories. In response to this tradition, Derrida asks whether it is possible to conceive of models of friendship and political belonging, in particular democratic belonging, which have no relation to the fraternal. Derrida does not answer this question, and the theme of friendship quickly disappears from his writings, suggesting that he may have decided that the concept was too closely tied to its masculinist history to be used in thinking democracy otherwise.

Derrida's central book on friendship is *Politics of Friendship*. Developing work pursued in his 1988–89 seminar of the same name and published in 1994, this text dates from the period when Derrida focused more directly on political and ethical themes, with other relevant publications of this time being "Force of Law," *Specters of Marx*, and *The Gift of Death*.[1] *Politics of Friendship* is a multi-faceted and complex work. It contains readings of a wide number of figures in the Western philosophical tradition, including Plato, Aristotle, Cicero, Montaigne, Kant, Nietzsche, Schmitt, Heidegger and Blanchot. The guiding thread of the text is a phrase quoted by Montaigne from Diogenes Laertius' *Lives of Eminent Philosophers*, "O my friends, there is no friend [*O phíloi, oudeis philos*]." This statement, which is attributed to Aristotle but does not appear in any of his works, is cited by almost all of the authors Derrida reads, binding together the particular tradition of writing on friendship he explores. It is a paradoxical statement, and as such emblematic of the way friendship is understood in this tradition.[2] For Derrida's contention is that the concept of friendship is contradictory, and that its contradictions cannot be resolved. In Derridean terminology, friendship is aporetic – it relies on opposing terms that remain in a necessary tension.

Derrida argues that there are several aporias in the concept of friendship, and the most prominent is found in the relation between two models which consistently recur. The first is "the Graeco-Roman model, which seems to be governed by the value of *reciprocity,* by homological, immanentist, finitist – and rather politist – concord" (PF: 290). This idea of friendship follows a logic of sameness and proximity, where friends resemble each other and share much in common. The second model is the first's opposite, based on "heterology, transcendence, dissymmetry and infinity, hence a Christian type of logic" (PF: 291). Rather than following a law of the same and commonality, friends according to this model are different from each other, sharing little or nothing in common, and are separated by distance.

In *Politics of Friendship* Derrida argues that the first model is dominant in the tradition, operating most strongly in Aristotle, Cicero, Montaigne, and Kant. The presence of the second is more subdued, and Derrida reads its clearest expression in Nietzsche and Blanchot. However, this division between models is not a clean one: as aporetic, friendship must involve both, simultaneously. Derrida demonstrates this through a series of close readings. He does not uncover a single template that repeats identically, but he does identify a recurring pattern, where each author, despite a tendency to promote one of the models, ends up relying on aspects of the other at certain crucial moments. Thus the authors read testify to the aporetic status of friendship, as all remain caught in the contradiction between sameness and difference.

Since I cannot adequately discuss all of Derrida's readings here, I will present one that is to some degree exemplary, that of Montaigne. The bulk of this reading appears in a long parenthesis after Derrida refers to the Aristotelian conception of a friend being "One soul in twin bodies" (PF: 177). Montaigne appeals to this definition when discussing what is shared between friends. "Everything is genuinely common to them both: their wills, goods, wives, children, honour and lives; their correspondence is that of one soul in bodies twain, according to that most apt definition of Aristotle's, so they can neither lend nor give anything to each other" (Montaigne 1991: 214). This description conforms to the dominant model in the tradition, based on commonality and similarity. Between such friends everything is shared. However, the tranquillity of this model is soon disrupted. For having claimed that nothing can be given, Montaigne qualifies his statement and asserts that giving is possible, albeit in an inverted pattern:

> In the kind of friendship I am talking about, if it were possible for one to give to the other it is the one who received the benefaction who would lay an obligation on his companion. For each of them, more than anything else, is seeking the good of the other, so that the one who furnishes the means and the occasion is in fact the more generous, since he gives to his friend the joy of performing for him what he most desires.
>
> (Montaigne 1991: 214)

In a perfect friendship, what each friend seeks the most is to do good for the other, to give to him. In receiving, the friend allows the other to perform this good. Receiving a gift is thus the greatest gift that a friend can give.

Derrida draws two consequences from these remarks. First, referring to his own analyses of the gift, he argues that Montaigne's description of giving introduces dissymmetry and difference into this understanding of friendship. Once the recipient is he who gives, a hyperbolic outbidding is set into motion, as each friend tries to outdo the other in giving him more opportunities to give through receiving. This "disproportionate inversion of dissymmetry" (PF: 179) disrupts the common measure, measured reciprocity, and equality that marks the friendship.

Second, Derrida underlines the implication of isolation that follows more generally from Montaigne's account. The description of 'one soul in two bodies' limits the friendship to an indivisible and closed couple. In Montaigne's words, "each gives himself so entirely to his friend that he has nothing left to share with another" (Montaigne, 1991: 214). A man can have only one perfect friend, for to that friend he gives all, amplifying the rarity of great friendships of which Montaigne had already spoken ('it is already something if Fortune can achieve it once in three centuries' (Montaigne 1991: 207)). Derrida argues that this singularity introduces another aporetic couple into Montaigne's account of perfect friendship, involving a dual relation to the political and the apolitical. On the one hand, the exceptional nature of such a friendship means that "no political project can predict, prescribe or programme it." The two friends are "heterogeneous to political laws," above the law, and so apolitical (PF: 182). But on the other hand, Derrida argues that this avoidance of the political is not fully achieved in Montaigne's text. While the singularity of such friendships is emphasised, they remain in one respect subordinated to political law. For Montaigne's perfect friendship, despite its singularity, must be in accord with virtue ruled by reason, and Derrida argues that "Reason and virtue could never be *private*. They cannot enter into conflict with the public realm ... In such a tradition, a virtuous reason or a rational virtue that would not be in essence homogeneous to the best reason of State [*raison d'État*] is unthinkable" (PF: 184). Montaigne's perfect friends are also model citizens, and so their friendship is to some extent programmed and prescribed by the reason of political law.

Thus from the assumption of the dominant model of friendship, based on symmetry and sameness, Montaigne introduces elements of the other model, based on asymmetry and difference. He thus appeals to both models, at once, despite their contradiction. However, in Montaigne's text these two logics are not in perfect balance, with each engaged equally. For Derrida argues that there is another thread of similarity underlying the whole of Montaigne's project, binding the contradiction together. This is constituted by Montaigne's consistent appeals to fraternity. Across the tensions and fissures of this theory of friendship, one constant remains – all of the friends are men. A perfect friendship seems impossible between a man and a woman, and between women. This holds despite the heterogeneity and dissymmetry on which Montaigne relies, for while friends gain distance from one another and indeed from all law, this distance is never so great as to cross the division of the sexes. Thus, Derrida writes, "That which ensures the mediation or the solder ... that which also relates to the exclusion of woman, if only in the form or the pretext of 'not yet', is the brother, and, more precisely, the name, the name 'brother' and the brother's name" (PF: 291). It is to the name of "brother" that Montaigne returns.

Why does Derrida emphasise the name? Initially because Montaigne states that "The name of brother is truly a fair one and full of love: that is why La Boétie and I made a brotherhood of our alliance" (Montaigne 1991: 208). He thus has recourse to the name 'brother' to capture the value of their friendship. But in addition, La Boétie's name appears in two key moments of Montaigne's account. First, in the context of his inheritance of his friend's papers, in particular of his friend's work *The Discourse on Voluntary Servitude* for which "On Friendship" was intended as the preface, Montaigne writes:

> Yet I am particularly indebted to that treatise, because it first brought us together: it was shown to me long before I met him and first made me acquainted with his name; thus preparing for that loving-friendship between us which as long as it pleased God we fostered so perfect and so entire.
>
> (Montaigne 1991: 207)

Montaigne came to know his friend first by his name, the name that signed the work whose reading constituted their first meeting. Second, Montaigne returns to this initial knowledge of names when searching for an explanation of their friendship's force:

> We were seeking each other before we set eyes on each other – both because of the reports we each had heard, which made a more violent assault on our emotions than was reasonable from what they had said, and, I believe, because of some decree of Heaven: we embraced each other by repute [*nous nous embrassions par noz noms*].
>
> (Montaigne 1991: 212)

Before meeting the two friends had heard of one another – each possessed a name of renown.

As Montaigne describes it, friendship, in its highest expression, is thus framed by inherited names and names of renown, and this framing ties it to fraternity and the exclusion of women. For in the tradition in which Montaigne lies, these are names that belong to men. Rarely passed on, and rarely renowned, the names of women have little place in such a scheme. "Under the two forms of this enframing (inheritance of the name and social renown) *this* history leaves less chance to the woman, to the daughter, to the sister. We are not saying *no* chance, but *less chance*" (PF: 292–93). It is in this way that the name binds friendship to fraternity, easing the transition to Montaigne's explicit exclusion of women:

> … women are in truth not normally capable of responding to such familiarity and mutual confidence as sustain that holy bond of friendship, nor do their souls seem firm enough to withstand the clasp of a knot so lasting and so tightly drawn … there is no example yet of woman attaining to it, and by the common agreement of the Ancient schools of philosophy she is excluded from it.
>
> (Montaigne 1991: 210)

Strictly speaking women can be friends, both with each other and with men. But it turns out that in the canonical accounts such as that of Montaigne and those he cites, they are not. At first this exclusion seems the result of chance, but this chance is quickly reinterpreted as a necessity.

It is thus through a constant if sometimes subtle reliance on fraternity that Montaigne returns his discourse to an economy of the same. In this way, the possibilities offered by the aporia of friendship are dramatically closed down – even as Montaigne introduces elements of dissymmetry and heterogeneity, he remains constrained by the name of the brother, implying that women will never be accepted within a perfect friendship. Translated to the political, such a model reinforces women's exclusion, for they can never attain the status of model citizens. This is the pattern that Derrida uncovers across the tradition. For Aristotle friendships of virtue must be between equals, but there is dissymmetry in his claim that it is better to love than to be loved (and Aristotle also prefigures the aporetic relation between friendship and the political, arguing that friendship is necessary in the *polis*, and that the best friendship lies above justice). Yet amidst these complications he similarly excludes women, confining their relation to men within friendships of utility. Kant also negotiates the logics of sameness and difference, avoiding the dangerous fusion of love by promoting distance through respect. But he too appeals to fraternity, using the brother as the figure for the friend of humanity. And Michelet states that "Fraternity is the law beyond the law" (PF: 182, 237), at the same time as positing it as the basis of equality and democracy. But he also claims that women are never fraternal enough.

Given that these authors all begin from the model of sameness, one might instead start from an idea of difference. Such is the path taken in the second strand of the tradition read in *Politics of Friendship*. It begins with Nietzsche's reversal of the Aristotelian phrase:

> Perhaps to each of us there will come the more joyful hour when we exclaim:
> 'Friends, there are no friends!' thus said the dying sage;
> 'Foes, there are no foes!' say I, the living fool.
>
> (Nietzsche 1986: 149)

Analysing these and other remarks in *Human, All Too Human*, along with the philosophers of the future named in *Beyond Good and Evil*, Derrida articulates a view of friendship based in solitude, distance, and difference. Such friends would share nothing in common, divided by space and time at an unbridgeable distance. This model, Derrida suggests, is at the root of subsequent theories of community found in Bataille, Blanchot, and Nancy, and he also sees it at work in Schmitt's understanding of the political. Derrida clearly has some sympathy for the Nietzschean approach.[3] In particular, he embraces the "Perhaps" which commences the citation above, arguing that it poses a strong challenge to the demand for constancy and permanence assumed in the Greco-Roman model. The perhaps opens the Nietzschean model of friendship up to chance and to risk, raising the possibility of a break with the tradition without this break being ever assured. The "perhaps" thus opens friendship up to the experience of the event, as Derrida understands it – as that which comes beyond all calculation and prediction.

But even given this promise, Derrida argues that those pursuing the Nietzschean model still return to the logic of the same by making their own appeals to fraternity. Thus, despite attempting to eradicate all commonalities in friendship, Nietzsche keeps the name of the brother in Zarathustra's reversal of Christian values. Schmitt makes the enemy the centre of his concept of the political, but he speaks of the absolute enemy through reference to the brother. And Blanchot pushes friendship in distance to an extremity beyond all those before him, yet he too retains the brother in describing relations to the other. While resisting the dominant tradition, these thinkers of difference thus remain trapped in the aporia of friendship, returning to the economy of the same through the figure of the brother. None breaks with this hegemony, and thinks friendship across sexual difference.

It is this limit point of the tradition that is Derrida's target, as he seeks to go beyond fraternity as an organising trope for friendship, and, by implication, for a democratic politics. As he asks at the book's end:

> Is it possible to think and to implement democracy, that which would keep the old name "democracy", while uprooting from it all these figures of friendship (philosophical and religious) which pre-scribe fraternity: the family and the androcentric ethnic group? Is it possible, in assuming a certain faithful memory of democratic reason and reason *tout court* – I would even say, the Enlightenment of a certain *Aufklärung* (thus leaving open the abyss which is again opening today under these words) – not to found, where it is no longer a matter of *founding*, but to open out to the future, or rather, to the "come", of a certain democracy?
>
> (PF: 306)

Derrida does not answer these questions, nor does he offer his own theory of friendship or democratic belonging that would break with all familial figures. The closest he comes to doing so is through fleeting invocations of "*lovence [aimance]*" in the text. He proposes this term to name what is beyond both love and friendship traditionally understood, suggesting that it is a minimal call to friendship, a call that one be heard, at work in every address to another. Perhaps, Derrida intimates, one could think politics wholly otherwise based on such a notion, outside of all the determined figures that are found in the tradition. But while courting this possibility, Derrida ultimately argues against using it to ground a new politics. Doing so, he asserts, would be to attempt to gain certainty and assurance, erasing the chance opened by the perhaps. Further, he questions whether there is always such a minimal call at work: "We cannot, and we *must* not, exclude the fact that when someone is speaking, in private or in public ... some force in him or her is also striving *not to* be understood, approved, accepted in consensus" (PF: 218). This possibility of failure, that a declaration "can always flip into its opposite," is essential and unavoidable – "Without the possibility of radical evil, of perjury, and of absolute crime, there is no responsibility, no freedom, no decision" (PF: 219). Thus, while Derrida at times speaks approvingly of *lovence*, seeing in it the chance for a wholly other politics, he holds back from pursuing it further, both in fidelity to the perhaps and because of the inevitable threat it harbours.

Indeed, when examining Derrida's writings after *Politics of Friendship*, one sees a clear turn away from the language of friendship. Never again does Derrida submit it to scrutiny, nor push further in thinking it otherwise. Instead he changes his vocabulary, focusing on other terms to engage political themes and issues and put pressure on the tradition's limits. Thus in the late 1990s Derrida examines hospitality to raise again the question of political inclusion, placing a special emphasis on the rights of immigrants and the stateless (Derrida and Dufourmantelle, 2000; Derrida, 2002b). Following a different path, his final seminars of 2001–3 interrogate sovereignty by way of the animal (BS1; BS2). And 2003's *Rogues* focuses squarely on democracy, exploring the meaning of and possibilities in the phrase "democracy to come." Even when Derrida explicitly continues his earlier analyses in this last work, interrogating at length Nancy's use of fraternity and reiterating his own resistance to the political use of the term, there is no mention of friendship (R: 42–62).

This suggests that, given the results of his research, Derrida may have decided friendship was of less use in the continued pursuit of his philosophical and political goals. It would be too tied to its exclusionary history, too dominated by a masculine understanding, to be successfully mobilised in an emancipatory discourse. Nonetheless, despite its somewhat brief existence in his oeuvre, the concept of friendship remains the key term in Derrida's most sustained and detailed work in political philosophy. It thus plays a crucial role in the last phase of Derrida's thinking, a phase dominated by an engagement with politics.

Notes

1 In its original French publication *Politiques de l'amitié* also included a second, shorter text, "Heidegger's Ear: *Philopolemology (Geschlecht* IV)." This appeared in English in 1993 in an edited collection on Heidegger and was not reprinted in the 1997 English edition of *Politics of Friendship*. Beginning with 'the voice of the friend' evoked in passing in *Being and Time* (§34), it analyses appearances of *phileîn* and *pólemos* across Heidegger's oeuvre. I will focus on the main text of *Politics of Friendship* since this contains the bulk of Derrida's reflections on friendship.

2 It is worth noting that the very syntax of the phrase in Diogenes Laertius' text is questionable, since, as Derrida discusses, including an iota subscript on the 'O [ὧ]' significantly changes its meaning (PF: 207–10). This is how it is taken in Hicks' English translation, rendering it as "He who has friends can have no true friend" (Diogenes Laertius, 1925: 465), but it has not been understood thus by Montaigne and others in the tradition Derrida reads (which happens not to contain any Anglophone philosophers). In any case, Derrida argues that the two versions, despite their apparent differences, both involve constative and performative dimensions and so partake in similar paradoxes (PF: 212–14).

3 This sympathy does not extend to Schmitt, who occupies a different place in Derrida's analysis of this Nietzschean lineage. Unlike his engagement with Nietzsche and Blanchot, there is very little in Derrida's reading of Schmitt that recuperates or develops his theory, and Derrida challenges him on several key points, including Schmitt's founding distinction between friend and enemy, his attempt to differentiate inter-state from civil wars, and his thesis of depoliticisation.

10 Sexual Immunities and the Sexual Sovereign

Penelope Deutscher

When I say wolf, you mustn't forget the she-wolf.

(BS 1: 9)

What is the sense in which a woman is substitutable for a beast, a slave, or a child?

Among the many different ways in which he thought about sexual difference, perhaps one could say Derrida had a quirk for thinking of women listed in a series – as with his reference to philosophical discourse which "marginalizes ... women, children, animals, and slaves" (Derrida with McKenna 2002: 121), or a remark made in *Beast and Sovereign*: that the beast has often been "the living thing to be subjected, dominated, domesticated, mastered, like, by a not insignificant analogy, the woman, the slave, or the child" (BS1: 66). Derrida notes that women have been serialised as "like" other subordinated others and they appear in such series in his work. But women were also mentioned in a different kind of series cited by Derrida, a series that indicated a concurrently perfectible and pervertible, auto-immune and paradoxical progress. He refers to the rights of man as having been expanded by being pulled out of their limits to include "the rights of women, the right to work, the rights of children, etc" (Derrida with Roudinesco 2004: 19); the description of the auto-immunity of democracy as "interminable in its incompletion beyond all determinate forms of incompletion, beyond all the limitations in areas as different as the right to vote (for example in its extension to women – but starting when? –to minors– but starting at what age? – or to foreigners – but which ones and on what lands [*sur quel terri-toire*]?" (R: 38–39)). Not initially extended to women, nor to the colonised, the rights of man also offered a language that could be so extended ("as", he proposes, "when a war for independence [is] waged in the very name of the political ideals extolled by the colonial power" (R: 34–35)). Similarly, women's rights have been claimed by means of a passage beyond previous limits. This is presented by Derrida in terms of the auto-immunity of universalist rights claims, for the language of the latter gave weapons to use against their own limitations (Derrida with Roudinesco 2004: 19). Insofar as they are mentioned by him as the auto-immunity of their own previous exclusion, I have been curious about the possibilities for interpreting historical claims for women's rights as auto-immune in the sense the term is used by Derrida: an obvious consequence of his remarks, but not one that he developed. We will find him reckoning with the beast in Hobbes and Rousseau, for example, but not in the work of eighteenth-century feminist philosopher Mary Wollstonecraft. So what might it mean to read Derrida's *Beast and the Sovereign* with Mary Wollstonecraft? The answer will give an opportunity to ask another question: what happens when women, claiming political rights, deem themselves the child, the slave, the beast, and how are the relations of the beast and sovereign differently sexualised?

The seeming substitutability mentioned by Derrida has a long history in the tradition of those who argued for women's rights, for example by the means of analogy with others previously denied rights, most obviously slaves. Since with Derrida I am going to make some reference to women's rights claims, and having mentioned a number of series proposed by Derrida, I will turn now to Wollstonecraft, and recall one of her references to series – her view that boys tend to acquire in childhood the habit of tormenting animals and her claim: "the transition, as [boys] grow up, from barbarity to brutes to domestic tyranny over wives, children, and servants, is very easy." (Wollstonecraft 1995: 268)

I hope to repeat with Mary Wollstonecraft a question I have directed at Derrida: how should we best understand such a series (here, brute, wife, child, servant)? This is a series in which Wollstonecraft also supposes a continuity: as the animal is treated, so will be by extension a wife, a child, or a servant. This is a serialisation occurring in the context of Wollstonecraft's ideal of making women less of a child, and, to use a formulation from *Politics of Friendship*, more a case of the brother (PF: viii). Her strongest image of an ideal relationship between men and women is the ideal of rational fellowship, a possible friendship that would take place inside and outside sexual relationships. Wollstonecraft hopes to make women a case of the brother, as immunity against the serialisation I mentioned (where the woman becomes the child, becomes the servant, becomes the brute). Such associations prompt a question not asked in *Beast and Sovereign*, but appropriate for that work and consistent with its interests – perhaps, one could say, strangely missing from it.

Derrida marked the importance of sexual difference to the relationship between the beast and the sovereign in the first seminar of that name and in *Rogues*, in a number of ways. The beast forming the copula to the sovereign (*la bête et le souverain*) was also analogised to the sovereign (*la bête est le souverain*) and it was also feminine, at least as "marked in the grammar of the definite articles" (BS 1: 2):

> as if we were naming in it, ahead of time, a certain couple, a certain coupling, marriage or divorce ... – not only between two types of living being (animal and human) but between two sexes ... making a scene.
>
> (BS 1: 2)

But since he elsewhere asked, what if the sister is made a case of the brother (PF: viii), perhaps we could also ask that question not asked in *Beast and Sovereign*: what if women were made, not just a case of the beast, but also a case of the sovereign?

I. Women, Hobbes and Arrant Wolves

Discussing Hobbes' state of nature, in *Beast and Sovereign* Derrida briefly returned us to a point made by Carole Pateman and any number of feminist readers of Hobbes (although none of these three puts the point in these terms) the mother in the state of nature must be no less the "arrant wolf" that Hobbes says man is to man. Hobbes does not specifically name woman in the state of nature as a beast, but he introduces no factor that would set her apart from the arrant wolves. In fact, he describes the mother as having "*Dominion*, i.e. *sovereign* power" over the infant in the state of nature (thus "every woman who gives birth becomes both a mother and a Mistress [*domina*]", (Hobbes 1998: 108). Hobbes comments.

> by *right of nature* the victor is *Master* of the conquered; therefore by *right of nature*, Dominion over an *infant* belongs first to the one who first has him in their power (*potestas*). But it is obvious that a *new-born child* is in the power of his *mother* before anyone else, so that she can raise him or expose him at her own discretion and by her own right.
>
> (Hobbes 1998: 108)

And woman may have been considered physically weaker but we are told in *Leviathan* that in the state of nature the weakest has strength [or cunning] enough to kill the strongest. Hobbes is quite clear that in a state of nature the war of all against all through which the life of each is exposed to others take place just as much between men and women: "There is not always that difference of strength, or prudence between the man and the woman, as that the right can be determined without War" (*Leviathan,* XX, 139). There will be sexual encounters between men and women in the state of nature, but there is nothing of the emerging gentle sentiments, or the pulls of pity described by Rousseau for the resulting mothers of the Hobbesian state of nature.

Discussing images in Hobbes of men as beasts and wolves in the state of nature, and the viciousness attributed to the original Hobbesian condition by Rousseau, Derrida does mention that in the state of nature (though not in civil society) "it is the mother, the only certain *generatrix*, who controls the child" (BS1: 29). This is *almost* to remind us that in this context women too must be classed among the Hobbesian wolves (with Derrida earlier proposing, not in this context, that we should not forget the figure of the she-wolf (BS1: 9). Derrida also reminds us that it is a different story in Hobbesian civil society, commenting, "when one leaves the state of nature through the civil contract, it is the father who, in a 'civil government,' has at his disposal authority and power" (BS1: 29) – over children, women, animals, what is figured as his household.

If humans leave the state of nature by establishing commonwealths specifically out of the aim of self preservation, we have also seen a reference to a threat to life posed to children by women in the state of nature. For one thing, no less than men they pose just as much a threat to adult life as any adult. But we also learn of the threat – not problematised in the same way by Hobbes – that they seemingly pose to the lives of their children. Newborns are described as under women's authority to be abandoned to death at their discretion. If we ask at whose hands we are at the mercy in the state of nature, it is certainly a case of all against all. But the view, mentioned in passing, is that the mothers may also abandon the children.

We know the Hobbesian sovereign offers, as Italian philosopher Roberto Esposito would put it, immunity against the risk to adult life feared by all (2012). But what happens to the original sovereignty of women over their children in the state of nature? Does the Hobbesian sovereign also offer immunity against these natural sovereigns, these women, even against the stated likelihood that they might well abandon their children? No answer of this kind is given by Hobbes, in part because this sovereignty is not problematised – to the contrary. But if we try to speculate how one might answer the question unasked, we could return to the oddity noted by Carole Pateman (1991) and seemingly by Derrida in his discussion of Hobbes in *Beast and Sovereign*. Men forming the civil contract are already contracting as fathers of families with their dominion somehow already in place over the mothers. In consequence, we are never offered an image of women, wives or mothers finding it rational to accord authority to a sovereign in favour of the life less nasty brutish and short. The women, as represented, make no such calculations. To the contrary, the civil contract seems to have retrospectively converted them into different kinds of beings who never will have had power to transfer. There is no moment in Hobbes's account of the state of nature where such a conversion is said to occur, no description of such a transfer of power. But from the point that commonwealths are described as established by "Fathers, not the mothers of the family," the women will have become those beings analogous to animals and servants insofar as they are under the authority of men. This, though it is not discussed as such, could even be seen as another function of the immunity conferred by the commonwealth: the capacity to make women into what will have been (in this different sense) analogous to the beast. So women will have been at least two kinds of animals in the state of nature. They will have been wolf-like, like men, to men (and presumably to other women). They will have been wolf-like to their children also. If so, it is because they have sovereign power over their children, with the capacity to exercise a wolf-like threat to life. Within the commonwealth established by fathers, they have become entities somehow already dispossessed of equality and authority over children. In the state of nature women are specifically not subordinate like the beasts, but they will have become so. This could even be called, to add to Roberto Esposito's reading of Hobbes, a double immunity. The Hobbesian contract offers immunity against the threat posed by all against all, but it also offers a supplemental immunity: some of those who had posed a threat become figures who could not have posed such a threat. They will become figures whose death threat has been cancelled not by reallocating what is described as their authority, right and power; rather, they are seemingly erased as figures who never could have had a power to re-allocate. At least, that is one way one could think of an immunisation against women's wolf-like lordship in the state of nature through this strange hollowing out mechanism. Given that "Hobbes posits the right of man over the beasts" (BS1: 29, citing Bobbes 1998: 105), women will have become in this quite different sense like the beasts: under the dominion of men. They are converted from one kind of beast, to those who will have been another kind of beast.

I have, of course, widened out this problem. Despite Derrida's reiterated interest in the sexual difference marked in the relation beast-sovereign and his references to the status of women in and out of the state of nature, he does not linger with this intriguing figure: the mother represented as possessing a sovereign power to expose her child.

II. The *Voyoute*

Derrida briefly mentions sexual difference in *Rogues* in the context of the difficulty he is describing of distinguishing between the good and the ills of democracy. Both liberty and dangerous license are simultaneously delivered in "the passage to democracy": for "*democratization* will have always been associated with license, with taking too many liberties, with the dissoluteness of the libertine, with liberalism, indeed perversion and delinquency, with malfeasance, with failing to live according to the law, with the notion that 'everything is allowed', that 'anything goes'" (R: 20–21). And so democracy's autoimmunity intertwines with its sexual divisions: "following in this vein of sexual difference, this long vein that runs, at least virtually, throughout the whole history of democracy and its concept, we would have to find the time to ask why *voyous*, if not *roués*, are almost always men" [R: 20].

The *voyoute*, conceived according to this reading, could be a more significant figure than Derrida allows. By the end of the nineteenth century and after WWI, he reminds us, a *voyoute* was a woman who dared "to declare herself just as free and master of her own life as a man ... a liberated woman ... who would do as she pleased with her body and her language ... man enough to give herself the air of a liberated feminist" (R: 67). Certainly the *voyoute* is considered a figure threatening to the orders of differentiated masculinity and femininity, legal mastery and legal subordination, and perhaps she prompts again that question asked by Derrida intermittently throughout *Politics of Friendship*: what happens when the sister is made a case of the brother (PF: viii)?

So if we ask the question – and what if the woman were a *voyoute?* – she would represent the point that Derrida makes about democracy: that it has always been difficult to distinguish the goods and ills of democracy. But she may also represent a question that circulated intermittently throughout Derrida's work when he speculated about the risks of feminism, and challenges made by the sisters to the brother's place. He claimed that feminism risked reproducing what it had meant to critique or transform. I return here to Mary Wollstonecraft, who certainly hoped to make the sister a case of the brother, who feared the risks of sexual license, who thought the former would give immunity against the latter, and in whose work, the great figure, representing all these possibilities was women's becoming animal-like.

Though she was not specific, about the civil, political rights, or the political participation she thought women ought to enjoy, Wollstonecraft, writing the *Vindication of the Rights of Woman* in 1792, decried the fact that women were "groping in the dark," "immured in their families," because they were "den[ied] civil and political rights" (Wollstonecraft 1995: 69), she claimed that they ought to have some direct form of political representation and some "direct share allowed them in the deliberations of government" (Wollstonecraft 1995: 237), and she decried the exclusion in 1789 of French women from the status of the active citizen. But the strongest claim she made in detail in *Vindication* was for the right to education, considered critical to women's emancipation. The cultivation and exercise and development of women's rational capacities and moral sense would elevate them definitively above the beast. In their current state Wollstonecraft claimed that a woman was "scarcely raised by her employments above the animal kingdom" (Wollstonecraft 1995: 102). She used an extensive animal metaphorics to make the point.

Metaphorically, she referred to women as patient drudges, analogised their work to that of workhorses, but also referred to women as like caged birds or pet dogs. Too long in such environments, and women come to be comfortable in their "chains," fit for nothing better (Wollstonecraft 1995: 161–62) So whether women were being treated as beasts of burden or as pets in cages, either way they were rendered in these two senses like brutes. But there was also a quite different sense in which they were said to be like brutes.

Lacking the environment that would allow them to cultivate benevolence and learn the bases for principled behaviour, women are said to be led by the senses, to be partial and unprincipled in their affections, so that even their affections are neglectful, damaging or vicious. This could lead to a number of different results, among them that women were putting their children at risk:

> The want of natural affection, in many women, who are drawn from their duty by the admiration of men, and the ignorance of others, render the infancy of man a ... perilous state.
> (Wollstonecraft 1995: 273)

In the absence of a foundation for principled behaviour women might neglect their children, or they might favour some at the expense of others, or they may be overly indulgent of their children. Not in a position to exercise good judgment, their affections could be partial and erratic, and often tinged with neglect and cruelty. It is not inevitable but it is possible for women to be selfish or insular in the forms of their devoted affection for their children. Not educated to be guided by principles, overall good, or a broad, collective or political perspective, they were equally as likely to neglect their children, or to show them a single minded, injudicious and equally harmful affection. This was also presented as a mode of the brute:

> The affection of some women for their children is, as I have before termed it, frequently very brutish; for it eradicates every spark of humanity. Justice, truth, every thing is sacrificed ... for the sake of their *own* children.
>
> (Wollstonecraft 1995: 243)

When women are rendered in these three senses brutes: workhorses, birds in cages, and unjust brutes, what then do men become? Let's recall that Wollstonecraft explains the subordination of women in terms of a history according to which "brutal force has hitherto governed the world" (Wollstonecraft 1995:108). Women's subordination is, in other words, a remnant of earlier days, figured as barbarous. Thus men revert to a putatively cruder earlier state of human development or, a law of the brutes, in other words they become brutes in rendering women poor brutes.

These images interconnect with a second analogical cluster. Women, especially *as* likened to animals, are connected by Wollstonecraft to a ubiquitous analogy in the history of women's rights. There are some eighty slavery metaphors in *Vindication* – they are as extensive as the animal metaphorics – with Wollstonecraft claiming, when these analogies are at their most literal, that women are brutalised like African slaves (Wollstonecraft 1995: 235). Meanwhile European men would concurrently be analogised, to slave owners; and, to return to the animal images, deemed all the more brutish, as such. This is a context in which all, brutal and brutalised, are considered sub-human.

Yet there is a more complicated version of each of these figures. Women ought not to be brought as low as animals, but in fact, so low are they brought that we will find animals are above them. When Wollstonecraft tells us that women become so unpredictable in their care for their children that they endanger their children, in fact what she claims is that the infancy of man is rendered "*a much more perilous state than that of brutes*"(Wollstonecraft 1995: 273, my italics). Similarly, women are said to be rendered as low as savages, but so low have humans become in contemporary society that we are told "savages" may show more benevolence, for example, to their animals, than do advanced Europeans (Wollstonecraft 1995: 268).

Similarly, women, like all humans ought to be above animals, but to give the point effect we are told that some women have become so immodest that animals may be superior to them: ("[French] women have treated as *prudish* that attention to decency, which brutes instinctively observe" (Wollstonecraft 1995: 67)).

I began with Derrida's suggestion of a possible serialisation – where the beast was "the living thing to be subjected, dominated, domesticated, mastered, like, by a not insignificant analogy, the woman, the slave, or the child," (BS1: 66). And I want now to place that comment in communication with another: Derrida also describes the phenomenon where "the supposed sovereign subject begins ... to look like the beast he is supposed to subject to himself ... we already know ... that in place of the beast one can put, in the same hierarchy, the slave, the woman, the child" (BS1: 33). These suggestions, both appearing in *Beast and the Sovereign*, are not the same. In fact they can be seen as troubling each other.

In this seminar, Derrida describes analogies between the beast and the sovereign: the literal beast may be figured as too wild, lacking reason, too low to recognise the law, and the sovereign may be set above the law – able to make the law, set it aside, set him or herself apart from it, higher, but in this respect both may be analogised to wolves (and the need for government might also be asserted because of the proneness of humans, deemed to have dominion over animals, to be vicious and wolf-like towards each other): "sharing this common being-outside-the law, beast, criminal, and sovereign have a troubling resemblance ... while seeming to be at each others' antipodes" (BS1: 17). So in a number of ways, beast and sovereign, high and low may be brought close and yet still opposed. Proposing that "analogy is always ... a calculus ... in which identity and difference coexist" (BS1: 14), Derrida suggests that the analogical play between beast and sovereign "now brings man close to the animal, inscribing them both in a relation of proportion, and now brings man and animal close in order to oppose them" (BS1: 14).

But Derrida has also proposed that sexual difference is embedded in the relation between the beast and the sovereign. He does not pursue this question far in *Beast and Sovereign*, and in that work he does not speculate on analogies between the woman and the sovereign. But we can add this question to the analogy he notes between the beast and sovereign: what happens when women begin to represent themselves as political animals, animals in relation to politics, animals below politics, animals who need education and politics? If the woman represents herself (to political ends, to the ends of claiming emancipation) as a becoming-animal, will we find that she also represents herself as a becoming-sovereign (or perhaps we will find that sovereign as a kind of becoming-woman)? In other words, we might ask, if analogy is always a calculus, what is the calculus in this case?

In Wollstonecraft's *Vindication*, I have suggested that there is a reiterated form, with respect to this analogical work, where we find that that which ought to be lower (the animal-like) is raised above the human, when the humans become like animals. I now return to the humans who become brutish by being trodden underfoot: the concurrent point is that cruelty is brutish, and one becomes brutish by being treated like brutes. Wollstonecraft connects the cruelty of young boys who mistreat animals, with the mistreatment by men of women, describing this as a "transition ... from barbarity to brutes to domestic tyranny" (Wollstonecraft 1995: 268).

But Wollstonecraft extends her argument that there are chain reactions of cruelty which lead to phenomena of subordination, literal violence and tyranny against women. She depicts women as becoming like tyrants in an exercise of dangerous and unregulated force, redoubling the representation of women. Although women are treated like brutes, deprived of an education, upbringing and environment that would cultivate human benevolence, morality, reason and justice, the women analogised to the harmless brutes who should appeal to benevolence can also *be* the brutes, and not only in the senses we have seen earlier. For, as we have seen, women's concern for weaker or subordinate beings is partial, unpredictable, unjust, and often cruel. Here, Wollstonecraft's images concern women of means, mistreating their own servants and horses, all the while that they decry the mistreatment of animals and manifest sentimental attachment to small birds (Wollstonecraft 1995: 269), or women who may have considerably more sentimental attachment to their pet dogs than their own children:

> she who takes her dogs to bed, and nurses them with a parade of sensibility, when sick, will suffer her babes to grow up crooked in a nursery ... and I own that I have been as much disgusted by the fine lady who took her lap-dog to her bosom, instead of her child; as by the ferocity of a man ... beating his horse.
>
> (Wollstonecraft 1995: 269)

The suggestion that women have become no better than the brutes, in the way in which they treat weaker creatures including the brutes, connects to the intermittent suggestion of a perverse result: what should be "lower" is in some respects higher. The brute might have more instinctive prudishness than the immodest French women. Women may well neglect their infants dangerously, rendering them in their capacity, in this respect, beneath the (unspecified) brutes. Thus cruelty is said to be savage, savages are said to treat women badly; men remain in both these senses barbaric; women are like animals in being so treated; subjugated women are both like slaves and like animals; and men are not only like savages but also like brutish animals in treating women like animals; women are like savages in their vanity. Yet the level of benevolence towards weak creatures seen in savages may well be superior to the level of that quality in civilized Europeans including women.

How might we best understand what I am proposing is a fairly complex web of analogical reasoning in this case made for women's rights? To return to the suggestion from *Beast and Sovereign* that analogy is always a calculus, I am asking, what sort of calculus is this, what is calculated?

It can be described as an "analogical aspirational subordination:" in other words, when women are analogised with those who are depicted as objects of mistreatment – animals and slaves in these cases – the analogy is deployed to feminist purposes but no less is a sly embedded subordination still operative. Wollstonecraft might argue that animals merit the benevolence whose cultivation is vital to the human future, but because her view is that animals are, in the order of creation, well below humans, she depicts an anomaly when humans do fall to, or below, brutishness, either in the cruelty with which they treat others, or in the cruelty with which they are treated. And staunchly anti-slavery as she is, she still retains a reference to the slave as that abject being with which women ought not be brought into proximity.

In other words, the analogy between humans (in this case, differently, women and men) and brutes does not bring them into proximity, and it does not level out humans and animals. To the contrary, it reinstalls the hierarchy of human over animal as it indicates just how low the author wishes us to understand that humans have fallen.

In Wollstonecraft's case, however, the animal, primitive and savage can work doubly. These have served as markers of that low level of proximity *to which* European humans can descend, to their supposed shame. But in Wollstonecraft's case, the animal, primitive and savage can be raised *above* the human serving not only as the marker below which humans can sink but also as the higher level to which they ought to aspire – in the one case the animal or savage would be benchmark of what the human can descend to, but in the other case a marker of what the human ought to attain. The savage will be both importantly better than, and the bottoming mark of, the dangerous regression or lack of perfectibility of an uncultivated humanity below the human. These are cases where, to return to one suggestion made at the outset, the analogy concurrently brings the parties into proximity and holds them at distance from each other, concurrently.

Whether it is Olaudah Equiano describing the evils of slavery through his account of how slaves are treated as animals (Equiano 2003: 60, 105, 109, 111, 232), or feminists from Wollstonecraft to Mill and Taylor arguing that women are treated as slaves, analogy has been a powerful means of staking rights claims. So, this gives me a first reason to question the suggestion that we should think of the beast as "the living thing to be subjected, dominated, domesticated, mastered, like the woman, the slave, or the child." The suggestion occludes the more specific form of this concurrent raising low and high. Each of the debased terms in the series is maintained as different and same. True, any analogy combines similarity and difference. But here, likeness indicates the aberrant: as when women claim they are like animals – but should not be. Not likeness, but hinges of aspirational analogical subordination capture better the revolving, concurrently high and low, subordinated and subordinating relationships in these series. When the claim that women are like animals or savages serves the interests of the argument that women should *not* be as low as savages, brutes and slaves, they are lowered to them, and the latter raised above; but women are also, concurrently, and aspirationally, held high above the same savages, brutes and slaves.

As we saw, in *The Beast and the Sovereign* Derrida discusses textual contexts in which "the supposed sovereign subject begins ... to look like the beast he is supposed to subject to himself [and he continues] we already know ... that in place of the beast one can put, in the same hierarchy, the slave, the woman, the child." My suggestion has been that, as figures of subjection, beast, slave, the woman, and the child, ought to present less as a substitutable series for the very reason Derrida is indicating. For Derrida is already describing the concurrently high and low. If beast, slave, woman, child are going to be in proximity, or substitutable in *this* particular regard (in their very capacity to be concurrently high and low) that gives a very different status to their proximity with each other. For when these terms can be themselves or their opposites, (to repeat Derrida's formula: the beast and the sovereign/ the beast *is* the sovereign ("*la bête et le souverain*", "*la bête est le souverain*"), BS1:18); our understanding of what could be substitutable for the beast as analogical other must change. Woman, slave, savage and animal will be concurrently subordinating of and subordinated by each other, concurrently.

I have mentioned Derrida's interest in the sovereign and brute coming to resemble each other. We have seen Wollstonecraft's argument that women are treated as brutes, which stimulates them to treat others as brutes – weak and inferior creatures such as children, animals, and servants. Similarly, she argues, children are exposed, but children also expose the brutes; they brutalise the brutes, and the "poor scare-crow of an usher," servants, the poor, those in a position of subordination. As we think of the analogical series we need to focus on the relations of subordination embedded within it. Some of these subordinated figures are also subordinating each other.

III. Women's becoming animal

To return to the themes explored by Derrida in *Beast and Sovereign*, and to the conversation such themes might broach with Mary Wollstonecraft, how might the beast and the sovereign be haunted by sexual difference in *Vindication*?

One could conclude there is no sexual difference in *Vindication of Rights of Woman*. Rather we encounter the travails of becoming animal-like. The only depiction of femininity we are offered is presented as a defective and aberrant version of the human. Moreover, it is consistently – if variably – associated with a range of forms of animality. In fact, Wollstonecraft problematises not just women's becoming feminine, but also men's becoming feminine, so we are offered very hostile accounts of men described as effeminate and vain. There is, arguably, no room for anything Wollstonecraft herself identifies as femininity in an account of a human she favours. This does not mean she defended an ideal of women becoming masculine. Rather she promotes a range of qualities – such as modesty, benevolence, and civic virtue. They are valued as sex neutral, praised where they appear in men, lamented where they don't appear in women.

But a curious form of sovereignty is going to be attributed specifically to feminine women, making their scene before men – it relates to the empire or sovereignty of sex. This form of the woman's becoming sovereign (becoming hyper feminine) is also presented as a kind of becoming animal, this time as less than human in the sense of not worthy of the human, as when she comments:

> How grossly do they insult us, who thus advise us only to render ourselves gentle, domestic brutes. For instance, the winning softness, so warmly, and frequently recommended, that governs by obeying. What childish expressions, and how insignificant is the being – ... who will condescend to govern by such sinister methods! "Certainly," says Lord Bacon, "man is of kin to the beasts by his body; and if he be not of kin to God by his spirit, he is a base and ignoble creature!"
>
> (Wollstonecraft 1995: 87–88)

While Wollstonecraft's elaborate analogical calculus may not occur in the same terms as Derrida's analysis, it prompts further thought about a question Derrida did in fact pose. How to understand some of the ways in which sexual difference can blur the relationship of the beast and the sovereign? And in thinking about the conditions of feminism, I have found it helpful to remember that "animal" is also a word (as is "slave," and "savage," and "primitive") that women have given themselves the right to give, and very elaborately, in the formulation of right's claims.

IV. Women and Sovereigns

Perhaps this might help us differently understand a curious phenomenon in the Wollstonecraft text – a further analogical work with which I will conclude. In Wollstonecraft's *Vindication*, it happens that women are also analogised with sovereigns in at least two ways. They are rather surprisingly analogised with monarchs (and by extension those holding aristocratic power), as are sovereigns with them. (Wollstonecraft writes this *Vindication* just three years after the French revolution, having just published, in 1790, *Vindication of the Rights of Men,* a rebuttal of Burke's *Reflections on the Revolution in France.*)

So, the substitutability to which I now turn is a curious one. Wollstonecraft is concurrently establishing the sovereigns, monarchs or more generally aristocrats, as animal-like, and of a particularly low kind, "swarms of summer insects that breed on putrefaction" (Wollstonecraft 1995: 226). In her account of the French revolution they are several times represented as ransacking cormorants, flocks of pigeons devouring [the] grain of the peasants, and as reptilian (*Origin and Progress of the French Revolution,* 1794). French aristocrats manifest:

> the habitual slothfulness of rusty intellects, or the depravity lulled ... on the laviscious couch of pleasure, man appears either an hideous monster, a devouring beast; or a spiritless reptile, without dignity or humanity.

At one point, they sink below also:

> vegetable tumours, which cannot exist without the sap of the plants they exhaust.
>
> (Wollstonecraft 1794: citing Abbé Sieyès)

Of course they are, at the same time, definitively subordinating figures, represented as "provided with food and raiment for which they neither toil nor spin" (Wollstonecraft 1995: 130) and to be sure, we have seen Wollstonecraft represent many hard-working women (analogised with horses and oxen), but as women come into analogical proximity with sovereigns, a different point in her mobile army of metaphors takes over. For Wollstonecraft does stress that there are women who profit from, and in particular act as tyrants through inherited advantages – beauty and the feminine arts. It is through these that they assume a sovereign role in the empire of sex. As we have seen, for Wollstonecraft nothing about the fact that women are without rights and subject to the tyranny of others means that women do not tyrannise others. She thought women in such circumstances were prone to tyrannise any available vulnerable candidates – children, animals. Women triumphed through sexual or sensual rule over men insofar as they could, lacking access to legitimate authority. And insofar as they may sometimes be able to exercise influence, women were described by Wollstonecraft as "like roman emperors, becoming depraved with power" (Wollstonecraft 1995: 130).

True, they are creatures of unreason, "exalted" she says in their inferiority", and she underlines and affirms this "contradiction," but she was willing to acknowledge that through a kind of sexual empire women might (stupid and inferior, *bête*, as they also were) find themselves exalted. She described monarchs, aristocrats and these kinds of women as ornamented, and likened them to heavily plumed birds, in fact in cages. Again, they are high and low, falsely praised, raised high, by society in and for their lowness, and achieving a limited reign of sexual tyranny. They are subordinated and yet they are tyrants.

This is an unjust sexual sovereignty not achieved through principle or reason, and the decadence, the failure to practice reason, the related ignorance, cruelty and stupidity, the arbitrary, unjust rule, is attributed by her to women and to sovereigns alike. Women are described as like other sovereigns in having a kind of power that is inherited (that is to say, it is not a power or authority earned or related to actual qualities, talents or capacities); they rule through the sovereignty of beauty. Other sovereigns rule by inherited, or seized unjustified power: women rule, insofar and where they do, by a kind of inherited or seized unjustified sexual power. Profiting from their hereditary honours, both of these kinds of sovereigns are incessantly flattered. This enfeebles them, and renders them incapable. Recall Derrida's proposal that we:

> unfold ... a double and contradictory figuration ... of political man as *on the one hand* superior, in his very sovereignty to the beast that he masters, enslaves, dominates, domesticates and kills, so that his sovereignty consists in raising himself above the animal and

appropriating it, having its life at his disposal, but *on the other hand*, (contradictorily) a figuration of the political man, and especially of the sovereign state as animality or even as bestiality. ... Political man as superior to *animality* and political man as animality.

(BS 1:26)

Could we add some interrogation of women's excluded status in relation to the political sphere, and in their claims to emancipation? For Derrida does mention in *Beast and Sovereign* the lurking role of sexual difference, in the copula and in the analogy: beast and sovereign (BS1: 32).

How has sexual difference marked some variants of the relations between the beast and the sovereign? One answer emerges by asking: what happens when women begin to represent themselves as animals in relation to politics, when they propose that the recognition of their rights will raise both men and women above what is claimed to be their own animality, when they aspire to be, as political, better than animals, and make these claims by asserting their likeness to animals?

Wollstonecraft appealed to the human pre-eminence over "brute creation" by virtue of Reason, virtue and knowledge, and she made promises with respect to what would ensue from women's emancipation: "Would men but generously snap our chains, and be content with rational fellowship instead of slavish obedience, they would find us more observant daughters, more affectionate sisters, more faithful wives, more reasonable mothers – in a word, better citizens" (Wollstonecraft 1995: 240). Yet was that a predictable outcome? For Wollstonecraft, suffrage, education and other rights (property rights, education, the means of earning income, worthwhile occupations) could give women (and the human race) a kind of immunity against the worst version of women and of humans, unobservant, unaffectionate, unfaithful, unreasonable, brutal, also subordinating, less than human. But she also suggested that a system of representation might well be (as she claimed of the system in contemporary England) "only a convenient handle for despotism" (Wollstonecraft 1995: 237). The capacity for political discourse, representation, property, income, education and activity could offer no guarantee that women would be good citizens, less beastly, and evidently it exposed women to the possibility they would be as bad as the men of Wollstonecraft's depiction. Moreover, though she would have offered a free or accessible education to all, Wollstonecraft did retain a commitment to class distinctions, embedding subordination in her vision of emancipation and so the likelihood of a continuity in the continuum of cruelty she described. The rights and education that could offer women a future whose contours Wollstonecraft thought could be reliably promised, also opened them to new poisons: think of how education, property, politics, political representation had functioned for men. One could ask: what if the conditions of Wollstonecraft's feminism also had the potential to undo its best hopes? She recognises this possibility when (in *Origin and Progress of the French Revolution*) she depicts politicised women in the French revolution becoming monstrous, violent beasts, their provisional liberty and political participation turned to unreasonable license.

I have used Wollstonecraft to develop further the suggestion raised but not developed by Derrida in *Beast and Sovereign* – and for which he may have needed different resources – not only that that (as he proposes) we not forget the she-wolves, but also that we think of the relations of sexual difference embedded in the relation between beast and sovereign. Developing this suggestion, I have used it to rethink the serialisation of the other that accompanies some of his references to women and women's rights. But I have also suggested a perspective Derrida could contribute to these rights claims. A deconstructive feminism could be characterised by its disposition to identify its own claims as auto-immune, and by the resources available for that analysis. Derrida affirmed that the political futures for which we hope could prove monstrous. He was particularly wary of the attempts to immunise those political futures in attempts to achieve a homogeneity and stability of political community. So the question we would bring to Wollstonecraft would concern the monstrous potential she did in fact acknowledge in the prospect of women joining the fraternity. The promise was that women would be raised above the beast. Yet Wollstonecraft appears to have acknowledged all the while that she disavowed that the future she articulated ran a high risk of reproducing the animality against which women's rights appeared to offer an immunity.

11 Democracy and Sovereignty

Alex Thomson

In his late work Derrida takes up key themes in political philosophy such as the nature of political authority, the relationship between politics, justice and law. However the style of his writing and thought in this period can make it hard to understand his project. In this essay I will use the example of Derrida's book *Rogues*, subtitled "Two Essays on Reason," to show the ways in which his analyses raise profound and troubling questions, but also function more directly as political interventions. Having looked first at the form of Derrida's thought, I will go on and consider the relationship between democracy and justice, before turning finally to the relationship between democracy and sovereignty, and finally at the idea of the promise. To understand the implications of both, we should keep in mind the links between them and the use throughout his work of this period of the phrase "democracy to come".

Democracy is a highly contested concept in both political theory and practice. Throughout most of its history the term has carried a pejorative meaning, but since the mid-nineteenth century it has come to acquire a central position in the modern political lexicon. As the political theorist John Dunn observes, the existence of "a single world-wide name for the legitimate basis of political authority" is "a startling fact" (Dunn 2005: 15). In *Rogues*, Derrida reminds us of this transformation. He lists a series of charges that have been levelled at democracy by philosophers over the centuries: it is unstable, anarchic, licentious, disordered. This can be traced in the history of philosophy. Because democracy presumes the basic equality of its citizens, it threatens to undo philosophy's promise to make distinctions based on excellence, and hence to identify the best regime. Because decisions are to be based on the counting of opinions, rather than the identification of truth, democracy will never live up to the philosophical ideal. This could lead philosophy to reject democracy – either by withdrawing from politics, or by seeking to overturn democracy in the name of truth, equating the power of reason with the power of authority. Derrida reminds us of some of this history, perhaps by way of a warning: "there are in the end rather few philosophical discourses, assuming there are any at all, in the long tradition that runs from Plato to Heidegger, that have without any reservations taken the side of democracy" (R: 41).

Yet in Derrida's thinking, the question of democracy has always been directly tied to that of philosophy. The term first acquires its distinctive emphasis in Derrida's work in a 1990 essay on the "right" to philosophy, a reflection on his various political campaigns to support the teaching of philosophy in French schools. There he notes in passing that "there is no democracy in general without [the right to philosophy]" and that conversely "democracy, the democracy that remains to come, is also a philosophical concept" (WP: 29). In principle, philosophy defines itself as the exercise of reason, the property of any person, hence presupposing both equality and universality. In practice, the concepts of democracy and philosophy that we inherit are both born together in ancient Athens. This brings us to the second problem alluded to above and developed in *Rogues*: the current worldwide hegemony of democracy as a name for legitimate politics. To affirm this dual inheritance is to give priority to "what is called the European tradition (at the same time the Greco-Christian and globalatinizing) that dominates the worldwide concept of the political" (R: 28). This is potentially a violent gesture. For Derrida this risk is justified however, because democracy is "the only name of a regime, or quasi-regime, open to its own historical transformation, to taking up its intrinsic plasticity and its interminable self-criticizability, one might even say its interminable analysis" (R: 25).

So the relationship between our concepts of democracy and philosophy is complex. Each implies the other, but each threatens the other. Moreover, each being universal in principle, and having spread across the globe in practice, both entail an apparent contradiction between their claim to do justice to the plurality of equal voices, and the fact that they can be construed as the dominance of one voice or tradition over others. Staking out this complex structure, Derrida locates himself within it: working within philosophy and affirming the ambiguity of its relationship to democracy, while reserving and affirming the right of philosophy to criticise democracy interminably. He acknowledges too that this is a political gesture, implicated in relations of force: hence inserting a question mark against the claim of either philosophy or democracy to be immune from the violence of political struggle.

This allows us to reach a preliminary understanding of the way in which Derrida sets about thinking about politics. In an interview given in 1989 he explains that his current seminar "is oriented towards a thinking of democracy. But a democracy for which the current concepts that serve to define democracy are insufficient. One might say that it's a deconstruction of what is always a *given concept of democracy*" (N: 178, Derrida's emphasis). So Derrida undertakes a questioning of the concepts we use to understand democracy, aiming to find or recover something against which we might measure not just the adequacy of our current democratic political systems, but the concepts by which we already criticise and understand democracy. This sounds very much like a form of critique in the sense first given to it by Immanuel Kant, and which still underpins the idea of a critical philosophy in general: an enquiry into the conditions of possibility of democracy, which allows us to define an ideal democracy towards which we might orient our own political activities. But we should bear in mind Derrida's warning in *Specters of Marx* that his thought takes the form of a *"radical* critique, namely a procedure ready to undertake its self-critique. This critique *wants itself* to be in principle and explicitly open to its own transformation, re-evaluation, self-reinterpretation" (SM: 88, Derrida's emphases). Radicalism means going back to the root (Latin: *radix*) and this means a return, not to destroy but to rebuild. As he states in the 1989 interview: "what interests me is to understand how the idea of democracy arose in the West and what can and should be conserved out of it" (N: 179). The openness to transformation of Derrida's hyper-critical thought means questioning the opposition of a democratic ideal to actual-existing democracy, while self-critique suspends the claim of the philosopher to have the answers to political questions, or to set a heading for society as a whole.

What Derrida's hyper-critical thinking about democracy uncovers is what he calls "democracy-to-come", the promise of a form of politics which exceeds existing democratic philosophy and practice. The phrasing signals a connection to the attention to time which runs throughout Derrida's work: that which is to come (*à-venir*) indicates the opening that characterises the form of time as such, so is not a specific future (*avenir*), or something that might arrive, but the open-endedness of history itself. At times Derrida links this experience of the promise to the idea of "messianism without messianism", signalling that his work may take the form of an act of attestation to or expression of democracy, but that this has to be distinguished from any certainty or even optimism that a particular improvement in our democracies is possible or likely. Throughout his work of the period his attempt to outline "democracy-to-come" is accompanied by a reckoning of the contemporary threats and opportunities for democracy, and the ways in which the contemporary transformation of political experience – for example through advanced communication technologies – is always the expression of this promissory structure: both the risk of less democracy, and the possibility of more. In *Rogues* he will go so far as to portray democracy as "suicidal," and in general Derrida's thinking intends to unsettle us. In one of his last major interviews, given immediately after the 9/11 attacks, Derrida links the future to the idea of trauma. Any event is traumatic because it involves scarring, changing, damaging the texture of history, the emergence of the new. This might suggest to us that in the phrase "democracy-to-come" we should hear not the security of a glorious democratic future guaranteed by the extension of global justice, but something more like the continued unfolding of a traumatic event of political struggle.

Turning to the earlier account of democracy in relation to the possibility of justice, Derrida begins by questioning the very concept of equality that underpins democracy. If the concept of equality is problematic, what does that mean for the political system defined in relation to it? In taking this as his starting point, Derrida can be seen to be developing themes from the thought of Emmanuel Levinas, who had challenged philosophical thinking in the name of ethics: our responsibility to others has a primary hold over us which challenges equality by demanding that we place the needs of others before our own; the equality of rational beings presupposed by philosophy would be radically inadequate to this experience of our ethical obligation. While seeking to avoid the establishment of a hierarchical priority of ethical experience over philosophy, Derrida insists throughout his work from the 1980s onwards, that the concept of responsibility presupposes something excessive: it must mean more than the mere completion of a finite set of duties, or it is nothing at all. But this excess in *practice* undermines the possibility of a rigorous analysis of responsibility in *theory*: moreover, in *practice*, the regulation of the social world by laws (whether customary, or legal) limits the infinity of my responsibility in ways which make it possible for me to live up to at least some of my responsibilities.

Crudely, we could take this as a description of the pre-given social and political world into which individuals are born. I am not equal to the demand of the other in both senses of the term: I cannot live up to so exigent an obligation, and to see myself as equal to others would already be an ethical failing. The situation in which we find ourselves is aporetic – a contradiction that we can experience but of which an exhaustive rational description is not possible. This aporia is an approximation to what Derrida calls justice: the unconditional and unfulfillable demand placed upon me by the fact of existing in a world of others, that is tempered by the existence of laws which place limits on what is expected of me, and grants me an equality with others that will always betray the dissymmetric call to treat others as more-than-equal to me. The significance of this problem for Derrida is such that in "Force of Law: The Mystical Foundations of Authority", he argues that "justice in itself, if such a thing exists, outside or beyond law, is not deconstructible. No more than deconstruction itself. Deconstruction is justice" (FL: 14–15). Readers of Derrida have not paid sufficient mind to this as an alternative entry point into his thinking of political philosophy: here the legitimacy of the law is established not on the basis of its justice, but in its forceful restriction of the demand of justice that makes possible anything like the existence of a social and political body.

In *Politics of Friendship*, a book based on his 1994 seminars, Derrida explores the question of the relationship between democracy and justice. Because it is the only political regime whose structure is directly tied to equality – as in the rule of all – democracy has a closer relationship to justice than the other two traditional regimes into which philosophy has divided political systems: aristocracy (the rule of the few) or monarchy (the rule of one). We can now see why democracy becomes for Derrida something more than one possible political regime amongst others, and something more like a name for politics itself. All three political forms restrict justice: by limiting political equality in the case of the latter two, and by limiting the political horizon to equality, in the case of democracy. Democracy may be closer to justice, but is still inadequate to it. The bulk of Derrida's project is to show how this structural condition – and limitation – of democracy surfaces throughout the tradition of political philosophy.

On the basis of detailed readings of writers from Aristotle to Nietzsche, he demonstrates that democracy has repeatedly been imagined or analysed in terms of the friendship between brothers. Derrida sees this as problematic on three grounds. First, friendship can imply the reciprocity of mutual relations, but my responsibility to others goes beyond exchange: the condition of love is its survival beyond the death of the beloved, hence it goes beyond any expectation of mutual or reciprocal benefit. Second, equality is universal but I can only have so many friends. Third, friendship can be elided into brotherhood, which substitutes a natural bond for a political bond, as if to show that the decision to restrict goods to those closer to me were not only inevitable, but pre-scribed by an external law. If we trace these out as an analysis of the state, we see a tension emerge. Democracy is the regime in which the constitutive conditions of political community are most openly brought to light, because both in practice and in theory democracy consists of a contradiction between the embrace of, and the restriction of, equality.

This understanding of democracy prescribes some of the practical political implications that Derrida develops in his writing. Although exorbitant, Derrida's insistence on justice should be considered realist rather than utopian. He is not asking us to do away with borders, but to recognise that no state can live up to the demands of justice. The institutions and practices, norms and laws of democracy both enable and limit the idea of equality: they can and must be criticised from the point of view of equality. He is regularly critical of and hostile towards nationalism and other forms of political identification that seek to justify or naturalise the restrictions implicit in democracy, while supporting struggles around immigration, and supporting cosmopolitan and international institutions. By heightening our awareness of this as a structural condition of democracy – that at the very basis of its logic is a conflict between the unconditional and the conditional – Derrida challenges our use of the term: we can never simply approve democracy, but nor can we dismiss it.

What distinguishes and privileges democracy in *Politics of Friendship* is that it connects to what Derrida calls *aimance*: the structural possibility of the friendship of anyone with anyone, and friendship as the dissymmetrical placing of the loved one before myself. We might see this as an idea of politics prior to any political or cultural identification. But just as in practice I can only have so many friends, this promise of democracy is only possible within certain limits; just as justice requires law, cities and states require borders and boundaries. This becomes axiomatic for Derrida: "there is no democracy without respect for irreducible singularity or alterity, but there is no democracy without the 'community of friends', without the calculation of majorities, without identifiable, stabilizable, representable subjects, all equal" (PF: 22). There would be no justice without political community, and the laws that guarantee equal rights to citizens. But a state is always *de jure* in breach of the demands of justice because it draws limits between citizens and non-citizens. This poses a significant challenge to our reliance on the idea of the state as the central source of political authority.

To think justice beyond the state must call the state into question. Derrida's questioning of equality goes even further however. Testing out the traditional Aristotelian definition of man as a political animal, and worrying away at the confidence with which we draw boundaries between human and animal, he asks in *Rogues*: "does this measure of the immeasurable, this democratic equality, end at citizenship, and thus at the borders of the nation-state? Or must we extend it to the whole world of singularities, to the whole world of humans assumed to be like me, my compeers [*mes semblables*]—or else, even further, to all nonhuman living beings, or again, even beyond that, to all the nonliving" (R: 53)? The radical demand of this question can be shown to be consistent with the extrapolation of insights from his earliest work. In *Of Grammatology*, he had argued that "[a]uto-affection is the condition of an experience in general. This possibility—another name for "life"—is a general structure articulated by the history of life" (OG: 165). Moreover, "[a]uto-affection constitutes the same (*auto*) as it divides the same" (OG: 166). In the language of his later work, the constitution of any identity must be characterised by an autoimmune tendency, by the violent denial of that on which it depends, by a forceful differentiation from its environment which can only be partial, provisional and fragile, and which can turn into the suicidal destruction of the self. The extension of this analysis in the political sphere carries the questioning of democracy and sovereignty beyond the political, narrowly considered, as the self-identity of any such field is recognised to be questionable, and poses challenges which we do not yet have the means to think: what is politics, what would politics be, once the border between human and animal comes under pressure, or that between the living and the dead? (Sure enough, *Specters of Marx* begins by reminding us that justice calls us to a responsibility "before the ghosts of those who are not yet born or who are already dead" (SM: xix).) So the problem of "the life or the living present of living in general" (R: 53) runs from the beginning to the end of Derrida's career, from *Of Grammatology* to *Rogues*, challenging us to think about the limits of politics.

Whereas his earlier work on democracy had linked it to justice, and tended to emphasise the promise implicit in the identification of justice with "democracy-to-come", in the last years of his life, Derrida begins to connect democracy to the problem of sovereignty. This might be seen as a further questioning of the limits of politics, pitting the unconditional sovereignty traditionally ascribed by philosophy to the power of reason against the equally unconditional sovereignty enshrined in the idea of the state. Sovereignty is the traditional name given by philosophy to the ultimate source of authority in a state, hence the basis for all compulsion to obey. Sovereignty is an exceptional force that has the power to make the law, and so is not subject to it. Philosophy has tended to insist that sovereignty be one and indivisible: hence removed from the messy sphere of democratic debate and deliberation. As Derrida shows in his seminar on *The Beast and the Sovereign*, and in *Rogues*, this is to understand sovereignty as bare, naked power, something more than human – beyond the law – but also savage, less than human – before the law. In a democratic system "sovereignty" is seen as the binding power of the law arrived at by democratic process over its members – the mutual subjection of each individual to the will of all. Because this appears to undercut our sense that democracy frees us in relation to our fellows, to approach democracy through sovereignty gives Derrida's discussion a darker tone than it has had before, and may indicate a response to external events. Just as his call to continue to think democracy critically comes in the wake of the fall of the Berlin Wall and the triumphalist claim by some democrats that the end of communism in Europe and Russia represented a vindication of democracy in its current form, he connects his discussion of sovereignty directly to the reshaping of world politics in the wake of the 9/11 attacks on the USA.

Derrida is forced back onto the terrain of the political because he fears that the critique of law (on the basis that its use of force is illegitimate) may result in a one-sided critique of law itself and of authority in general; he seeks to affirm the necessity and dignity of politics as the regulation of competing forces, *and* of philosophy as a space for critical reflection on politics, the latter requiring as its complement a challenge to the authority of philosophy itself. This entails a partial change of emphasis in relation to the account of democracy in *Politics of Friendship*, in underscoring the *a priori* violence constitutive of political and social order, and hence of our experience of democracy, but not a change of position. Taking up the definition of democracy in terms of the sovereignty of the people – not the equality of all, but the rule of all – Derrida stresses the permanence of power and of the force required to maintain it, underscoring tensions within democracy such as that between liberty and equality, and between the calculation required to reach a majority decision and the need to protect minorities from the tyranny of majority. Rather than hearing the *demos* in democracy, the equality of all with all, now Derrida asks us to hear the word *kratos*, rule. Within law, force cohabits with the promise of justice. The (political) attempt to distinguish "good" states from "bad" states will obscure the permanent disjunction between politics and justice: "there are thus no longer anything but rogue states, and there are no longer any rogue states" (R: 106). This is because "there is something of a rogue state in every state. The use of state power is *originally* excessive and abusive" (R: 156).

Derrida's late work on sovereignty remains obscure, but light can be shed on it by returning to the link he sees between democracy and philosophy. Because "sovereignty is first of all one of the traits by which reason defines its own power and element, that is a certain unconditionality" (R: 153), reason offers a basis from which to criticise political violence – and as we have seen, even politics *as* violence in the name of the idea of justice as unconditional (if unimaginable) peace. This allows for a revision of the philosophical challenge to the *autonomy* of democracy: not on the grounds that philosophy can offer a "truth" unavailable to public reason, but in terms of the right of reason to question politics in the name of unconditional justice. If it is the *ipseity*, the very identification, of the state that is troubling, if its sovereignty depends on its completion or self-enclosure, then sovereignty is always challenged and crossed, conditioned, by reason. This figure makes more sense described in terms of distinguishable (if not rigorously distinct) spheres, and hence separate forms of sovereignty. Philosophy reserves the right to limit politics; but politics has the right to override reason with force. Limiting each other, the sovereignty of neither can be completely assured, and so the sovereignty of both is breached or compromised.

So although he disputes the self-enclosure and autonomy attributed to sovereignty – "pure sovereignty does not exist; it is always in the process of positing itself by refuting itself, by denying or disavowing itself" (R: 101) – Derrida has to defend sovereignty in order to safeguard the inheritance of both philosophy and democracy: "one cannot combat, *head-on, all* sovereignty, sovereignty *in general*, without threatening at the same time, beyond the nation-state figure of sovereignty, the classical principles of freedom and self-determination" (R: 158, Derrida's emphasis). This double bind gives his reflections on democracy and sovereignty their characteristic knotty texture. It also leads to a further circular recoil. Thinking this division of the idea of sovereignty against the tradition, Derrida also finds himself reasserting his own philosophical lineage. In *Rogues* he underlines once again that he sees his work "an unconditional rationalism that never renounces—and precisely in the name of the Enlightenment to come, in the space to be opened up of a democracy to come—the possibility of suspending all conditions" (R: 142). Moreover, the wolves who figure bestial sovereignty throughout Derrida's final works remind us that political philosophy itself was born as a response to the question posed to Socrates by Thrasymachus, his "wolfish" interlocutor in Plato's *Republic*, who challenges him to prove that justice can mean more than the right of the strongest (336d) (c.f. R: 92).

12 On Time, and Temporisation;
On temporalisation and history

Joanna Hodge

1. Mode of analysis/modes of givenness

Derrida's analyses and enquiries always take place inscribed within and between the texts of his predecessors, and interlocutors. It is thus exceptionally difficult to determine where his thinking begins and ends, and where the thought of the other arrives. This holds with especial force in the domain of a thinking about time, where an inarticulable time of the unconscious, a time before the genesis of conscious life, is a precondition for, and repressed component of conscious thought. Derrida thus sets up one kind of text as the placeholder for the unrecognised and unrecognisable conditions of possibility for another kind of text whereby a temporality, which cannot be acknowledged in the one, is articulated in the other. This procedure is especially in evidence in *Of Grammatology* (1967) and in *The Post Card: from Socrates to Freud and beyond* (1980), for which time and its temporisation are key concerns. The connection between time, and its temporisation, in modes of givenness, conscious and unconscious, is very much a theme for phenomenological enquiry, one which Derrida puts in question by indicating that in advance of any thesis, there must already be available a system, or systems, of formulation and presentation, of inscription, and transmission, providing a prosthetic enablement, in which to register and communicate any such thesis about time, and its temporisation. This notion of an originary prosthesis comes to the fore in Derrida's biographical text, *The Monolingualism of the Other: Of the Original Prosthesis* (1997), but is detected by Bernard Stiegler, in his extended study *Technics and Time* (2001) as at work already in *Of Grammatology* (1967).

Temporalisation and history, by contrast, arrive in the modes of publicly given time, and of collective experience, to which institutions and nations bear witness. This is a time of community and inter-subjectivity, with the possibility of conflicting accounts and structures, of an originary *polemos* concerning time and being. Here already an originary prosthesis comes into contact with an originary *polemos*, and both are held in place, or suspended, between meaning and meaninglessness by the question concerning the meaning of time. Derrida's discussions of time and of history are thus held in place by the play between these various forces, as complicated by Martin Heidegger's intervention concerning being and time. In *Being and Time* (1927) Heidegger describes how a failure to provide an adequate analysis of time leads to a forgetting of the question concerning the meaning of being, from which philosophy begins. As a result, metaphysics takes its fixed form, attempting to provide an atemporal and omnitemporal specification of what there is: being, as the mode of givenness of what there is, gets covered over again. By doubling the questioning of time by a questioning of its mode of givenness (temporisation), and by doubling this question about temporisation by questioning temporalisations (the modes of givenness of history, which include all the forms of writing and inscription, archaeology and decryption), it is possible to open up a form of enquiry in which this forgetting can be thematised, without eroding its status as forgetting, opening it up for discussion and analysis. This Derrida achieves by respecting an autonomy for literary, for psychoanalytical and for political economic descriptions alongside the supposedly master discourses of the philosophers, or encyclopaedists. Derrida can thus read Kant and Hegel, Husserl and Heidegger, Freud and Levinas alongside each other, without reducing the terms of the one to the terms of the other. These are the strategies adopted to provide modes of analysis which can respect a many layered structure of time, with alternating and conflicting modes of grasping what time is, rather than imposing a single systematic structure.

Temporalisation provides motivations for the framing of histories, and their participants, as falling into certain phases; history frames the passage of time by marking up certain events and processes for attention. Thus, attention to temporalisation and to history draws attention to ways of breaking up the otherwise even flow of a passage of time into certain phases or epochs; palaeolithic and neolithic, Greek and Roman, Christian and Moslem. The obviously political register of the latter recedes in the attention to the detail of conscious processes in the former; by implication, the play of forces (which make some voices more powerful than others) is relegated to the margin. Derrida underlines the manner in which a certain history of philosophy covers over its own political heritage, in a disavowal of political heritage. The prosthetic moment of enablement privileges the transmissions of one set of texts and enquiries, in one set of languages, under the apparently neutral description, the love of wisdom. He also points out how this history and transmission has repeatedly been rescued from immobilisation and irrelevance, by opening itself up to the disruptive forces once excluded from it. He reads the possibility of his own inclusion within that history and transmission as evidence both for the possibility of such opening, and of the strength of the forces that continually seek to resist such opening. This is the context for his reflections on time and history, and on the distinct play of forces in temporisation: the arrivals, delays, and de-synchronisations of time, and in temporalisation, the assigning of meaning to time, in the construction of historical frameworks. The phenomenology of Edmund Husserl can be seen to attend more to the constitution of time through the processes of temporisation; that of Hegel to the constitution of history through the attending and giving meaning to the processes of framing temporalisations.

2. Twentieth-Century Context

Derrida attends to a series of responses to the presentations, and representations of time provided by Hegel and by Kant, and to thematisations of time offered in phenomenology, starting with the close study of genesis in Husserl's phenomenology. For some versions of these, those not informed by a transcendental turn, there is a privilege granted to the immediate contents of consciousness, and a presumption that at some level all such consciousness is alike. The challenge posed to this last presumption, under the various titles of otherness, alterity and post-coloniality reveals the hidden political stakes of the Derridean discussion of time. These two modes of registering time, as presentation and as representation are explored by Kant and by Hegel, and the history of twentieth-century philosophy may be inscribed in the gap which opens up between them, into which the Husserlian notion of the *epoche* (bracketing taken-for-granted evidences), the Heideggerian *Ereignis* (the turning in which determinate order and meaning arrives), the Levinasian trace and Derridean *differance* arrive to complicate any sense that there is some choice to be made here. Neither the monumentalising of a definitive *Darstellung* (of presentation), nor the serial self-modifications of corrigible *Vorstellung* (or representation), can do justice to the workings of time, nor yet to the manner in which the entire framework within which time is conceived rotates in the course of the twentieth century, from a renunciation of any special status for the Christian inheritance in thinking about time at the beginning of the century, to a recognition in the last years of the century that there is an inheritance here to be discussed. This provides the backdrop for Derrida's discussions with

Jean-Luc Marion on the gift, and with Jean-Luc Nancy on touching, and makes possible an opening up to a non-European, non-Christian, non-metaphysical exteriority. It is this movement of opening to which Derrida attends in his patient readings of the texts of the tradition.

3. Early Moves

There are three key early texts which provide an orientation for Derrida's discussions of time, temporisation, temporalisation and history: the lectures *"Différance"*, and "The Ends of Man", delivered in January and April, 1968, respectively, and the long essay *"Ousia* and *gramme*: Note on a Note in *Being and Time"*, also first appearing in 1968, all of which are subsequently published in *Margins of Philosophy*, the collection of essays and lectures from 1972, which arrived in English in 1982. The essay, *"Ousia* and *gramme"* is especially noteworthy since it inserts, into a footnote in Heidegger's *Being and Time,* a discussion of Heidegger's attempt to frame an entire history of thinking, into the passage between Aristotle and Hegel. *"Ousia"*, meaning unchanging properties, and *gramme*, the letter of *Of Grammatology* (1967) are juxtaposed by Derrida to suggest that while thinking may seek to reiterate the one true thinking of substance, as *ousia*, arriving in a "now" of comprehension and formulation, the *gramme* (point, line, trace, or letter) of its formulation or presentation introduces an irresistible slippage of meaning, marking up a passage of time. The essay thus draws attention to the paradox, or aporia, of presupposing a privilege to this "now" time of time, in order to provide a non-restricted account of time. From a possible thinking of time as the source of meaning, time is reduced first to a ready-to-hand resource, and then to a present-at-hand marker of position. While discussions of the contrasting analyses of time and of history provided by G.W.F. Hegel (1770–1831) and of Martin Heidegger (1889–1976) are of course pivotal here, the trajectory of Derrida's thinking makes sense only if set into the wider frame of the subsequent discussions of memory and mourning, of the pre-discursive "thing" and "real" of psychoanalytical observation, and in relation to the writings of Maurice Blanchot, and Paul de Man. Derrida develops analyses of the disputed givenness of time, death, and meaning, in the trio of texts, *Donner le temps (Given Time: 1: Counterfeit Money)* (1990), *Donner la mort (The Gift of Death)* (1991, 1999) and *Aporias: Dying-awaiting (one another at) the limits of truth* (1993); and he invokes the anticipatory structure of the *a-venir*, as early as the essay: "Of an apocalyptic tone recently adopted in philosophy", a title citing a remark of Immanuel Kant (1724–1804). This last was delivered by Derrida at the conference concerning his work, under the title "*Les fins de l'homme*", at Cerisy la Salle, France, in 1980.

These discussions of time and temporisation, temporalisation and history also need to be placed back into the ongoing encounter with Husserl's phenomenology, starting in 1954, which Derrida states in his thesis defence, "Time of the Thesis; Punctuations" (1980), had never ceased to be important for him. This encounter returns to inform his response to Jean-Luc Nancy in *On Touching: Jean Luc Nancy* (2000), as it does his discussions with Jean-Luc Marion, of the donation and the gift of time/death and with Bernard Stiegler, concerning technicity, as originary prosthesis. The implication that every thesis, or *noesis* (as lived experience or mental content), grounding themes and meanings, is preceded by an implied and unexamined prosthesis, or pre-predicative impression is plain. In the background there is also an important dispute concerning the status of Marx's writings, as political analysis, and of Marxism, as an account of history. Derrida adopts a certain distance to Marx and the various available versions of "Actually Existing Socialism" and of Communism available before the fall of the Berlin Wall, and the dissolution of Soviet Russian, adopting a more direct engagement after 1989, notably in *Specters of Marx: The State of the Debt, the Work of Mourning and the New International* (1993). There Derrida analyses the claim that Marxism has not yet happened, with a circulation of debt and exchange to be displaced in favour of an analysis of an undischarged work of mourning, anticipating a new dawn, in the New Internationalism of the title. The key here is to situate Derrida's interventions in a conjuncture of this thinking of time, of mourning and memory, in the unconscious, or pre-conscious modes of registration, as pursued by Freud, Husserl, and indeed Levinas, with disputes concerning the status of a concept of history, which arrives more emphatically in the context of the writings of de Man, Blanchot and Jean-Luc Nancy.

There are three distinct logics through which the discussion of time is pursued by Derrida: a logic of beginnings and ends; a logic of the gift; and their impossible conjugation in a logic of that which happens, the "*a-venir*", of a messianic time without messianism. This articulates an inherited disjunction between a thinking of time, as pure moment, and a thinking of history, as pure event. The cumulative effect of Derrida's encounters with these various other thinkers, of his writings and of his enquiries more generally, is to reveal that what happens is the impossible future reconciliation of the contrary forces of a breaking open of time, in which meaning arrives, with a history of the continuities in which meaning is embalmed. There now follow two sections exploring in more detail a logic of morning and evening, beginning and end, first and last, as analysed in these three earlier texts; and a logic of the gift: on time, death, mourning, which, as Derrida remarks in the Foreword to *Given Time: 1: Counterfeit Money*, comes to the forefront of his thinking in the course of the seventies.

4. Morning and Evening, Beginning and End, First and Last

The lecture *"Différance"*, 1968, introduced the neologism, which cannot be heard, but can be detected only when written. This device invited its audience to consider the manner in which an understanding of what has been said arrives only with a lapse of time, and, in this case, only when the written version becomes available, such that the acoustic ambiguity can be resolved. "The Ends of Man" was delivered to a conference in the United States, in April, 1968, and it invites a thinking of the contrast between two notions of ending: the end as completion, in a Hegelian teleology of concepts; as opposed to an end, as break up of continuity, in a triumph of global technology, envisioned in Heidegger's analyses of a movement of nihilism. These contrasting notions of ends are twinned by a fleeting invocation, at the end of the lecture, of contrasting notions of *la veille*, the vigil, night watch, wake, or day before, in which there arrives either the completed Hegelian concept, at the flight at dusk of Minerva's owl; or the new day of a Nietzschean self-overcoming; or, implicitly, the day of days, the last judgment, *jungste Gericht*, of the Book of Revelations. The implied reading of Heidegger is split between these two notions of end, as completion, or end, as inauguration, or indeed as both together, for Derrida emphasises that there can be no question of choosing between them. For Heidegger, in the mode of *Gelassenheit* (an abandonment of entities by the being from which they spring) there is an end of philosophy and completion of metaphysics, which marks a new inception, in an "other beginning".

These contrasting concepts of beginnings and ends, the temporising of philosophy, are then complicated by Derrida's questioning of the temporality of concepts: are they given in time, are they marked by the passage of time, or are they immune to time's transformative effects? Plato's concept of *psyche* works as a device ensuring a moment of eternity in human reasoning, giving human beings access to timeless truths. Freud's re-theorisation of the temporality and constitution of *psyche* thus acquires philosophical significance, once it is granted that the processes through which concepts acquire determinacy are themselves in process of acquiring determinacy. This doubling of the question of the temporalisation to which concepts and meaning, reasoning and understanding are prone, is addressed in one way by Hegel (1770–1831) and in another by Husserl (1859–1938). The central contestation of "The Ends of Man" is then to reveal an implicit appeal to the finite time of human lives, in a covert humanism, at work in the phenomenologies of Hegel, of Husserl and even of Heidegger, and which is then put in dispute by a confrontation between the analyses of Jean Paul Sartre (1905–80), as humanist Marxist, and of Michel Foucault (1930–84), as genealogist of the present, whose *Les Mots et les Choses (The Order of Things)* appeared in 1966. Thus the lecture "The Ends of Man" provides a reading of these competing strands of phenomenology into which it is possible to place the discussion of time and meaning provided for a more specialist audience in the earlier lecture: *"Différance"*. A non-finite time of conceptual determinacy, it is suggested, is covertly derived from, or dependent on a finite time, of the temporising of human existing, and the temporalities of human histories.

"The Ends of Man" also sets up contrasting readings of Immanuel Kant's account of the status of moral concepts and imperatives: whether or not conceptual determinacy in these matters is available to human beings in history, or whether it is available only at the level of the stance of eternity. Out of the dynamic generated by these contrasting readings of Kant, Derrida subsequently derives his distinctive logic of impossible conditions of possibility: for beings in time, such as human beings, only what falls into time is available as determinable objects of thought, but such objects of thought are transient, not fixed and determinate, and are thus not determinable objects of thought. In "The Ends of Man" Derrida frames the discussion by putting into play the contrasting readings of Kant and of theorisings of time, of temporality and of history offered by Sartrean Marxism, and by Foucauldian genealogy; it invokes the contrasting notions of endings and beginnings, in play in the writings of, at least, Hegel, Husserl, Heidegger, Kant, Nietzsche, Sartre and Foucault. However, this list of authorities in dispute is complicated in advance by the alternate list provided in the first published version of the lecture *"Différance"*, which offers an implicit genealogy for the concept of that in which this thinking is formulated, the gramme, or "trace", which prompts the inauguration of this term, 'neither a word, nor a concept', *différance*. In the preface to that lecture, published, but not pronounced, in the original 1968 version Derrida invokes the writings of Nietzsche and Freud, de Saussure and Levinas, and Heidegger; he then goes on, in both the published version and in the lecture as delivered, to contrast the two senses of the Latin term *differre*, as a slippage of meaning within a given temporal structure, and as a slippage in the temporal structure itself, where a time lapse is constitutive of the effect or meaning in question. The emphasis on the "A" of *différance* functions as a marker of an ambiguity, which cannot be heard, but which must be read to be understood. This difference within *differre* operates from the start: that is, from the beginning of the very system of inscription, the alphabet. This beginning however is restricted from the start to those systems of meaning that make use of the Latin, Greek and Hebrew scripts, with the letters "a", alpha, aleph.

For Kant, temporal ordering has the markers of simultaneity, succession and co-existence, rendering it linear and disambiguated. According to the Derridean reception of the notion of the trace, this temporal ordering is to be complicated by allowing for the workings of chance, of delay and of a necessary incompletion. He challenges the Kantian notion of time as the form of inner sense: he surmises that the temporisations of understanding, as a series of impressions, are already spatialised in a way that threatens the linearity, both of time, and of the results of the working of the understanding. Derrida shows that the orderliness of these results is secured and maintained only when they are committed to writing, with the added implication that the processes of formulation as written record contributes substantively to that ordering, and to setting up the resulting marks of consistency and completeness. In the place of time and space, as the forms of inner and outer sense, securing and ordering the results of the workings of the understanding, Derrida substitutes the temporisation of those processes, in which an inheritance of claims to knowledge is preserved, transmitted and received only in the writings to which their inventors have consigned them. Those results are then subject to the vagaries of the adequacy of their formulation, the stability of the meanings of the terms in which they are formulated and the capacity of the inheritors to understand what is transmitted. This then is the originary prosthesis that permits time to appear linear and ordered.

Derrida marks up a link in the writings of Freud between processes of inscription and those of a delayed impact (*Nachtraeglichkeit*), conveyed in the dreamwork and in writing as the transmission of meaning. These considerations then provide a context for responding to the third source, the essay "*Ousia* and *gramme*: Note on a Note in *Being and Time*". The note in question is from the closing pages of *Being and Time* (1927), Heidegger's incomplete treatise under that title. In the reception of Greek thought, as organised through the Christian reception, *ousia* (which may remain concealed), is standardly contrasted to a notion of *parousia*, used to capture the distinctiveness of the coming of Christ, in which the Godhead is revealed as flesh. In *parousia*, what might remain concealed in the mode of *ousia* is made evident in an actual appearing. Here, the temporising of philosophy is marked up in a Christian retrieval of a

Greek term, in the newly forged context of Christian faith. This then introduces the notion of the modes of givenness of time, and of being, which constitutes the main preoccupation of the various phenomenologies of the last century. While these various phenomenologies pay attention to the manner in which distinct modes of temporisation inflect the workings of consciousness and the formation of meaning, the analysis of literary activity, by Blanchot and by de Man, reveals how time is captured in the formulations of the literary text. This meaning then acquires the contrary status of a fixity and determinacy, by contrast to the fluidity distinctive of the processes of its initial formulation. The move from unfixed, to a fixing of meaning is to be contrasted to a move from a fixity of self-evidence about the passing and constitution of time, to a dissolution of such fixity in Husserl's texts. This unfixing leads into the radical disruption of all thinking, in the aporetics of time, as traced out by Heidegger, Levinas and Derrida. These contrary movements are powerfully at work in Derrida's texts on the gift, on death and on mourning.

5. The Debt/Gift: on time, death, mourning

In *Given Time 1: Counterfeit Money*, there is a discussion of the logic of the gift as marked from the beginning by the distinction between restricted and general economy, and by the inflections on the notion of the "*es*" in the Heideggerian phrase "*es gibt*" ("it gives" or "there is"). Derrida refers back to his own essay on *ousia* and *gramme*, and explores how this logic binds together the analyses of Heidegger on time and being to the reflections of Georges Bataille and of Freud on a distinction between self-preserving restricted economies, and self-abandoning general economies in which an initiating '*es*' is not preserved. The economy of an exchange of value, in which the gift is returned, and a potlatch economy, in which what is given is dispersed, ties the analysis up to Marx's analyses and disputes concerning the functioning of capitalism: whether it functions through exchanges of value, supported by the extraction of surplus value, or through a willingness to push the system to the point of the destruction of value. These three strands, that of Marx, those of Freud and Bataille on the death drive that annihilates its bearer, and the logic of life, requiring a complete emptying out of energy, leading not to death but to an end of life itself, and that of Heidegger place the enquiry on the level of one about the very viability of humanity and its history. This suggests that there is no guarantee of a continuation of time and of history, in which conflict and meaning may work themselves out. This context is then complicated in *The Gift of*

Death by the arrival of a dispute between Judaism and Christianity on how to understand Abraham's willingness to sacrifice his only son, Isaac, at the behest of his God. A singular status is claimed by Kierkegaard in his analyses in *Fear and Trembling* (1844) for this sacrificial dedication of all creation to its creator, in which a religion is founded, and it then also marks the possibility of a re-founding of religion, a re-dedication of creation to its creator, in the New Covenant of Christianity.

This singular status, and its possible repetition, is distributed by Derrida across all experience, under the gnomic phrase: *tout autre est tout autre*: all otherness is wholly other, the title of the fourth section of *The Gift of Death*. There is no commonality, least of all a shared time of experience; there is no common moment of a founding sacrifice. Religious bonds are revealed to be contingent, not binding. This is then underlined by the logic of mourning, where one always predeceases the other, subverting the sense that there is at least some co-existing in time. The dispute would then be whether to read *Aporias* (1993), or *Specters of Marx* as the third text in the triad, or whether rather to read them in conjunction. For *Aporias* revisits Heidegger's analytic of *Dasein*, from *Being and Time*, and seeks to demarcate a difference between a metaphysics of death, reading death as that which might determine an essence of *Dasein*, and Heidegger's own delimitation of the existential analytic by marking up *Dasein's* relation to itself as determinately thrown projection, stretched out between birth and death. *Specters of Marx* opens up the horizon of Marx and Marxism, not as piece of history, a nineteenth-century contribution to political economy, and a twentieth-century reinvention of revolution, but as a promise of another kind of futurity. Thus in *Specters* a messianic time of transformation, without the messianism of either Judaism or of the various available Christianities, is marked up as the contribution to an innovation in thinking time, which might form a commonality between Marxism, those of both Marx and Lenin, Engels and Stalin, and phenomenology, that of both Husserl and Heidegger, of Nancy and Marion. Derrida situates a thinking of time on the edge of the known conjuncture between limited modes of enquiry and given forms writing: the literary, and the psychoanalytic, the political, and the economic, the religious, and the philosophical. There is thus for Derrida no concept of time; there are texts in which the traces of a possible futurity are to be marked in tenses which have not yet been inscribed within received systems of conjugation.

13 When it comes to mourning

Michael Naas

When it comes to mourning, it is always tempting to want to begin at the end, as if mourning began only right after or perhaps just before the death or disappearance of the one we love, cherish, or admire. Unable myself to resist this temptation, let me begin this brief essay with some of Derrida's reflections from right near the end of his life, on the threshold, so to speak, of death, when the question of mourning appears to have been foremost in his thoughts. In a public discussion with Jean-Luc Nancy and Philippe Lacoue-Labarthe in Strasbourg on 9 June 2004, that is, just four months before his death, Derrida speaks of inheritance, survival, and, thus, mourning from the perspective of someone who seems to have known that the end was near.[1]

> In my anticipation of death, in my relation to a death to come, a death that I know will completely annihilate me and leave nothing of me behind, there is just below the surface a testamentary desire, a desire that something survive, get left behind or passed on—an inheritance or *something* that I myself can lay no claim to, that will not return to me, but that will, perhaps, remain. ...
>
> (D2 93: my translation)

Nothing would seem to be less extraordinary, more ordinary, than this desire to be remembered and, thus, mourned by means of the traces or memories we leave behind. Though keenly aware that what will be remembered and mourned will not be *him* exactly, since death, as he says, will annihilate the self to whom such memories could ever again be attached, Derrida nonetheless desires to leave traces behind him, traces and, thus, heirs to inherit and to mourn. These traces would of course include his many books, articles, and interviews, the many marks he will have left on the history of philosophy, but also, Derrida goes on to say, "ordinary or everyday gestures," anything that might bear witness to him or retain the memory of him when he is "no longer there."

In the summer of 2004, therefore, just months before his death and more than a year after he had been diagnosed with pancreatic cancer, Derrida spoke of the trace and the testament in relation to his own death and the mourning and scenes of inheritance he imagined would follow it. But Derrida goes on in this dialogue in Strasbourg with his two long-time friends to say something much more general about the trace, something about its very "essence" or "structure". "Every trace is in essence testamentary [*toute trace est d'essence testamentaire*]", he goes on to say, and it is this testamentary "structure of the trace" that has "always haunted" him (D2: 93). Hence Derrida moves in these extemporaneous remarks from an expressed, personal *desire* to leave traces behind him to a *claim* about the structure of the trace in general, a claim he first made nearly four decades earlier in *Of Grammatology* (1967) when he said in words that are almost identical to those spoken in Strasbourg in 2004: "all graphemes are of a testamentary essence [*tout grapheme est d'essence testamentaire*]" (OG: 69).

Derrida's reflections in the summer of 2004 about the trace in relation to the testament thus surely did not originate out of his anticipation of, or anxiety before, a death he suspected to be near, even if the proximity of these remarks to his death gives them a particular poignancy. Having claimed from the very start that the trace is in its essence testamentary, Derrida will have been from the very beginning a thinker of legacy and inheritance, and, always inseparable from these, of mourning.

This same movement or oscillation between a personal desire to leave traces behind him and general claims about the nature of the trace can also be seen in Derrida's final interview, published in *Le Monde* in August 2004. Just before evoking what he there calls his "passion" for leaving "traces in the history of the French language" (LLF: 37), Derrida evokes a general theory of the trace in relation to the testament. Whether we want or intend it or not, the traces we leave behind are never simply ours but are already and from the very beginning beyond us and outside our control. Whether "spoken or written", "all these gestures", says Derrida, "leave us and begin to act independently of us", like "machines" or like "marionettes", acting in essence without me, that is, after me or in my wake, after my death or at least *as if I were dead* (LLF: 32).

My death is thus not some contingent event that may one day befall the trace I produce, marking it from that moment on with my death; rather, my disappearance or my death is the very condition of the production of the trace and the structure it subsequently comes to bear. Hence Derrida can argue that "the trace I leave signifies to me at once my death, either to come or already come upon me, and the hope that this trace survives me. This is not a striving for immortality; it's something structural" (LLF: 32). Again, it is not by chance but *by structure* that the trace survives me, even if only briefly, indeed even if it is *in fact* immediately destroyed or erased after its production. With the question of the immortality of the self or the soul off the table, and with the sober recognition that no trace can survive forever, survival seems to be limited in its very structure to an indeterminate, finite, and always uncertain and threatened future. It is at this point that Derrida gives us—bequeaths us—one of his simplest and most poignant definitions of the trace and of the uncertainty that conditions every legacy:

> I leave a piece of paper behind, I go away, I die: it is impossible to escape this structure, it is the unchanging form of my life. Each time I let something go, each time some trace leaves me, "proceeds" from me, unable to be reappropriated, I live my death in writing. It's the ultimate test: one expropriates oneself without knowing exactly who is being entrusted with what is left behind. Who is going to inherit, and how? Will there even be any heirs?
>
> (LLF: 32–33)

In these simple, no doubt deceptively simple, words, spoken, as I said, by someone who suspected that the end was near, Derrida seems to lend credence to the simple version of inheritance and of mourning I evoked at the outset: one lives, one leaves things behind—a piece of paper, a final interview, a corpse and a corpus, traces and memories—and then one goes away, one disappears, one dies, and those who remain are left to inherit and to mourn. Nothing seems more self-evident or ineluctable. As Derrida says, "it is impossible to escape this structure".

But this simple version of inheritance and of mourning is complicated when Derrida goes on to say that this structure is "the unchanging form of [his] life". He does not say, and the difference is significant, that this structure is the unchanging and unavoidable *trajectory* of his life, the fate to which he—like all of us—must one day succumb. He says instead that this "structure" is the "unchanging form" of his life, as if life first had to be thought on the basis of the trace and not the other way around. Once again, it is the very structure of the trace that implies the death or absence of the one who leaves a trace behind, but then also, as we will now see, the death or absence of the one who might inherit that trace, the one whom we might have naively assumed to be fully living and present to mourn the one who has gone.

In his 1971 essay "Signature Event Context," Derrida is even more explicit and detailed about the way the trace is in its essence and by structure testamentary. Whether written or spoken, every trace, every mark, must be readable in its structure, Derrida argues, in the absence of both the addressor and the addressee. It "must continue to 'act' and to be readable even if what is called the author of the writing no longer answers for what he has written, for what he seems to have signed, whether he is provisionally absent, or if he is dead" (MP: 316). The trace must remain readable in the absence of the one who produced it. But insofar as it must be able to act independently of any act of production or reproduction, any attempt to reanimate it through reading or inter-pretation, it must also be able to act in the absence of the one for whom it was produced. Derrida thus goes on to say, placing emphasis yet again on *structure*: "a writing that was not structurally readable—iterable—beyond the death of the addressee would not be writing" (MP: 315). What Derrida says here about "writing" holds for every mark, every trace. Insofar as it must be able to "act" in the absence of both the addressor and the addressee—a bit like the machine or the marionette Derrida spoke of in his final interview—every trace implies the "death," the possible or virtual death, of both the one who produced it and the one destined to receive or inherit it.

The result of this understanding of the trace—of every trace, written, spoken, and even unspoken, as in a gesture—is that death is no longer simply exterior to life, what supervenes at a moment in time upon life in order to surprise or seize it in its purity. A certain death—what Derrida would come to call "life-death"—would be originary, constitutive even, of all life or all survival. In short, it is "life-death" that is, for Derrida, "the unchanging form" of our life, a thesis that will come to have pro-found implications for the scope, temporality, topology, and even the possibility of mourning. For if death does not simply follow upon life, if life is never simply and completely distinct from death or the possibility of death, then—contrary to the commonsense view of things outlined at the outset of this essay—mourning is perhaps already there at the origin.

I leave a piece of paper behind, I go away, I die: the going away or the dying is not some contingent event that will *eventually* but has not yet come upon the one who leaves a trace behind. It is, we now see, co-extensive with the very production of the trace—and thus with life itself. Hence Derrida in the fifth of the fifty-nine periods or periphrases or, indeed, breaths of "Circumfession" can write, "I posthume as I breathe" (C: 26).[2] With this aphorism Derrida seems to be suggesting that with every breath he takes he is already posthumous, surviving beyond him-self, "living on" in marks or traces emptied of all living breath.

"Posthume", says Derrida in a neologism, because every letter he *posts,* every trace he sends out, is already and from the beginning post him, past him, already a letter from beyond the tomb, posthumous to him even when he was still living and breathing. The posthumous, then, would be the very air we breathe, the very form of our lives, so that mourning becomes possible not simply at the moment of another's "actual death" but already with their first mark, which will have always been produced *as if he or she were already dead.* As the unchanging form of the life of the one who bequeaths the trace as well as of the one destined to inherit it, there is, as Derrida put it in that final interview published in *Le Monde* in August 2004, "an 'originary mourning' ... that does not wait for the so-called 'actual death'" (LLF: 26).

In the beginning, then, there is mourning—an originary mourning or melancholy that is not nostalgia for some lost presence but an affirmation that the testamentary trace and a mourning for the other is the unchanging form of our lives. Derrida will thus say in an interview from 1990: "I mourn therefore I am" (P: 321). More originary than death or being-towards-death, mourning for the *other,* or at least the structural possibility of such mourning, begins not at death but already at the beginning of life, already with the first trace.

But this reference to the *other* should lead one to suspect that this brief analysis of the testament and of mourning in Derrida's work has thus far been rather one-sided, approached almost exclusively from the side of the one who faces his or her "own" death in the trace or knows he or she must die, rather than from the side of the one who must at some point face and experience the death of a friend, colleague, or family member, or who must live with the knowledge that a friend, colleague, or family member is destined to die. Such an emphasis on the testamentary structure of the trace and its implications for "my own" death is, however, no accident. To begin with "my own" death is yet another temptation of the philosophical tradition that runs from Plato (who defines philosophy as the "practice of dying") to Heidegger (whose *Being and Time* is first and foremost the analysis of *Dasein's* own "being-towards-death"). But as we have seen, it is not only my own death that is implied in the trace but the death of the other, and our earliest and most common experiences of death involve not our own deaths but the deaths of others and the pain we feel in mourning them. In the interview cited above in which Derrida seems to affirm in mock-Cartesian fashion his *own* existence through mourning—"I mourn therefore I am"—he goes on to say:

> I mourn therefore I am, I am—dead with the death of the other, my relation to myself is first of all plunged into mourning, a mourning

that is moreover impossible. This is also what I call ex-appropria-
tion, appropriation caught in a double bind: I must and I must not
take the other into myself; mourning is an unfaithful fidelity if it
succeeds in interiorizing the other ideally in me, that is, in not
respecting his or her infinite exteriority.

(P: 321)

In this interview from 1990, Derrida appears to make two distinct
though related points about death and mourning. First, my relation to
myself, to my life as well as my death, seems to be conditioned less by an
experience of my own death than by the death of others or of the other.
Derrida will thus go so far as to affirm that "I can have this experience
of 'my own death' by relating to myself only in the impossible experience, the experience of the impossible mourning at the death of the
other" (P: 321). But that would then mean that the *possibility* of a relation to my own death is conditioned by an experience of the "*impossible*
mourning" of the other. Mourning would be "impossible", on this
account, even though it would be one of our most common and unde-
niable experiences.

For Derrida mourning does indeed take place, indeed it happens all
the time, it is, in essence, the "unchanging form of our lives". But
because mourning can never be completed or be completely successful,
it can never be completely distinguished from melancholy and the
aporias that define it. Whereas Freud in his 1917 essay "Mourning and
Melancholia" (Freud 2005) opposes a successful mourning that results
in the eventual incorporation of the lost love object within the psyche
to an unsuccessful mourning (or melancholy) that is unable to bring
about such an incorporation, Derrida argues in several key works that
this incorporation is at once impossible and undesirable and that, as a
result, *all* mourning is and indeed must remain unsuccessful and thus
to some extent melancholic. As Derrida puts it in one of his most
important texts on the subject, "cryptic incorporation always marks an
effect of impossible or refused mourning (melancholy *or* mourning)"
(Derrida 1986b: xxi).[3]

Because the other whom one mourns is not, for Derrida, a lost object
that might be incorporated or interiorised within the psyche but an
"infinite exteriority", mourning is at once originary and impossible.
Better, mourning is and must forever remain caught in the aporia or
"double bind" of having at once to appropriate the other (so as not to
abandon them to indifference) and not appropriate them (so as to respect
their singularity and infinite exteriority). Hence mourning is given over
to an "unfaithful fidelity" where mourning can succeed only by failing,

where it can succeed only by interiorising or incorporating an absolute singularity or a unique other that must remain in its singularity or uniqueness exterior and unincorporated. Derrida can thus speak in the interview from 1990 cited a moment ago of "the attempt, always doomed to fail (thus a constitutive failure, precisely), to incorporate, interiorize, introject, subjectivize the other in me. Even before the death of the other, the inscription of her or his mortality constitutes me. I mourn therefore I am ... " (P: 321). Just as the trace is testamentary by structure, in essence, and not because of some contingent event like the death of the author, so mourning is doomed to fail not because of some contingent weakness or shortcoming on the part of the one who mourns but because such failure is structural—as well as "constitutive" of the one who mourns. I am who I am because of this relation to an other whom I can never simply make my own. As Derrida says again in the interview from 1990, "This carrying of the mortal other 'in me outside me' instructs or institutes my 'self' and my relation to 'myself' already before the death of the other" (P: 321).

This theory of "impossible mourning" is developed in many texts of Derrida, from "Fors" to *Memoires for Paul de Man* to *Specters of Marx* to, most powerfully and poignantly, *The Work of Mourning*. Beginning in the early 1980s and continuing almost right up until his own death in 2004, Derrida wrote a series of memorial essays or funeral orations on the occasion, so to speak, of the deaths of friends, mentors, and colleagues from Roland Barthes, Paul de Man, Louis Althusser, and Michel Foucault to Sarah Kofman, Jean-François Lyotard, Emmanuel Levinas, Gilles Deleuze, and Maurice Blanchot. In these works, Derrida at once elaborates a theory of mourning, its logic, rhetoric, codes, and rituals, and finds both this theory and himself put to the test by these unique events of personal mourning. First published in 2001 in English under the title *The Work of Mourning* and then in 2003 in French under the title *Chaque fois unique, la fin du monde*, this series of essays develops in an even more detailed and performative manner the enigma or aporia of a mourning that is at once originary and impossible.

As Derrida makes clear in each of these works of mourning, the death of a loved one or friend is absolutely singular, unique and incomparable, unable to be synthesised, dialectised, or interiorised. And yet, because *each* of these deaths is unique, because all these unique, singular deaths have come to form a *series*, a series that, alas, grows only longer with time, mourning always finds itself caught in the double bind of having at once to recognise the uniqueness of the friend for whom one mourns and to compare this death to others. By having to mourn for more than one friend, and by having to do so in the same rhetorically codified way, often by means of the same gestures, the same words, one betrays the unique singularity of the dead friend.

But it is not only through its repetition in other deaths that the unique death gets betrayed. As we have already seen, insofar as mourning for the other begins already with the trace, the death of each singular other is similarly multiplied, the absolutely unique event of their death already repeated. Mourning for the friend continues—gets repeated—long after their actual death and it begins well before it. As Derrida argues elsewhere, "the melancholic certainty of which I am speaking begins, as always, in the friends' lifetime" (SQ: 140). If the posthumous is the very air we breathe and the testamentary is the very structure of the trace, then mourning is the very element in which friendship grows. Derrida writes in one of the essays gathered in *The Work of Mourning*:

> To have a friend, to look at him, to follow him with your eyes, to admire him in friendship, is to know in a more intense way, already injured, always insistent, and more and more unforgettable, that one of the two of you will inevitably see the other die.
>
> (WM: 106)

Contrary to the commonplace view with which we began, mourning does not wait for the actual death of the friend to take place; the death of the friend—and thus mourning for the friend—begins already at the beginning, already with the first trace, instituting at once friendship with the other and, as we have seen, my own self relation.

At once absolutely unique and yet inevitably put into a series, repeated, the death of a friend is always, to cite the title of the French edition of *The Work of Mourning*, "*chaque fois unique, la fin du monde*", that is, "each time unique or uniquely, the end of the world." As Derrida puts it elsewhere, "each time, and each time singularly, each time irreplaceably, each time infinitely, death is nothing less than the end of the world" (SQ: 140). While common sense tells us that no matter how painful the death of a friend may be the world continues on for us the living, Derrida claims the contrary. This is not rhetorical hyperbole but, once again, the very structure of mourning and of the "subject" who mourns. Inasmuch as the other's death cannot be incorporated or interiorised, *comprehended* within or against the backdrop of an already established horizon of the world, what we experience at the death of a friend is not simply the death or end of someone *within* the world but the end of the *world itself*. Because my own self-relation within the world is constituted through the other and my mourning of the other, then the death of the other can never be just another event within the world, or just one death among others within the world, but the end of what opens up the world itself. And since this singular and unanticipatable event is, as we have seen, repeated, it is *each time*, each time uniquely, the end of the world. This is no doubt why Derrida could write in one of his most controversial and easily misunderstood statements that "there is no common measure adequate to persuade me that a personal mourning is less serious than a nuclear war" (Derrida 1984: 28).[4] Each time unique, a personal mourning is nothing less than the end of the world.

The scope and stakes of mourning could thus not be greater for Derrida. Not just one subject or theme among others in his work, mourning is inseparable, as we have seen, from Derrida's thinking about the trace and the testament, time and repetition, self and other, friendship and world, personal loss and the end of the world.

When it comes to mourning it is always tempting, as I said at the outset, to want to begin at the end. But to think mourning with Derrida we must understand that the end will have already been there from the beginning, that mourning will have begun with the first trace. This structural necessity does not, of course, occlude, negate, or suspend the surprise, the wound or the trauma, of the event of the end when it does "actually" arrive, the moment, each time unique and always as if for the first time, when mourning comes.

Notes

1 Derrida died during the night of 9 October 2004.
2 It should be noted that Derrida is playing on the common French expression *"tu mens comme tu respires,"* "you lie as easily as you breathe."
3 I am simplifying in the extreme here a long and complicated argument regarding the topology of this incorporation and the putative difference between it and introjection. (See Derrida 1986: xvi-xvii).
4 Jacques Derrida, "No Apocalypse, Not Now (full speed ahead, seven missiles, seven missives)," trans. Catherine Porter and Philip Lewis. *Diacritics* (Summer 1984): 28.

14 Race

Claire Colebrook

It might seem at first as though Derrida's explicit intervention into race was a minor, occasional and possibly even inadequate gesture. Unlike Deleuze and Guattari (1987), whose theory of life and its emergence by way of mutation, transformation and the genesis of tribal and racial inscription has race at its centre, Derrida's "Racism's Last Word," is a short piece in response to an art exhibition. There is a very glib, but still pervasive, understanding of deconstruction as being primarily rhetorical in its politics, and having little to do with the real world. Indeed, this accusation was directed at Derrida in response to "Racism's Last Word": after a translation and publication of the short piece Anne McClintock and Rob Nixon wrote a criticism of Derrida's approach and suggested that had he looked "beyond the text" he would have been mindful of a whole series of hard political facts that would render his approach clumsily monolithic, as though a scholar such as Derrida focused on "logocentrism" or "Western metaphysics" could really have nothing to say about race in any meaningful way (McClintock and Nixon 1986). In response Derrida, among many other ripostes, seemed to reinforce the minor nature of his intervention, which was to comment on an exhibition. Or, rather than use the word "minor", which suggests a logic that opposes the essential and universal to the inessential and insignificant, he uses the word "singular" and then raises a temporality of the text and its force to remain through time and not be contained by the site or occasion of its emergence. The art exhibition itself was, or aimed to be, highly specific at a historical or strategic level: the exhibition was in response to the South African government's policy of apartheid, which was officially instituted in 1948 and was gradually dismantled in the 1990s but which was still ongoing at the time of the exhibition. Derrida refers to the exhibition as a satellite, not only because it is sent into orbit or circulation beyond the sphere of its creation, but because the sending of a text into the future might make us then imagine the present not from its own timeframe or context. Whatever the force of the present, there is another textual/temporal force that cannot calculate what will come into being:

> In order to respond to this singularity or, better yet, to fling back an answer, the singularity right here of another event takes its measure. Artists from all over the world are preparing to launch a new satellite, a vehicle whose dimensions can hardly be determined except as a satellite of humanity. Actually, it measures itself against apartheid only so as to remain in no measure comparable with that system, its power, its fantastic riches, its excessive armament, the worldwide network of its openly declared or shamefaced accomplices. This unarmed exhibition will have a force that is altogether other, just as its trajectory will be without example.
>
> Its movement does not yet belong to any given time or space that might be measured today.
>
> A satellite is a guard, it keeps watch and gives warning.
>
> (RLW: 293)

I want to suggest that there is something significant – racially significant – in the notion of some essays being local and minor while others speak to universal themes. Derrida's strategy of reading texts and words as satellites, and as declared "last words" does not remove the hierarchies or differences that mark all forms of politics, including racism, but it does open any supposed essential, universal or central term to a time that might end, or that might be sent into a future in a manner that cannot be calculated. One way of thinking about art objects and texts is not that they present what is universal or major, but that their role is institutional. Rather than ask what a text means or presents one might ask what it inaugurates: might this exhibition some day be marked as the point at which racism could be named and set aside in a completed past? If this were to be the case then the logic of what counts as true and universal would have to change. If the text succeeds it will redistribute what will (in some future) count as major, universal or essential; but part of what constitutes a text's textuality – or the fact that it can be sent into the future, repeated, copied, transformed and misquoted – is that one cannot determine in advance how it will operate or what it will present. Derrida refers to the "wager" of the exhibition, that it imagines a time in the future when "apartheid" will be the name for what will have been the last instance of racism in the West. Derrida takes a local event, an exhibition that is already a response to a historical moment – apartheid – and then asks what it might mean to think of the possibility of such an event truly coming to an end, or being able to be named as the last word of racism. If apartheid were to come to an end then a radical shift in politics and thinking would have occurred, because "apartheid," or a logic of pure apartness is what has contaminated the West, enabled racism and anti-racism, and cannot itself be fully presented precisely because it is the logic of presence (the logic that truth, humanity, what is, essences could be presented). Thus Derrida's essays calls for a future where "apartheid" might be a name of something that could be definitively set apart:

> APARTHEID – may that remain the name from now on, the unique appellation for the ultimate racism in the world, the last of many.
>
> May it thus remain from now on, but may a day come when it will only be for the memory of man.
>
> A memory in advance: that, perhaps, is the time given for this exhibition. At once urgent and untimely, it exposes itself and takes a chance with time, it wagers and affirms beyond the wager. Without counting on any present moment, it offers only a foresight in painting, very close to silence, and the rearview vision for which apartheid will be the name of something finally abolished. Confined and abandoned to this silence of memory, the name will resonate all by itself, reduced to the state of a term in disuse. The thing it names will no longer be.
>
> But hasn't apartheid always been the archival record of the unnameable.
>
> (RLW: 291)

Of course, Derrida's piece is of historical interest, if read today after apartheid, and after an era in which the dominant figure or word for racism was "apartheid." But part of Derrida's argument is to say that if apartheid were indeed to become something of the past, something that we could look back upon and separate ourselves from, then we would need to have taken part in an entirely unforeseen mode of politics, quite different from the political order of the West today which is essentially complicit with apartheid:

> ... the name of apartheid has managed to become a sinister swelling on the body of the world only in that place where homo politicus europaeus first put his signature on its tattoo. The primary reason, however, is that here it is a question of state racism. While all racisms have their basis in culture and in institutions, not all of them give rise to state-controlled structures. The judicial

simulacrum and the political theater of this state racism have no meaning and would have had no chance outside a European "discourse" on the concept of race. That discourse belongs to a whole system of "phantasms," to a certain representation of nature life, history, religion and law, to the very culture which succeeded in giving rise to this state takeover. No doubt there is also here – and it bears repeating – a contradiction internal to the West and to the assertion of its rights.

(RLW: 294)

For this reason his piece is entitled "Racism's Last Word," playing on the notion that there will be a time when we might be able to say that the language of racism has come to an end, and that in many ways racism will have the last word precisely because the very inscriptive system and sense of the human that made racism impossible is the same system that has the resources to imagine racism's end. Or, put far too simply: racism is only possible because of a textual system (including language and literature in the narrow sense) that discriminates, constitutes essences and creates the ongoing sameness of identity through time; to appeal to a new humanity, after racism, when "we" might be able to name racism as something that definitively has come into being and then can be labeled requires the same logic of essential politics that allows racism to come into being. This is why Derrida begins by referring to the art exhibition as a wager: whatever is other than or after racism cannot now simply be presented, for every attempt to talk about and distance ourselves from the system of apartheid must (now) use the same logic of "apartness" and separation or even purity that characterises racism. What we can do, from within the very logic that generates racism, is take a bet on something other than racism. Derrida's occasional piece on this art exhibition therefore deploys three highly significant strategies to do with time, to do with the archive and to do with politics.

The idea that there will be a last word of racism suggests – among many things – that both the notion of the last word (final, definitive, clean, essential, delimited) is what enables racism, and that if racism were to end it might be the logic or temporality of the word that would also need to end. It is true that apartheid has a specific political and historical beginning, as the policy of the national party beginning in 1948 (and one might, in turn, want to trace subtle shifts in uses of political language after "apartheid" was explicitly named as a policy). Derrida makes several maneuvers with regard to the relation between this word and time. He begins his essay, insistently, with a performative: "may that

remain the name." He writes this at a time when even though the
national party in South Africa started to use different rhetoric, racism
and the policy of separation or "apartness" was still in force. So Derrida
asks, wishes and imagines that there might be a day when it would be
possible to name apartheid as a thing of the past. But once he does that –
once he raises the stakes beyond criticising this policy here and now by
asking what would it mean for apartheid no longer to be present, but to
be named and situated in the past – he goes on to look at the broader
conditions of apartheid. These conditions are historical but not just in
terms of historical events, such as the events of South African politics,
but have to do with the history of which the exhibition and the call for
racism to end are also a part. How was and is apartheid possible? It was
part of a European venture of colonisation and globalisation, which is of
a highly complex and contradictory nature. One crucial feature was the
Christian logic of sovereignty in which the one and true power was
whole and indivisible, and it is this feature that allowed at one and the
same time for the imposition of rule over non-European peoples, and a
sense of the rightness of separation and the natural birthplace of nations.
Derrida therefore raises the question of what it would mean, from
within this history, and using this history's own logic of human rights,
to name an end or to declare a definitive separation from its racist and
contaminating possibilities. The very possibility of history, of the tracing
out of progress (or decline) through time, of the final declaration of
human rights, and the call to end apartheid in the name of a humanity or
justice that can see beyond apartheid's "apartness" nevertheless is also
part of the same inscriptive system of temporality and promise:

> Europe, in the enigmatic process of its globalization and of its
> paradoxical disappearance, seems to project onto this screen [of geo-
> political computation], point by point, the silhouette of its internal
> war, the bottom line of its profits and losses, the double-bind logic
> of its national and multi-national interests. Their dialectical evalua-
> tion provides only a provisional stasis in a precarious equilibrium,
> one whose price today is apartheid. All states and all societies are
> willing to pay this price, first of all by making someone else pay. At
> stake, advises the computer, are world peace, the general economy,
> the marketplace for European labor, and so on. ... With great fan-
> fare, they are trying to make the world forget the 1973 verdict –
> "crime against humanity." If this verdict continues to have no effect,
> it is because the customary discourse on man, humanism and human
> rights, has encountered its effective and unthought limit, the limit of
> the whole system in which it acquires meaning. ...

Beyond the global computer, the dialectic of strategic or economic calculations, beyond state-controlled, national or international tribunals, beyond the juridico-political or theological-political discourse, which any more serves to maintain good conscience or denegation, it was, it will have to be, it is necessary to appeal unconditionally to the future of another law and another force lying beyond the totality of the present. ...

Referring then to the exhibition, Derrida says,

Even the future perfect can no longer translate the tense, the time of what is being written in this way – and what is doubtless no longer part of the everyday current, of the cursory sense of history.

(RLW: 298)

Derrida, here, is neither being relativist in saying that apartheid is one political system among others, nor nihilist in saying that the West as a whole is really ultimately racist. On the contrary, he is waging, betting or calling for – from within a political logic of nations, citizenship, sameness, essences – another logic. This might perhaps suggest another mode of time, not a time in which "we" innocently look on South Africa and imagine that racism can be held there, apart from us. Perhaps there will be another logic, and "apartness" will be the last word, racism's last word.

This brings us to the second strand of Derrida's essay which has to do with text, archive and inscription. Derrida argues that racism is textual, which is not only to say that it is linguistic and inscriptive – that it requires institutions which label, discriminate, essentialise and narrate – but that also any event of racism, such as South Africa's apartheid policy, is caught up in multiple and multiply complex relations, times, forces and possibilities that preclude us from, say, locating it as a single event with its own unique meaning.

As already mentioned, after Derrida published "Racism's Last Word," in translation in *Critical Inquiry* Rob Nixon and Anne McClintock corrected and criticised both Derrida's strategy, for focusing on language or textuality rather than going "beyond the text," and Derrida's account of the word "apartheid" which was no longer the official name for South Africa's policy. Against this Derrida makes two rigorous points about language, which have broader implications for deconstruction and its supposedly "textual", "literary" or non-empirical nature. Derrida insists that he continues to use the word "apartheid" precisely because one should not see the force of words or textual strategies as tied to their origin or supposedly governing intention; apartheid explicitly named a strategy of segregation and apartness that remains; to keep using the word, while also imagining that there will be a last use of the word, is to deploy a textual strategy. The word apartheid originally used as an explicit policy can still be used in a war on the word "apartheid", especially if the strategy of not using the word would allow the process of apartness to continue by way of other policy terms. So Derrida takes something seemingly local and singular – South Africa's historically specific name of "apartheid" – and looks at the ways in which this word and force of apartness, of naming apartness, cannot be cleanly set apart, but that one might send a text into the future, such as his own essay, that would imagine that "apartheid," become something apart, past, or a last word. So for Derrida a textual strategy is at least twofold: allowing a word, such as "apartheid," to contaminate and render problematic our simple political sureties and senses of innocence, and also writing in the manner of a wager, to write or speak as if the word apartheid were to become a name, for something that had been.

Derrida therefore responds harshly, rigorously and humorously to McClintock and Nixon's criticism of his textual strategy. First, he insists that "text" does not refer narrowly to books on library shelves, and so to say that there is "nothing outside the text" is to say that anything we consider (whether it be a word, a policy, a body, a violent event or a sculpture) is caught up in relations that can never be exhausted. Nor can one close down or determine what a proper context or relation might be. It is as legitimate to look at apartheid in terms of European globalisation and the civilising mission of an essential truth and humanity as it is to trace the day by day shifts in the South African government's policies and rhetoric. Indeed, as Derrida responds to Nixon and McClintock, their accusation that his strategy is textual and misguided would consign him to his own segregated area of literature while they supposedly take on the work of real politics; this would amount to a form of apartheid or demarcation:

> … text, as I use the word, is not the book. No more than writing or trace, it is not limited to the paper which you cover with your graphism. It is precisely for strategic reasons (set forth at length elsewhere) that I found it necessary to recast the concept of text by generalizing it almost without limit, in any case without present or perceptible limit, without any limit that is. That's why there is nothing "beyond the text." That's why South Africa and apartheid are, like you and me, part of this general text, which is not to say

that it can be read the way one reads a book. That's why the text is always a field of forces: heterogeneous, differential, open, and so on. (BB: 167–68).

To conclude, though, we need to see that Derrida is not only saying that politics cannot be cordoned off in some distinct domain of the real apart from the complexity of networks of rhetoric and relations beyond full presentation or comprehension, for there is something about apartheid, race, racism and textuality that might prompt us to adopt a counter-political strategy. Let us say that racism would not be possible without the textual strategies of naming and demarcating, and that the problem of racism is not that it discriminates but that it doesn't discriminate enough. Humans are grouped into nations and granted a sameness, and perhaps a separateness. If one appeals to humanity, or global and universal justice one is not only, also, deploying textual strategies – there is also a certain temporality of naming. It is as though language were the name for some presence that might be grasped and retrieved as unique, present and indivisible: "the history of apartheid (its "discourse" and its "reality," the totality of its text) would have been impossible, unthinkable without the European concept and the European history of the state, without the European discourse on race-its scientific pseudoconcept and its religious roots, its modernity and its archaisms-without Judeo-Christian ideology, and so forth" (BB: 165).

This has been the logic of right, sovereignty and nationhood, as well as racism and apartheid. To take textual politics seriously would be to deploy or allow oneself to be overtaken by a different temporality. The very word that names and delimits apartheid has the capacity to survive and act beyond apartheid, but could there be another survival that is not that of naming, and not where words are seen to be names or signs of presences that they merely label? This is what Derrida sees the art objects of the exhibition as having the potentiality to do. Within a system of apartheid, of naming, of presentation, the objects in the exhibition do not label what is present, but instead send themselves into a future where there may no longer be the logic of naming and presentation. This would not be a politics that stepped outside the text to grasp the true, real or material world, nor could it be a politics that simply opposed itself to a Western logic of naming and saming. One could not say or present what this post-apartheid politics would be. It could not be a pure apartness, and it could certainly not be post-racial in the sense of finding, once and for all, the humanity that lay waiting for racism to be over.

15 Auto-Affection

Leonard Lawlor

Auto-affection refers to self-experience. It is not, however, the experience opened up by a deliberate act of reflection through which an object called the self is given in a representation. Below reflection is a basic self-awareness, such as the experience of my own thoughts. "Of my own thoughts" is an important phrase since it tells us immediately what is at stake in auto-affection. It is an experience of sameness and selfness. "Auto" in Greek, of course, means "self" and "same," as in "auto-mobile", which literally means "self-moving" or in "tautology," which means a sentence that says the same thing twice. The idea of auto-affection seems to enter philosophical discourse when Plato, in the *Theatetus*, defines thinking as interior monologue (189c–190a). More recently, we see it functioning not only at the root of Descartes' "I think therefore I am" – it is the same "I" on both sides of the "therefore" – but also at the root of Kantian autonomy: I give the law to myself. It is auto-affection therefore that supports not only theoretical foundations but also moral foundations. Because auto-affection has this grounding function, Derrida has made it the object of his deconstructions. Indeed, it is possible to say without exaggeration that every deconstruction Derrida has ever written targets auto-affection. Deconstruction aims to show that all auto-affection, however it is conceived, is really and fundamentally hetero-affection. All the neologisms or redefined terms that Derrida developed throughout his life (from "différance" to "anachronism") attempt to name this aporetical relation between sameness and otherness to which the deconstruction of auto-affection leads us.

I. Derrida's Appropriation of Three Phenomenological Ideas

In order to understand Derrida's deconstruction of auto-affection, we must examine the first and most important deconstruction of auto-affection that appears in Derrida's 1967 *Voice and Phenomenon*. This is a difficult book. It looks to be a simple criticism of phenomenology, even a rejection and dismissal of phenomenology. It is not. From this book onward, Derrida embraces and indeed never retreats from three phenomenological ideas. It is impossible to understand *Voice and Phenomenon* without pausing over these three phenomenological ideas.

The *first* idea is perhaps the greatest innovation of phenomenological thinking: the *epoché*. Based on Descartes' idea of methodical doubt, the *epoché* suspends all belief in a world that exists independently of experience. It reduces all being "in itself" to subjective experience, to "phenomena." However, the *epoché* is more radical than Cartesian doubt insofar as it reduces subjective experience itself. The *epoché* must be strictly universal, which means that it even includes me as a psychological person within all the data that is reduced. The universality of the *epoché* opens up a pre-personal, even pre-subjective experience. For Derrida, when one moves through a deconstruction, one ends up at this profound level of experience, a level that Derrida, in *Voice and Phenomenon*, calls "ultra-transcendental" (VP: 28). The *second* idea concerns the composition of the ultra-transcendental level. Following Husserl (and Heidegger), Derrida conceives this level as temporal. We shall return to this idea in a moment since it is central to Derrida's deconstruction of auto-affection in *Voice and Phenomenon*; moreover below, we shall also see that the composition of the ultra-transcendental level is a complicated relation of forces. However, for now, we must note that, when Derrida appropriates the phenomenological idea that all experience is fundamentally temporal, he demonstrates that temporalisation is a movement of differentiation. The present is always being differentiated into pastness and futureness so that the present is itself always in a process of division. The present is fundamentally composed therefore of a gap or a hiatus that can never be closed or reconciled. The *third* idea, closely connected to the second, comes from Husserl's descriptions in the Fifth Cartesian Meditation, his descriptions of the experience of the alien (Husserl 1963).[1] When Husserl describes the experience of alterity, he recognises that this experience differs from self-experience. Indeed, the difference he discovers is a genuine phenomenological insight (rivaling the innovation of the *epoché*). When I experience myself, according to Husserl, my own self is given to me in a presentation (a *Gegenwärtigung*). In other words, my experience of myself is immediate. In contrast, when I experience you, you are given to me in a *Vergegenwärtigung*. There is no precise English word that is equivalent to the German "*Vergegenwärtigung*." It is usually translated into English with the neologism "presentification," but the prefix "Ver-" clearly indicates a kind of duplicity, as in the "re-" of "representation" which is also a possible English translation of "*Vergegenwärtigung.*" The prefix indicates however that the way you are given to me is mediated. More strongly, it indicates, and this is really Husserl's great insight, that the interior life of another is never given to me as such. In the experience of the other, there is a kind of absence or non-presence that differs from the usual kind of non-presence one encounters in perception. The perception of a three-dimensional object always includes absence insofar as there are hidden sides to every spatial object. Yet, these hidden sides can be brought into presence if I move around the object. Unlike the absence of the back-side of a table, the non-presence of the other, however, remains no matter what I do, no matter how I move about. Husserl thinks that this experience of the other happens only with the other. Derrida in contrast thinks that, *even in self-experience*, we find *Vergegenwärtigung*, that is, non-presence and mediation. In other words, Derrida generalises the experience of the other to all forms of auto-affection. Now, let us examine the specific arguments against auto-affection that we find in *Voice and Phenomenon*.

II.   The Deconstruction of Auto-Affection in *Voice and Phenomenon*

The precise argumentation deconstructing auto-affection appears in Chapter Six, "The Voice that Keeps Silent." But the argumentation relies on what Derrida does in Chapter Five, "Signs and the Blink of an Eye." We shall start with Chapter Five. In the first four chapters of *Voice and Phenomenon*, Derrida had been trying to show that when Husserl, in the *Logical Investigations* (Husserl's first truly important book), wants to isolate logical meaning, that is, expression, from the contingent and factual meanings of everyday communication, that is, from indication, Husserl resorts, through a kind of epoché, to the experience of soliloquy, to what above we called "interior monologue" (Husserl 1980). According to Husserl, in soliloquy, the meaning of the words I am using seems to be immediately present in the moment, in "the blink of an eye." Because Husserl speaks of the moment (the German word for moment is "Augenblick," which literally means "blink of an eye," hence Derrida's title for Chapter Five), Husserl seems to be presupposing some view of temporal experience. Therefore in Chapter Five, Derrida turns to Husserl's descriptions of temporalisation, even though Husserl himself had not yet presented his famous lectures on time until some years after the publication of the *Logical Investigations* (VP 68).[2] In the lectures (called *The Phenomenology of Internal Time Consciousness*), Husserl attempts to describe the experience of time (temporalisation), but especially the experience of the present as I live it right now: the "living present." As Derrida reads it, *The Phenomenology of Internal Time Consciousness*, on the one hand, indicates that the living present seems to have a *center,* which is the now point. But, on the other hand, the time lectures indicate that the living present seems to be *thick*; it includes the immediate memory (called the "retention") of the now that has just elapsed and the anticipation (called the "protention") of the now that is about to appear. For Husserl, the retentional phase is different from memory in the usual sense, which he calls "secondary memory"; the usual sense of memory is defined by representation (*Vergegenwärtigung*). Because of the thickness, what is at issue, for Derrida, is precisely the kind of difference that one can establish between the retentional phase of the living present and secondary memory. In other words, what is at stake is the kind of difference we can establish between *Gegenwärtigung* and *Vergegenwärtigung*, between presentation and re-presentation. We anticipated this discussion above when we referred to Husserl's insight in the Fifth Cartesian Meditation. While Husserl shows in *The Phenomenology of Internal Time Consciousness* the irreducibility of *Vergegenwärtigung* to *Gegenwärtigung*, Derrida nevertheless interrogates – without questioning the demonstrative validity of this distinction – "the evidentiary soil and the *milieu* of these distinctions, ... [that is] what relates the terms distinguished to one another and constitutes the very possibility of the *comparison*" (VP: 72, Derrida's emphasis). It is important to recognise that Derrida is not claiming that there is no difference between retention and secondary memory (or between *Gegenwärtigung* and *Vergegenwärtigung*). Instead, because Husserl at one point (in §16 of *The Phenomenology of Internal Time-Consciousness*) calls retention a "non-perception," Derrida argues that there must be a *continuity* between retention and secondary memory such that it is impossible to claim that there is a *radical discontinuity* or a *radical difference* between retention and re-presentation. Therefore because the living present is thick, because the now cannot be separated from retention, there must be no radical difference between re-presentation and presentation or between non-perception and perception (VP: 72). As Derrida says,

> As soon as we admit this continuity of the now and the non-now, of perception and non-perception in the zone of originarity that is common to originary impression and to retention, we welcome the other into the self-identity of the *Augenblick*, non-presence and non-evidentness into the *blink of an eye of the instant*. There is a duration to the blink of an eye and the duration closes the eye. This alterity is even the condition of presence, of presentation, and

therefore of *Vorstellung* in general, prior to all the dissociations which could be produced there.

(VP: 73)

Within the duration, there is an alterity, a heterogeneity between perception and non-perception which is *also* a continuity. Between retention and re-production, there is only a difference between two modifications of non-perception (VP: 73). Therefore, as Derrida concludes, the alterity of the blink of the eye "cuts into, at its roots," the argument concerning the immediacy of meaning (expression) in soliloquy (VP: 74).

We have been considering the argumentation found in Chapter Five, but, as we said above, the argumentation against auto-affection really occurs in Chapter Six. In fact, Chapter Six is the heart of *Voice and Phenomenon*. Chapter Six concerns the voice of the title *Voice and Phenomenon*, the voice in soliloquy or interior monologue. For Husserl, according to Derrida, meaning (a thought) is generated from a stratum of silence, "the absolute silence of the self-relation" (VP: 77). Sense must be generated as an object repeatable to infinity (a universality) and yet remain close by to the acts of repetition (proximity). In other words, sense must be simultaneously present in the sense of an object (the relation to the object as over and against) and present in the sense of the subject (the proximity to self in identity, as close as possible). In order for this to happen, a specific medium or element of expression is needed; that medium or element is the voice (VP: 85). Sense is going to be generated by means of hearing-oneself-speak, by means of this specific kind of auto-affection (VP: 88). In effect in Chapter Six, Derrida provides a phenomenological description of hearing-oneself-speak.

Here are the basic features of that description. When I speak silently to myself, I do not make any sounds go out through my mouth. Although I do not make sounds through my mouth when I speak silently to myself, I make use of phonic complexes, that is, I make use of the forms of words or signs of a natural language. The use of natural phonic forms seems to imply that my interior monologue is an actual (not ideal) discourse. Because however the medium of the voice is temporal – the phonic forms are iterated across moments – the silent vocalisation endows the phonic forms with ideality (VP: 86). Thanks to the phonic forms utilised in hearing-oneself-speak, one exteriorises the ideal sense (a thought). This exteriorisation – ex-pression—seems to imply that we have now moved from time to space. But, since the sound is heard by the subject during the time he is speaking, what is expressed seems to be in absolute proximity to its speaker, "within the absolute proximity of its present" (VP: 85), "absolutely close to me" (VP: 87). We see how the element of the voice seems to satisfy the two requirements for the constitution of an ideal meaning: the silent expression objectifies the sense (universalises it) and yet it remains in proximity to the one expressing. In other words, the subject lets himself be affected by the signifier, but apparently without any detour through exteriority or through the world; or, as Derrida says, apparently without any detour through "the non-proper in general" (VP: 88); the subject seems to hear his *own* voice. Hearing-oneself-speak seems to be an absolutely pure auto-affection (VP: 89). What makes hearing-oneself-speak seem to be a pure auto-affection, according to Derrida, is that it seems to "be nothing other than the absolute reduction of space in general" (VP: 89). This apparent absolute reduction of space in general is why hearing-oneself-speak is so appropriate for universality (VP: 89). Requiring the intervention of no surface in the world, the voice is a "signifying substance that is absolutely available" (VP: 89). Its transmission or iteration encounters no obstacles or limits. The signified or what I want to say seems to be so close to the signifier that the signifier seems to be "diaphanous" (VP: 90).

Yet, the diaphaneity of the voice is only apparent since, now reverting back to the argumentation found in Chapter 5, it is conditioned by temporalisation. Temporalisation indeed makes the voice ideal, but by doing so it also makes the voice (the phonic forms) repeatable to infinity and therefore beyond the acts of expression taking place right now. As repeatable, the phonic forms have the possibility of not being close by. They are able to function as referring to something that is still to come; they are able to refer to non-presence, which turns the voice into an opaque murmur. In other words, the phonic forms are able to function indicatively – within the silence of expression. So, even in the auto-affection of hearing-oneself-speak, we find that we are not able to exclude impurity and impropriety. In short, temporalisation results in auto-affection being always and necessarily hetero-affection.

III.   The Two Forces of Event and Repetition

The argumentation we have just reconstructed from *Voice and Phenomenon* implies something about the composition of the ultra-transcendental level. It is composed of two kinds of forces: event and repetition. This is what Derrida says in "Typewriter Ribbon" (which dates from 1998): "Will this be possible for us? Will we one day be able, and in a single gesture, to join the thinking of the event to the thinking of the machine? Will we be able to think … , at one and the same time, both what is happening (we call that an event) and the calculable programming of an automatic repetition (we call that a machine)" (WA: 72)? The event is one of the forces. For Derrida, the idea of event refers to the force of the living being. The living being is spontaneous and self-moving. Insofar as it affects itself, it seems to be based on nothing but itself. It is singular. The first force is the force of singularisation. But also, as the living being affects itself, the affect gets "inscribed," as Derrida says, "right on some body or some organic material" (WA 72). The idea of an inscription leads Derrida to the other force. Here we have something like an inorganic matter, a machine, the machine of memory or retention. The machine that inscribes is based in repetition: "It is destined, that is, to reproduce impassively, imperceptibly, without organ or organicity, the received commands. In a state of anaesthesis, it would obey or command a calculable program without affect or auto-affection, like an indifferent automaton" (WA: 72). The automaticity of the inorganic machine is not the spontaneity attributed to organic life. These two forces, for Derrida, appear to be antonymic, incompatible, and yet inseparable. The thought of them together – joined and yet at war across the hiatus we mentioned above, the hiatus now resembling a sort of battlefield – opens up a new logic, an unheard of conceptual form, another kind of thinking than what we have seen in the history of philosophy. While the traditional form of thinking had opposed and separated, as Husserl opposed and separated expression and indication, the force of the event and the force of repetition, this new logic gives up "neither the event nor the machine, [it] subordinates neither one to the other, neither [does it] reduce one to the other" (WA: 74). At the beginning, we mentioned that Derrida's neologisms attempt to name the aporetical relation between sameness and otherness. Now we see that his neologisms or reconceived terms (from "différance" to "anachronism," and onto to "democracy") really refer to the logic of forces of event and repetition.

IV.   Conclusion: The Deconstruction of Sovereignty in *Rogues*

The logic of forces disturbs the theoretical foundations (as in Descartes) since the subject, we see now, is based in temporalisation. The present singularity of the "I think" is in fact contaminated with repetition coming from a past that it cannot remember and heading toward a future that it cannot predict. It also disturbs moral foundations (as in Kant) since autonomy – I spontaneously give the law to myself – is contaminated with the machinic repeatability of heteronomy, making the moral subject resemble animals. The argumentation against auto-affection and the logic of forces that emerges from it, however, go further than the theoretical and the moral. They also disturb political foundations. Derrida's later reflections on sovereignty flow from this argumentation. We shall conclude therefore with the deconstruction of sovereignty as it appears in *Rogues* (which dates from 2002).

The argumentation in *Rogues* is remarkably similar to that found in *Voice and Phenomenon* (more than thirty years earlier). According to Derrida, sovereignty, pure sovereignty, the very "essence of sovereignty" (R: 100), is silent. It does not have to give reasons, it "always keeps quiet in the very ipseity of the moment proper to it, a moment that is but the stigmatic point of an indivisible instant. A pure sovereignty is indivisible or it is not at all" (R: 100–101). "Ipse" is the Latin translation of the Greek "auto." Thus we see already how sovereignty seems to rely on auto-affection. What defines sovereignty is the indivisible possession of power; sovereignty does not share power. Not sharing means contracting power into an instant—the instant of action, of an event, of a singularity. When power is contracted into an instant, it is withdrawn from temporalisation; it has no "thickness." Recall Derrida's examination of Husserlian temporalisation: the "thickness" of retentions and protentions. Such a withdrawal explains why sovereignty is always silent; it tries to keep its power secret. If power is to be sovereign and indivisible, it cannot participate in language, which introduces universalisation and sharing. Sovereignty is incompatible with universalisation, with the force of repetition, which divides the instant and opens up the distance of the hiatus. And yet the concept of sovereignty calls for universalisation. If it is to be effective, sovereignty must communicate its power, its freedom, its decisions. It must necessarily enter temporalisation and more concretely history. It must speak. Yet, "as soon as I speak to the other, I submit to the law of giving reason(s), I share a virtually universalisable medium, I divide my authority" (R: 101). As soon as there is sovereignty, there is abuse of power since sovereignty can reign only by not sharing its authority. And yet there can be no use of power without the sharing of it through repetition. More precisely, as Derrida says, "since [sovereignty] never succeeds in [not sharing] except in a critical, precarious, and unstable fashion, sovereignty can only *tend* [Derrida's emphasis], for a limited time, to reign without sharing. It can only tend toward imperial hegemony" (R: 102). The tendency of which Derrida is speaking means that the event of sovereign power is always to come. It is an impossible event, but, as Derrida would say, the only event worthy of the name. Yet, the tendency to the event opens up a new investigation. How are we to imagine this tendency? Is it a tendency toward the worst or the best? More precisely, is the tendency moving toward a perfect sovereign, a god who would save us all? Or is the coming of a perfect sovereign the very worst violence in which all sharing with other living beings would end? Or is it possible to move the tendency toward something else, even though we do not know what that something else might be? Is it a tendency toward the least violence, in which all living beings would be allowed to be sovereign? Or, is this tendency toward letting all living being be sovereign itself, it too, the worst? Derrida of course cannot answer these questions, further questions that his thinking pushes us to ask. He has, of course, passed away. These are questions only for us, for those of us who still undergo the need to think of a future that keeps coming and without end.

Notes

1 The experience of the other is central to the argumentation found in *Voice and Phenomenon*. But it seems Derrida first emphasised the experience in his 1964 "Violence and Metaphysics: An Essay on the Thought of Emmanuel Levinas," in *Writing and Difference*. See especially WD: 123.

2 Although Husserl wrote some early texts on time prior to the 1900–1901 *Logical Investigations*, Husserl's time lectures really begin in 1905. Derrida had no access to these archival texts from the 1890s. In *Voice and Phenomenon*, he refers to Husserl's lectures as edited by Martin Heidegger (Husserl 1928). Derrida cites the Dussort translation. At the time *Voice and Phenomenon* was going to press, in 1966–67, the archival material on time appeared, but probably too late for Derrida to take into account (Husserl 1966).

16 Literature

Jeffrey T. Nealon

The question of literature in Derrida's work is, by necessity, entangled with the question of philosophy. Like so many other binary oppositions that Derrida deconstructs throughout his career, literature seems initially to occupy the place of the subordinate term in this philosophy vs. literature opposition, excluded by the dominating metaphysical ambitions of philosophical discourse (at least since Plato's banishment of the poets from the republic). However, in the end, Derrida works time and again to thematise literature not as philosophy's excluded binary opposite, but as a rival mode of theoretical engagement: literature as philosophy's secret partner and enabler.

In fact, Derrida confesses to have been interested as a young man primarily in literature rather than philosophy. As he admits at his thesis defense, looking back from 1980: "my most constant interest, coming even before my philosophical interest I should say, if this is possible, has been directed toward literature" (Derrida 1983b: 37). Indeed, he writes voluminously about literature throughout his career, and his work was first received into the English-speaking academy primarily as a kind of literary criticism, before (or at least in addition to) deconstruction's disciplinary identity as a philosophical discourse. The standing appointments that Derrida held at Yale, Irvine, NYU were housed in literature departments, not philosophy departments; and much of his work on literature was strategically aimed at questioning the totalising pretentions of philosophical discourse, its inability or unwillingness to deal with a certain kind of excessive writing practice that might be most economically characterised as "literary." As Derrida puts it in a 1983 interview, "My 'first' inclination wasn't really toward philosophy, but rather towards literature – no, towards something that literature accommodates more easily than philosophy" (I: 73).

This tension between philosophy and literature is played out in much of Derrida's early and mid-career work, but perhaps nowhere more intensely than in 1974's *Glas*, his two-column opus that quite literally plays the sober philosophical discourse of Hegel against the excessive literary productions of Jean Genet. In one column of the text we read about Hegel's incessant interest in religion, the family and the proper – Hegel's dialectic as guarding the productive channels of desire and the education of spirit, incorporating alterity and making it useful. In the second column, Derrida confronts this philosophical discourse par excellence, Hegel's discourse, with Genet's queer embrace of transgression – Genet's almost pure affirmation and expenditure, the improper in all of its guises. With this two-column arrangement of the text, Derrida's *Glas* quite literally asks the question: Given that dialectical philosophy aspires to include or sublate everything, to gather up all that remains and make it productive, what can this all-inclusive project have to say about Genet's discourse of joyous expenditure without return? Where do the lyrical languages and queer desires of Genet fit within the world of absolute spirit? In short, *Glas* stages for us the faceoff between philosophy and literature.

So perhaps philosophers will be pardoned if many of them have shared Jurgen Habermas's objections to deconstruction. In *The Philosophical Discourse of Modernity*, Habermas (1987) suggests that Derrida's work consists of a long series of attempts to reduce philosophy to literature, or at least to treat philosophical texts in a "merely" literary way – with obsessive attention to their style, metaphorics, and language usage, rather than their argumentative "content." In fact, it is this suggestion (that the whole of philosophy for Derrida is "literary" in some way – metaphorical, excessive, bound to language and its inherent slippages) that has led many philosophers to assert that in the world of deconstruction, there's nothing but literature: because slippage and indetermination are everywhere, and literature is the proper name for this undecidability, then everything is literature within the project and practice of deconstruction. This, at least, is a common way of understanding Derrida's infamous statement in *Of Grammatology*, "There is nothing outside the text." And in turn, it is a commonplace to suggest that deconstruction does nothing but endlessly restage the fight between literal and figurative language, between literature and philosophy. The major difference, of course, being that when deconstruction referees the bout, the poets win every time.

Derrida, however, most strenuously objects to this characterisation of his work as privileging literature over philosophy, or (even worse) reducing philosophy to a demonstration of endless indeterminacy. He takes particular issue with Habermas's (as I suggest above, quite representative) critiques of deconstruction in *The Philosophical Discourse of Modernity*:

Although I am not cited a single time, although not one of my texts is even indicated as a reference in a chapter of 25 pages that claims to be a long critique of my work, phrases such as the following can be found: "Derrida is particularly interested in standing the primacy of logic over rhetoric, canonized since Aristotle, on its head. ... the deconstructionist can deal with the works of philosophy as works of literature. ... In his business of deconstruction, Derrida does not proceed analytically ... Instead, he proceeds by a critique of style." That is false. I say false as opposed to true.

(LI: 156–57)

Likewise, and as an even more sharp rebuke to the dominant interpretation which suggests that he sees literature everywhere all the time, Derrida in fact quite pointedly says exactly the opposite: "there is no— or hardly any, ever so little [*à peine, si peu de*]—literature" (D: 223). So maybe at this point we need to follow Derrida's deconstructive practice and retrace exactly what literature is – how it functions – in Derrida's work. And hopefully this will help us to understand how, far from being "everything" or everywhere in his work, literature in Derrida's sense is in fact quite rare.

First, we need to recall the definition of "literature" at work in Derrida's texts. Contrary to the Manichean understanding of literature that many people carry into their reading of deconstruction (literature as the trans-historical binary opposite and "other" to the literalist dreams of philosophy – literature as the name for any indeterminate, highly metaphorical language usage), Derrida has a quite precise and historically bounded version of the concept. When asked by Derek Attridge what he means by literature, or what it meant to him to be invested in literature as a young man, Derrida answers: "literature seemed to me, in a confused way, to be the institution which allows one to say everything, in every way. ... The institution of literature in the West, in its relatively modern form, is linked to an authorization to say everything, and doubtless too to the coming about of the modern idea of democracy" (AL: 37). A couple of things we notice right off the bat here about Derrida's sense of literature: first, and most surprisingly, we see that for Derrida, literature is not the long-suffering "other" of philosophy (its oldest enemy, literature as the proper name for the undecidability that always and everywhere haunts the totalising pretentions of philosophy). On the contrary, what attracts Derrida to literature is not its corrosive, anti-Platonic recalcitrance, but the ways in which literature comprises its own alternative form of "totalisation": literature for Derrida is quite literally that which "allows one to say everything, in every way."

Second, we note here that Derrida's conception of literature is a distinctly modern and Western one, tied to the political rise of European democracies in the nineteenth-century. More than that, "literature" for Derrida very specifically signifies Western European avant-garde writing in the mode of aesthetic high modernism: "Let's make this clear," Derrida replies to Attridge with a kind of uncharacteristic candour: "What we call literature (not belles-lettres or poetry) implies that license is given to the writer to say everything he wants to or everything he can, while remaining shielded, safe from all censorship, be it religious or political" (AL: 37). When pressed to expand on his sense of literature, Derrida clarifies: "The name 'literature' is a very recent invention. ... Greek or Latin poetry, non-European discursive works, do not, it seems to me, strictly speaking belong to literature. One can say that without reducing at all the respect or the admiration they are due" (AL: 40). So it turns out that literature, far from being everything or everywhere in Derrida, is in fact very specifically confined in his work to describing the Western European avant-garde project of aesthetic modernist writing over the past 150 years or so, one which specifically tries to "say everything" in a form that rivals, rather than merely undermining or abandoning, the philosophical inclination toward totalisation.

We can at this point perhaps better understand Derrida's attraction to modern writers of great stylistic ambition – those who, in their own singular idiom, try to "say everything": Joyce, Genet, Ponge, Mallarmé, Kafka, Artaud. Indeed, it is this sense of literature as the idiomatic attempt to say everything that Derrida suggests is the reason he could never bring himself to write about Samuel Beckett's work – because Derrida's concept of literature as a uniquely exhausted but inexhaustible voice that tries to say everything is most intensely on display in Beckett's work. As Derrida says about Beckett, "precisely because of this proximity, it is too hard for me, too easy and too hard ... as though I had always already read [Beckett] and understood him too well" (AL: 60–61). And if something of the stylistic and conceptual ambition of a Joyce or a Genet is what qualifies as literature in Derrida's sense (a singular idiom harnessed to the project of saying everything), this likewise helps us to understand how or why there is very little literature: first, the field itself is relatively small – essentially, Western European high modernism; second, from within that relatively narrow aesthetic and historical field of possibilities, precious few writers approach the magisterial "say everything" ambition of Derrida's chosen canon on literature.

So we are now in a position to circle back around to one of the quotations from Derrida that we began with: "My 'first' inclination wasn't really toward philosophy, but rather towards literature – no, towards something that literature accommodates more easily than philosophy" (I: 73). In the end, then, it is not so much that literature rests in a simple binary opposition to literature in Derrida's thought, but philosophy and literature are two projects or performative forms that enact two distinct relations toward totalisation. It is not, as we have seen, that literature wallows in being open-ended and indeterminate, while philosophy thirsts after rationalist totalisation; but that both literature and philosophy comprise their own modes of totalisation, differing attempts to say everything. What separates them is not their nature, or even their project, but the performative and idiomatic ways in which literature "accommodates more easily than philosophy" the necessary failure of the project of saying everything – its inevitable limits, as well as its productivities.

And for Derrida, literature – avant-garde Western literature of the modernist era – takes both its form and content from that kind of necessary hesitation. With Beckett as its template and most intense example, literature doesn't merely abandon form, or relinquish the desire for completion; but literature does endlessly accommodate itself to the fact that the very possibility of its "say everything" project is simultaneously the condition of its impossibility: trying to say everything will inevitably fail. As Beckett puts it in a most compact fashion, "I can't go on. I'll go on." For his part, Derrida summarises the literary conundrum at a bit more length: "All those problems which are traditionally called 'formal' are what interest me most. To that extent, I think of myself as a sort of writer. But I'm unhappy with the boundaries between, let's say, literary writing and philosophical writing. I'm not a writer, but writing to me is the essential performance or act. I am unable to dissociate thinking, teaching, and writing. That's why I had to try to transform and to extend the concept of writing" (Derrida 1990: 4).

In other words, there is a sense in which Derrida wants to treat philosophical works in a "literary" manner, but that is only to say he is drawn in the text of Western philosophy to those moments of hesitation, *aporia*, and uncertainty: where the texts of the otherwise confident philosophical tradition fold back on themselves, those moments when they begin to accommodate themselves or bargain with a certain kind of possibility (the project of accounting for everything) that shows itself simultaneously as an impossibility. Literature, if there is such a thing (as Derrida is fond of saying), is the proper name for that (im)possibility of totalisation enacted as a mode of writing: literature comprises a singular idiom or form of engagement (different each time) that is rare in its ability to move forward in the project of saying everything, while simultaneously acknowledging its own limitations.

17 Politics

Niall Lucy

The Australian Labor Party government (a party of the so-called left, or a so-called party of the left) recently signed an asylum seeker deal with the government of Malaysia, a country that is not a signatory to the United Nations refugee convention, which would have seen 800 asylum seekers in Australia sent to Malaysia for "processing" in return for Australia's acceptance of 4,000 already "processed" and "legitimate" refugees from Malaysia. The full bench of the Australian High Court, however, has since found against the government's proposed deal, reasoning (by a majority of six to one) that a foreign country could not be declared a site of off-shore refugee processing "unless that country is legally bound by international law or its own domestic law [Malaysian internal policy does not recognise refugees], to provide asylum seekers with effective procedures for assessing their protection needs; protect the asylum seekers until their refugee claims are determined and also protect them until they return voluntarily to their homeland or are resettled in another country" (Kirk 2011). The Australian government may yet pass a bill to circumvent the High Court's decision by increasing the powers of the federal immigration minister, but in the meantime let's take this for a good example of a political event involving at least the following features: an elected government's right to determine citizenship and to police its national borders; the right of a judiciary to decide the legality of government policy by an appeal to international law; and the question of the official and unofficial status of refugees.

But the lesson of deconstruction, as it were, might be that in order for such an event to be seen as "political" it must not be reducible to a programmable decision arrived at from within a determinate system. "Guaranteed translatability," Derrida writes in *Specters of Marx*, "given homogeneity, systematic coherence in their *absolute forms*" would each or together be "what renders ... the future—in a word the other—*impossible*" (SM: 35). Hence a political decision that was immediately and universally translatable—perfectly homogeneous and coherent from within a politico-philosophical *system*—would *not* be a decision in Derrida's sense. This is already to rethink the political in terms of what might be regarded as secret, mysterious or undecidable. "Politics excludes the mystical," as Derrida puts it in *The Gift of Death*, which is to say that for politics (as for philosophy and ethics) there are "no final secrets" (GD: 34; 63). For politics to be on the side of a certain relation to the future and to others, then, a new concept of the political is called for that would be characterised by its inclusion of whatever politics in the standard sense excludes: namely, everything belonging to the structure of the secret that might be said to be foreign or heterogeneous to knowledge.

A possible candidate for such a concept might be the popular expression that "everything is political," a claim both totalising and unfalsifiable: there is nothing that could not be used as evidence to support it. If, to take a seemingly trivial example, I chose the larger of two remaining portions of cake at a dinner party, knowing that at least one other guest wished for cake, I could be accused of making a decision that was not simply impolite or selfish, but "political," since it was exercised on behalf of my own interests at the expense of another's. Even had I taken the larger slice unwittingly, oblivious to anyone else who may have desired it and who had no less right to it than me, by choosing the bigger portion I deprived others of the chance to do so; hence I acted to my own advantage by deciding, wittingly or unwittingly, not to acknowledge a responsibility to consider the interests and welfare of others. My action may have been a breach of etiquette, then, but it could also, in the context of the terms I am using here, be called political for being an expression of my *power* to act in such a way, so that it was in my power to decide to take the larger slice or to disregard the rights of others to it because of my age, say, or my gender, ethnicity, social position and so on, or simply because my proximity to the cake tray afforded me an opportunity to pick the bigger piece.

Who would have thought a slice of cake might have had so much blood in it? Yet if this were allowed to count as a political example for now (thereby politicising my decision to use it), it might be seen to unfold the political as a site of contestation: as a condition never quite *belonging* to an event, but which is produced or postulated by an act of reading or interpretation. Hence there would not be *one* political discourse, but a multiplicity of discourses (heterogeneous, contradictory, historical, etc.) on or around the identity of politics as a concept that is never indivisible and therefore never pure, and therefore always already in deconstruction. If it is possible to refer, say, to the "politics" of table manners, then surely it would seem that everything is political and politics is a concept with no outside. On this view, while there may be things other than politics, nothing would be essentially contrary to politics as such. Precisely, then, because politics is multiple and divided, it does not belong exclusively to matters concerning the management or government of a state, or to international relations between states, and so we may speak of institutional, domestic, corporate, cultural, sexual, industry, religious, gender, personal, generational and many other forms of politics.

These other forms, however, are mere supplements to the official or classical understanding of politics as the science of government or, following Aristotle, as the field to which "affairs of state" properly belong. But every supplement (Lucy 2004: 135–41) can always function either as a substitution or an addition, by replacing a supposedly originary essence or presence or by adding something to it, and if this is true of *every* supplement, then what exactly "is" the function that supplements perform? Consider the example Derrida works with in *Of Grammatology* (but not only there): writing as the supplement of speech. If written language can substitute for spoken language, how could anything belong to speech as something "proper" to it; and how could spoken language be authentic or originary? If, on the other hand, writing adds to speech, what did spoken language lack from the beginning? What is essential to speech such that writing may substitute for its essence; and what is an essence inhabited by a lack?

The logic of supplementarity is not only a matter for philosophical contemplation; it also poses a political problem. For if the identity of a thing is not assured, but porous, how would we know where or whether to intervene on behalf of minority causes or marginal interests? For a certain concept of the political, however, this would not be a question because politics proper (*Realpolitik*, as it were) would always be distinguishable from its sectional or supplementary 'copies'; and yet if Derrida's work may be said to describe a political project, or perhaps to open a political theme, dating from "Force of Law" (1989) through to *Specters of Marx* (1994), *Politics of Friendship* (1997), *Philosophy in a Time of Terror* (2003), *Rogues* (2004) and beyond to the two volumes of *The Beast & the Sovereign* (2009 and 2011), its point would be to render unthinkable any notion of a purely political discourse or a pure concept of the political. This theme is played out in Derrida's later work through a biological figure, autoimmunity, the features of which resemble those associated with the earlier figure of the supplement.

Autoimmunity refers to the inherent capacity of every immune system to turn upon itself and suicide, mistaking the self (the body's own cells) for the other or the non-self (foreign antigens). Just as the logic of supplementarity reveals the relationship between speech and writing to be non-oppositional in structure, so the logic of autoimmunity causes trouble for the idea that self and other are opposed. It is important to note, however, that supplementarity and autoimmunity are situated among a series of Derridean terms or figures (*pharmakon*, parergon, *differance*, iterability, etc.) that put the identity of a thing in deconstruction, and so while they may not be fully interchangeable they are also not fundamentally different from one another. What causes Derrida to turn to autoimmunity (without turning away from supplementarity, etc.) when it comes to politics, especially regarding the possibility of thinking politics otherwise, has to do with the ways in which the breakdown of the biological self offers a metaphor for the deconstruction of the body politic.

As a particular kind of language game that legitimates certain sets of practices and identities while denying legitimacy to alternative sets, every politics seeks to immunise itself against external threats. Typically, then, hostility is the hallmark of a political response to others. The modern expression of what might be called this antagonistic function of the political is owed to German philosopher and jurist Carl Schmitt, who famously defined politics in his 1932 book, *The Concept of the Political*, as "the distinction between friend and enemy" (Schmitt 2006: 26). For Schmitt, then, a politics without enmity would be impossible, but for Derrida it is precisely this impossible "politics of friendship" that must be allowed to permeate the borders of a concept whose purity would be defended at all costs, including the lives of others. As a kind of immune system for the protection of friends against the intrusion of foes, Schmitt's politics operates only at the public level (there could be no private enemy according to Schmitt) and does so, moreover, on behalf of a scarcely concealed ethnocentrism: the word "friend," he reminds us, referred originally to "the friend of blood, the consanguine parent or again 'the parent by alliance' through marriage, oath of fraternity, adoption or other corresponding institutions" (Schmitt 2006: 104). Schmitt's friends, in short, constitute a family, a *Volk*.

In the first volume of *The Beast & the Sovereign* (being in part the posthumous continuation of Derrida's dialogue with Schmitt), Derrida points out that philosophers of politics are always at the same time citizens, and that what they say about politics is always "implicated and exposed in the national political field of their time" (BS 1: 51). In Schmitt's case, his implication extended from his membership of the Nazi Party to his appointment as State Councillor for Prussia and his professorial chair at the University of Berlin, positions he owed to Nazi patronage. Indeed, as the architect of the Weimar Republic's Article 48, which granted absolute power to the executive in the event of an emergency, Schmitt made it possible for Hitler to establish the dictator-ship of the Third Reich by providing him with the constitutional means to suspend democratic rights in Germany in 1933. As implications go, Schmitt's could not have been more unequivocal; his political "philoso-phy" was mired in the politics of fascism, although it would be wrong to think that fascism as a political philosophy was conceived in opposition to democracy. The first official fascist document, after all, the "Platform of the Fasci di Combattimento", published in Mussolini's *Il Popolo d'Italia* newspaper on 6 June 1919, calls for the implementation in World War I-torn Italy of recognisably democratic social rights including uni-versal suffrage and "eligibility for women"; lowering the voting age to eighteen; a minimum wage; an eight-hour working day; proletarian management of industries and public services; and the *"seizure of all goods belonging to religious congregations* and the abolition of episcopal revenues, both of which represent an enormous liability for the nation and a privilege enjoyed by the very few" (Schnapp 2000: 5–6).

The Third Reich's political birth from within a democratic constitu-tion serves as a historical reminder that fascism is not quite external to democracy; hence the paradox of autoimmunity—what would protect us, destroys us. For democracy this paradox proceeds from the extension of rights, which must include the possibility of suspending those rights, but Derrida insists that autoimmunity is not an exclusively destructive process:

> ... autoimmunity is not an absolute ill or evil. It enables an exposure to the other, to *what* and *who* comes—which means that it must remain incalculable. Without autoimmunity, with absolute immu-nity, nothing would ever happen or arrive; we would no longer wait, await, or expect, no longer expect one another, or expect any event.
>
> (R: 152)

While autoimmunity opens us to threat, in other words, it also opens us to chance. Without autoimmunity, without this exposure to who or what knows may come from elsewhere than within the self, the self would not *be* itself. Our selfhood or self-identity, then, is not defined by absolute immunity, but by the condition of our unconditional openness, to others. The self is not fixed, but fissured.

If immunity leads to hostility, to the protection of borders from the threat of external penetration, autoimmunity may lead to the possibility of *hospitality*, of receiving others without demanding they should be or become like us or on condition only that they are or must become our friend. In this way autoimmunity would be the general economy of a new concept of the political, as distinct from the restricted economy of "political immunity" that a nation state may bestow on certain others as an exception that is the very expression of sovereign power. "It is precisely the exception," according to Schmitt, "that makes relevant the subject of sovereignty, that is, the whole question of sovereignty" (Schmitt 2006: 5). Sovereignty is thus the power to decide exceptions, but, as Derrida notes, it would be wrong to suppose that so-called norms (laws, say, or rights) are immune to this logic:

> ... sovereignty, like the exception, like the decision, *makes the law in excepting itself from the law*, by suspending the norm and the right that it imposes, by its own force, at the very moment that it marks that suspense in the act of positing law or right. The positing or establishing of law or right are exceptional and are in themselves neither legal nor properly juridical.
>
> (BS2: 81)

The law, that is to say, exempts or excepts itself in order to invent itself as the norm. By an originary act of violence it gives itself the right to decide what is normal or exceptional, and in maintaining this right the law is caught in an autoimmune paradox of using violence to guard against violence. Neither legal nor juridical, sovereign power exempts itself from the law in order to invent the law as the arbiter both of normality and exceptionality.

Typically, the expression of this power is associated with totalitarian, theocratic, dictatorial or other anti-democratic forms of statehood, often referred to as "rogue" or "outlaw" states. As Derrida observes, though, a "rogue state" is not a transcendental category, but rather a term used to designate an enemy of US economic, political or military interests. "A rogue state is basically whomever the United States says it is" (R: 96). But since America cannot quite label its Schmittian enemies the enemies of America per se, it defines them as states operating as exceptions to international law; and by asserting its exceptional power to decide these exceptions, the US becomes the most sovereign rogue of all:

> The first and most violent of rogue states are those that have ignored and continue to violate the very international law that they claim to champion, the law in whose name they speak and in whose name they go to war against so-called rogue states each time their interests so dictate. The name of these states? The United States.
>
> (R: 96)

American exceptionality immunises it from official censure, not least due to America's membership as one of only five permanent nations of the UN Security Council. The democratic internationalism of the United Nations, in other words, is haunted by the autoimmunity of the super-powers, China and the US, together with the other permanent Security Council members, Britain, France and Russia. A small group of nations therefore has the executive power to decide, on behalf of an idea of the international, where and when a violation of international law has occurred, and what force to use in response to it: "it is the Security Council, with its veto power, that has all the power to make binding or enforceable decisions, that wields all the force of effective sovereignty" (R: 98). The sovereignty of the United Nations owes its democratic force to the sovereign sovereignty of the Security Council; democracy depends on the violence it would oppose.

But while US foreign policy may appear to confirm Schmitt's defini-tion of the enemy as always public, its post-9/11 domestic policy gives the lie to Schmitt's insistence that enemies always pose an external threat. Since 9/11 and the declaration of the war on terror, indeed, it is not only the identification of enemies but also a whole set of political terms of reference which has become increasingly problematic, such that the "war" against "terrorism" cannot be understood according to the traditional concept of a war between nation states. The "rogue" states accused by the US or the UN of aiding terrorists "do not do so as states" (Derrida quoted in Borradori, 2003: 101), and as for the location of ter-rorist networks—these foreign cells are as likely to be found within one state (the US, for example) as another. The terrorist, then, conforms not to the appearance and identity of Schmitt's enemy, but to the ghost of Hamlet's father, a figure that puts the very concepts of appearance and identity into question. What is that figure's being, its sovereignty, its time? If it may be thought to exist at all, to *be* at all, how may it do so in a time other than the present?

From Al Gore to Al-Qaeda, politics today has no choice but to respond to spectres; and yet it is not the spectre of environmentalism, but of terrorism, to which today's political systems (especially those calling themselves democratic) have chosen to be most responsive. The risk of environmental no less than that of terrorist annihilation threatens to rain down an apocalyptic future that would bring the future to an end, but it is only the threat of the spectre of terrorism that causes democracies to act in ways that violate what might be called shared democratic principles of free expression, free passage and free assem-blage. There is no "more visibly autoimmune process," Derrida insists (R: 39), than the repression of these principles in the aftermath of 9/11, in the name of state or national security. Democracy would appear to have no immunity against its own autoimmune suspension:

> One can thus do little more than regret some particular abuse in the a priori abusive use of the force by which a democracy defends itself against its enemies, justifies or defends itself, of or from itself, against its potential enemies. It must thus come to resemble these enemies, to corrupt itself and threaten itself in order to protect itself against their threats. Inversely, antithetically, so to speak, it is perhaps because the United States has a culture and a system of law that are largely democratic that it was able to open itself up and expose its greatest vulnerability to immigrants, to, for example, pilots in training, experienced and suicidal "terrorists" who, before turning against others but also against themselves the aerial bombs that they had become, and before hurling them by hurling themselves into the two World Trade Towers, were trained on the sovereign soil of the United States, under the nose of the CIA and the FBI, perhaps not without some autoimmune consent on the part of an administration with at once more and less foresight than one tends to think when it is faced with what is claimed to be a major, unforeseeable event.
>
> (R: 40)

Yet how "unforeseeable" was it, given that in retrospect we might say that *Specters of Marx*, written well before the event of 9/11, scripted the very conditions of possibility for such an event? It did so, for example, by alluding to the "worldwide power of those super-efficient and properly capitalist phantom-States that are the mafia and the drug cartels on every continent", which have "infiltrated and banalized themselves everywhere, to the point that they can no longer be strictly identified" (SM: 83). If today, then, "Al-Qaeda" operates rhetorically in the West as a quasi-nation state, its phantasmagoria is owed not exclusively to 9/11, but also to what Derrida calls "tele-technic dis-location" (SM: 82).

Precisely because the terrorist, like the phantom, may appear anywhere at any time, the US puts everyone under suspicion—including those who would be the victims of terrorism. When, like the phantom, or like members of the mafia or drug cartels, the terrorist is neither identifiably inside nor outside the state, what is there for the state to immunise itself against? But since autoimmunity cuts both ways, security is always vulnerable to hospitality; in the case of democratic states, national security is always to some extent limited and compromised by an openness to difference that extends beyond the borders of a nation and the idea of nationhood. The autoimmune effect of such hospitality is the condition of what Derrida calls the "new international," described as "a link of affinity ... without coordination, without party, without country, without national community" (SM: 85). As "the friendship of an alliance without institution" (SM: 86), the new international would be the politics of friendship as an event that was not reducible to a time and place—the Occupy "movement," perhaps, or for example. Without the autoimmune threat to the security of a democratic nation from effects of hospitality, a nation would not be democratic: the others whom a democracy would keep out, it must also welcome. Hence there could be no such thing as a democratic nation since democracy would always be international:

> ... democracy has always wanted by turns and at the same time two incompatible things: it has wanted, on the one hand, to welcome only men, and on the condition that they be citizens, brothers, and compeers, excluding all the others, in particular bad citizens, rogues, noncitizens, and all sorts of unlike and unrecognizable others, and, on the other hand, at the same time or by turns, it has wanted to open itself up, to offer hospitality, to all those excluded.
>
> (R: 63)

The autoimmune effects of internationalism (even in the restricted sense of international trade or tourism) put every nation at the risk of suicide. By opening themselves to global media networks and the Internet, nations must welcome even "dangerous" ideas and possible links of affinity that may threaten the very foundation of a national identity. There is no outside the media or outside-mediation, as it were (Lucy 2011). Such effects, however, are not confined to their impact on national identities, but extend to the very identity of a thing "itself". Consider the example of the present book, whose identity would claim for "it" a certain unity or autonomy; yet what is the unity of a book that is divided and dispersed by the autoimmune inclusion of a set of bibliographic references? What is a book that is not constituted by a network of relations to an outside in the form of writing or textuality in general?

If these questions conjure the spectre of an "early", "playful" Derrida, they might also be taken as an injunction to read or reread deconstruction as political philosophy from the very beginning. The view that Derrida took a political turn in his later work, in other words, may not have its source in those works as such, but in their indissociability from the political field of their time; a field that stretches from at least the first Gulf War to beyond 9/11, when the phantom suicide bomber reappears as Hamlet's ghost. When there is no border that can separate the inside from the outside, whether of a text or a nation; when there is no absolute precaution that could be taken to protect a concept of self-identity, politics could be only what happens in the thick of things. There, in media res, the political would be revealed as the work of case-by-case decision-making in the absence of a prescriptive system of laws. In this way the political would be always already divisible and deconstructible, such that we may entertain the politics of table manners; which is why, precisely, we may entertain the politics of friendship.

18 Reading: Derrida and the Non-Future

Tom Cohen

1. Future Readers

It is interesting to think of Derrida's readers not as they are today but as they may be, beyond the current generation of relays, handlers, and nostalgiacs, *tomorrow*—whether that time ever arrives or not. But let us assume the event of Derrida can be *pinged*, and let's assume that reading as we know it remains, and that the episode that Derrida represents persists. Such future readers would be heirs to the present, including the present's wilful blinds, in diverse ways. They would not form some imaginary progeny that would continue as a "school." They would inherit the remainder: devastated resources, mega-debt, irreversible climate change and accelerations. It would be easy enough to say, too abruptly, that the tendency to want to identify (or identify with) various official versions of "Derrida", real and manufactured, had gotten in the way of genuine reading—much as had his own, late tendency to generate and play with various *personae*. It gets in the way, this algorithmic dandyism, becoming a way of managing a spectral empire and an imagined future readership. Derrida's self-presentation concealed immense disguised melancholy perhaps, producing dolphin flips in rhetoric that would make "deconstruction" seem almost too assimilable, too appropriable, too fangless to be resisted. In the "later" Derrida we hear ethics, religion, "politics,"—and of course the closet affirmation of Eurocentrism and, ultimately, a sort of "Yes, Yes," that became a little bit too indiscriminate and, well, roguish. Since this imagined readership of the non-existent future (a definition of "future" here) will emerge fundamentally in a different set of co-ordinates, it will likely look back upon the legacy of twentieth-century thought, inclusive of "deconstruction," and ask two questions. Why were the "revolutionary" mavens of twentieth-century critique seemingly blind to the arrival, and implications, not of social and mnemonic contexts, forces of human historical justice, or the relation of war to technics, but the mass extinction events under-way, and accelerating, of twenty-first century climate change? Was Der-rida, after all obversely, tied *not* to metaphysics (which turns out never to have existed as such, but rather to be a hermeneutic reflex practiced more broadly today than ever), but to the "anthropo-narcissism" which, he remarks in *Specters of Marx*, would be a primary target of something referred to in the third person as "deconstruction"?

2. Endings

Where did Derrida seem, despite so many overturned structures, to stop short nonetheless? What does this imagined reader of a non-existent future extract from Derrida's text once all the tricks, traffic, doubling-back, and self-stagings no longer appear as relevant? One must add, at this point, that such an inquiry is not only about the "future" readers but responds to the present wake of Derrida's work. However assimilated a certain set of tags are, and however the word "deconstruct" circulates in popular media today (which has come to mean nothing more than to display inner contradictions), it is clear that Derrida always knew he had a problem with "legacy;" and so he tried to rehearse it all again and again in advance. Today, despite earnest energies, there seems to be a surprising failure of "deconstruction" to assure the relevance of itself, or Derrida, to twenty-first-century readers. So the problem is not imagin-ary, nor can it be fully unfolded in a brief note like this.

3. Archive

A "note like this" assumes a certain familiarity, on one's own terms, with this trajectory. But one can suspend the genre of interrogating Derrida's text, or an imaginary "Derrida," which one would read with or re-inscribe or "extend" or repeat—as if a persona were essential to side with (or against). One can rather use this "future" as an index to read back, separate out or extract and revive. That is, rather than aim for familiarity and fraternity with a Derrida one would imagine as the *real* Derrida, one might already abandon that gesture and look back at Derrida, as if from afar. That "future," whatever it looks like in a few decades, will produce some wonder at the passive disorientation or "inattentiveness" (Stiegler 2010) of the most recent *fin de siècle*. Wonder will be directed not only at their (our) spellbound irresponsibility, infantilism, and corruption (the "turn-key totalitarianism" of compara-tive comforts and consumer options), or the lack of critical innovation or any political trenchancy at all, but that the decade of tipping points passed should be missing from the philosophic traditions, from Derridean *ecriture*. They are going to be pissed, and probably dismissive of moaning about legacies, mourning, ghosts, and so on—which will seem, by then, distractions.

4. Promise

This future is likely to focus on the implications of an early Derrida, an unfinished opening, in which a certain "materiality" of mnemonic structures was definitively exposed and linguistically put on display—irreversibly, except not quite. Derrida's generation would never quite engage the biological epochality released by the hydrocarbon era, but rather roamed within it. One can identify many points of crossing in Derrida, and each reader will find her own; but his recurrent instinct was to work the borders, to restitch archival forces, to incorporate the newsreel of contemporary investments—to stage deconstruction as a pedagogic performance (and self-commentary). This staging produced so much debris, so many fractals. What one does *not* have is the destructive "one-way street" evinced by Benjamin, or practiced by de Man; in the end, Derrida's affirmations creak a bit (Benjamin 1979; de Man 1986). So this "future" reader might, say, return to the opening question which Derrida's work poses, and regard episodes of the subsequent work as one or more virtual trajectories, or as miscalibrated, while other moments would be of more interest to a different reading scene or community. (And yes, by the time Derrida allowed himself tropes like "deconstruction is justice," he seemed to abuse his rhetorical powers.[FL])

5. Bet

The question, really, is what Derrida understood his *wager* or gamble to be, or what risk he took in moving foward, and why he pulled back repeatedly? It has been suggested that this absence, repression or occlusion of "climate change" and eco-catastrophics in late Derrida, – when it should certainly have appeared – provides the clue to a strategy, once we step back from the omission's obvious fronts and rhetorical regressions. By re-citing the Levinasian formulae he had, early on, seemed to foreclose (WD), he not only prestidigitated a weird "ethics," and colluded with a diversion of attention away from accelerating ecocide to invoked "others", he also deflected attention away from the problem of the limited materiality of his own archive. So, we must imagine this future reader as unencumbered during her time and context, without the fetishisations of the name or need for crafted personae. For her, the overriding question would return to what Derrida had, at his inception, discovered: that the very orders of cognitive and neural programming were associable with marking systems, and the hypothesis that a certain type of intervention, a certain type of reading, would interrupt the machine and re-set the inscriptions out of which modernities seemed generated. This focus, I think, is one Derrida perhaps once dreamed of.

6. New

To speak of future readers is not quite the same as "new" readers, those picking up Derrida today,—though these latter do so in a bewildering enough environment. It points toward an absent reader, which the Derrida who brooded over his legacy would gesture to (uniquely, in his last interview, by disavowing his contemporaries' and scions' reading of him [LL]). So outside of the conundrum that was once to be speculated upon, as if protesting too much, about "*deconstruction's*" *futures*, we might ask instead why there seems to be a general sense (a decade after Derrida's death) that the forces he set in play have mothballed, and that this is so despite (or *because*) of the efforts of a select group of institutional promoters? Any *direct* extrapolations of a "deconstruction" legacy has largely run aground, in particular with regard to any interest it draws from the "nextgens." To speak of Derrida's readers tomorrow is not to flag the endless (clearly anxious) conferences once given for Derrida on deconstruction's "futures," but is another question entirely: something else, technically beyond the life spans of much in the present generation. This reading, nonetheless, would be generated from a certain position seeded within Derrida's work.

7. Work

I say Derrida's *work* because I think, by then, even a few decades hence, all the residual traces and paradoxes of how Derrida staged his living signature(s) would have vaporised, along with the weak mourning for imaginary "Jacques" in the current generation (where that exists). One would also be removed from the tedium of twentieth-century polemics and pre-occupations, academic schools and factions, along with the rhetorical compromises he thought he could outwit by being "Derrida." That is, a future reader would have emerged, in this not too distant future, amidst an entirely different set of referents from the late twentieth-century traditions provided in the tribal preoccupations and hopeful versions of "politics." After all, by and large across the board, these twentieth-century thinkers, Derrida among them, were *not* alert to twenty-first century climate change—which casts the whole game-board, outside of the Euro-centered fetishization of "metaphysics," into a "speciesist" perspective. And from this later moment, decades hence, one can anticipate traits (at least), which suggest how "deconstruction" may be taken up or re-viewed. I will return to these. But by then this game-board of virtual readings would no longer be a thought experiment, but more like a mathematical deduction. What if the premise upon which Derrida staged himself rhetorically involved a twentieth-century platform which, rhetorically, would fade, be hollowed out or replaced, altering the mode of reading that would crystallise?

8. Presence

I would like to speculate from this point of view on Derrida's words, for a portmanteau translation (and do so as an obverse echo of Geoffrey Bennington's master-stroke in *Jacques Derrida* of foregoing citations). The genius here was a move that was at once popularizing, disowned (by Derrida of course), and an abandoned (dis)incorporation. There has always been a covert paralysis as regards incorporating Derrida while "alive," that was held in check by Derrida himself. But let's put aside whether "deconstruction" (this third person "it" that Derrida liked to conjure) had any mission of its own (or, like psychoanalysis—a more successful *branding*—could feign the prestige of being a science). That is, pretending that "metaphysics" was a starting point: was what was to be "deconstructed," something more than a collective Western cultural programming, and one which we very much have with us still? Was what Derrida targeted as "metaphysics of presence" not rooted more in cognitive and interpretive conventions—conventions that are not simply found but perpetually generated? This, *sotto voce*, or hint that "presence" was not simply a topic of high philosophy was the nudge that Paul de Man offered to Derrida, which was declined, but which seems to offer a much firmer starting point for a twenty-first century "reading" of Derrida.

9. Climate Change

This "future" reader of Derrida, from a position clarified by the advance of mid-twenty-first century climate change (which has been the missing factor, and blind, of twentieth-century philosophic and socio-revolutionary traditions) might well set aside some Derridean strategies as too cloying, or as tactical detours. Once this future reader set aside the grand gestures of self-archiving, she might then draw out those left standing.

At a certain "heart" of Derrida's writing machine there was a gamble on a transformation, a mutation, that would institute a wholly different import, model, and scene of action in reading, aka, the policies of mnemotechnic worlding; this gamble would occur at a time, in a sense, when "reading" itself were to be both generalised and marginalised, in ways accelerated by the explosions of digital circuitry and data streams. This anarchic mutation of reading would be the first thing rejected as the point of resistance to Derrida—to be deflected by the import of focusing on language, text, that there is "nothing" outside "text," and so on. And of course, as the "world" moves into mass-extinction accelerations (with no pathos intended here, for a destruction that seems to be pre-inscribed in archivization as we know it), this "textual" strategy seemed even less relevant. Yet this never goes away: the core interface between human cognitive organisation and its anteriorities, inscriptions, "truths," and stupidities, all bound to institutionalised cognitive-cronyisms undifferentiated from telemarketing in many ways—or, for that matter, the "short-circuiting" (Stiegler) that has yielded a Potemkin "capitalism" and a "proletarianization of the senses" and of critical strategies. It is not accidental that the "post-theory" menu of start-ups has proven systemically regressive while narrating themselves as provincially "post-human" (return to phenomenology, return to affect, pretend ethics is finding another other to ventriloquize animals?), extend and pretend. To recover a perpetually explosive side of Derrida's wager, which had no "use by" date, is to reframe what is, or would be, transformed. And it might mean allying the Derridean pulsion *with what looks back from the temporal disorders that the realities of climate change provide*—a succinct displacement of the "anthropo-narcissism" that Derrida targeted? Today of course, "2014," witnesses geographically diverse societal breakdowns and insurrections, resource wars, and wildly destructive weather anomalies. It is the same date, from some non-future, that will be marked as a cipher in two related ways: one, is that the dust-clouds following the 2008 "financial meltdown" settled to reveal the most astonishingly engineered mass wealth shift since Genghis (digitally enhanced), with some 86 individuals owning the assets of the lower 50% of the population (7 billion people). It is also the year, quietly signalled, when the Western states (U.K., Europe, Australia), set aside their carbon reduction goals before economic pressures (the eco-eco catastrophe dance), just as increasingly dire reports of passed tipping points proliferate—and climate denialism rises (in the Anglo or Murdoch media nations). That is, it would be the year in which the corporate states affirm irreversible global warming and the prospect of mass (and possibly auto) extinction events. This new mass "proletarianization" of global middle classes spawns a two-tier world or what the financial analyst Catherine Austin Fitts terms a "breakaway civilization" or economy. If you are on a wasted planet with too many people for the resources, rapidly deteriorating, you do one of two things: you either come together as a "global civilization" to do a re-set (Copenhagen), in full awareness of the consequences—but at the cost of ruining the economies and their own political regimes; or, you accelerate forward, planning for a survivor group that controls hard assets and new technologies (nano-technics, genetic engineering, nextgen robotics). In short, the outline, on a dying planet, of an engineered species split going forward, whose mantra will be *adaptation* (retiring sustainability and mitigation) *and* the profit of engineering schemes. Straight out of Hollywood, but at least it's a plan. So this is an interesting date in some ways, if one is paying attention (which is difficult with cultures enforcing ADD).

How might such "reading" (after the foreclosure of reading) proceed? Reflectively, selectively.

10. Ethics

One might focus on an unlikely thread here—perhaps the unlikeliest in Derrida: "Ethics." There is no greater failure of the rhetoric of ethics as a pretense than its inability to function collectively, as regards its future, before climate change. In fact, the entire model of ethics as directed to an "other" should be abruptly jettisoned as a transient vestige of late twentieth-century humanism.

This motif and pre-occupation of the "late" Derrida can be tied to a complicity and rhetorical regress, placating the intellectual mood and modus of contemporaries: the post-colonial hangover, the affirmations of "cultural" others, the responsibility of the (blind) "decision," and so on. It is in this bouillabaisse which some point to as where Derrida erred, prestidigitated too much, spawning at best a cozy subset of "decon-structive" carriers bonded to the idea of some sort of good, bleeding into the political and the religious. These are topoi that "early" Derrida had been accused of sterilising his thought toward (that is, as "politics," or "religion," or "ethics" had been deployed). In the end, everything rests, we noted, on a mnemonic intervention, a wager, a re-ordering of incompatible times. Yet the *irreversibility* of this gesture is one Derrida would retrace his way to again and again, but seldom choose to cross. So the "ethical" would find itself feeding off the (then) contemporary readership's need to identify as a "good," to bond around, to pretend to access "the otherness of the other" in zombie-reviving Levinasian formulae which the early Derrida had, supposedly, decimated.

11. 21st Century

The question is: does "Derrida" re-assemble, necessarily, differently from a twenty-first century "tomorrow," or in the face of climate change, resource depletions, and a disappearing "future"? The absence of a discourse of climate change or a critique of ecolographics in his work, it has been remarked, is too egregious to be accidental—and designates, by its absence, a translational node we can supplement today. I would suggest that the present generation, and above all those hung-over with twentieth-century master-thinkers, with various promises of revolution and revelation, has proven itself uniquely blinded and unprepared, critically, for the turn that was handed to it. Like the political systems today, and like a post-democratic West whose corporate media ensures that no "leaders" will arise capable of individual decision (evidenced by the absence of climate change from the recent presidential elections in the U.S.), the *critical culture* had been quietly gutted. As noted, what Stiegler terms a "proletarianization of the sensibility," a numbing take-over of inscriptions by a relentless short-circuiting of reference, extended to a proletarianization of critical maneuvers—unable to step outside of local default "we's" or hermeneutic algorithms that never part with the *eco*, and return to pre-critical premises – miming past memes for currency, the way Putin regurgitates being seen as Czar, or China as "Maoist," or the U.S. as an "age of affluence," all 20th century covers. This critical culture had not yet (or still) separated itself from the machinations that brought about a span of a decade or so in which, according to the numbers, the futures of species would be negatively decided (and irreversibly). It is more obvious today that "metaphysics" was never discrete, and did not name an ontological mutation. If anything, it would be a by-name for the blind acceleration of an arc of late anthropoid imperialism and hyperconsumption that would cap a short, recently over-populated trajectory enabled by the discovery of hydro-carbon fuel. It is the brevity of the so-called human or civilized "histories," or the length of its immersion in unrecorded pre-histories (when perceptual settings would be hewn), that makes the pre-historial post-contemporary. Finally one might choose to re-direct the "ethical" impulse, but only *after* the artefaction of the "good" has been deleted (it really takes only a key-stroke) as a machinal effect of interpretation allied to the anchor of reference, grounds, origins, organic models, and other gods. Today, the introduction of the ecocidal thought advances this prospect, the affirmative calculus that any model of recovery, mitigation, sustainability, and so on—any latent organicism or, for that matter, hope in dodging "X" catastrophe on its way like a Hollywood asteroid—is not only over-written but itself fed the acceleration. Moving from the ecological thought to the ecocidal thought is not, however, as the reaction formation dictates, "pessimistic," cynical and so on.

12. Generation

I confess, as a reader, to find conflict in Derrida that disappoints in some ways—generating "Derridas" for purposes of consumption, survival, seduction, occasion. One may shake some of that out or off from this "future" vantage point of reading – assuming, that is, that reading itself, like attention, will not have been altered *at its core*. One might also concede, on a structural-mnemonic level, that "Derrida" was a contrarian episode in an otherwise atrophying malaise of reading that would fuse neural pathways irremediably. One must be mindful of the shadow logics at work here though. Derrida's turning or folding back at rhetorical borders did not guarantee him integration into the arterial mainstreams, but it did detract from what the ensuing critical culture would or could do—and to what degree his algorithms could be redeployed. That is entirely do-able, stripped of personae. Nor is it innocent that Derrida chose not to address bio-morphic collapse—since the occlusion mimes that of the mainstream media and the management of a denialist cloud. It is interesting, in this regard, that this parallels his occlusion of cinema as a zone to write to or on: each represents an extreme in the spectrum of anarchivism—the one by bio-morphic systems and the inorganic (no, imaging a cat scoping you out does not do this, in fact, the opposite), the other by convoking an organization of mnemonics and perceptual regimes, what Stiegler names *archi*-cinema (*as if* older than archi-writing) and finds initiated in cave-paintings. Each exceeds at either end of the spectrum the premises of the deconstructive performance framed by an existing archival (textual) legacy. Derrida, who could easily have been the key resource for post-anthropocene thought, chose to turn back at these borders to maintain rhetorical purchase and legacy leverage. He short-circuited in doing so. Given how epochally he defined his name with transforming archival memory, with language, his withdrawal from this dare and the hopelessness of the community he left in place to tend to and regressively "canonize" his script, he left a hole. When attention withdrew from him following his death, as he assumed, and was only compounded by the scurrilous academic rituals of closing ranks to somehow enshrine or restitute, that would effectively close access for the discourse on climate change, extinction, and even bio-ethics, where there would be a turn away from "language" and hence the core inscriptive habits of the global hermeneutic, just when that mattered most. That is, there is no addressing of this zone without accessing the perceptual memes, referential settings, and cognitive regimes pro-grammed variably: even on the surface, the appalling mix of infantile metaphors and scientist trope and romantic aesthetics awash in the debris of environmental discussion has been a sham to begin with. Only the terrain of a Stiegler, inventing out from Derridean incisions, leads into this space, much as a provocateur like Timothy Morton does in opposite terms by indexing eco-catastrophe to a misreading of Romantic aesthetics—Morton, the Emerson of the Anthropocene. One would want to put in contact in this regards the thinking of hyper-technics (Stiegler) with the errant performative claim of hyperobjects.

13. Touch

So let's turn the *skein* in another direction—and suspend all efforts to engage, tailor, celebrate, identify or identify with one of a number of *personae* generated from Derrida's writing. Put it in eclipse. What one witnesses may seem to be possessed by several algorithms. In certain of these Derrida directs all returns to capturing and dislocating memory programs (long installed), generating a deconstruction of "anthropo-narcissism" at a limit, and here is what bonds a certain Derrida to this "future" reader. One witnesses, again and again, a *rhetorical* choice to turn back at the point this reading community would be dissolved, its very "we," instead turning back to engage a working through of its terms, its investments, and its citational trends (again). An example of this, one of many, is Derrida's pedagogic handling of the hand and touch in his polemic with Nancy (OT: 135)—where he would choose to turn back and tutor the "deconstructors," rather than proceed on the path of dissolution that pokes through repeatedly (perhaps in the costume of "absolute mourning," the mourning of the abandonment of mourning as an organizing trope). This is what allows late Derrida to appear at once as a supposed extension (to the world, politics, ethics, and so on) and also, to some eyes, as regressive, as if miming positions before the early Derrida's "trembling" intervention. Yet today's disassemblage of "anthropo-narcissism" arrived as if from without (by way of poisoned foods, diminishing climate timelines, mutations of bio-systems, extinc-tion events and so on), in advance of "deconstruction's" somehow having accomplished the *destructive* side of its itinerary. Perhaps Derrida thought there was a continuity with 20th century time that projected generations for him to work through the entrails of the global archive. It puts the late personae of Derrida in a corrupt position, contaminated, as he would acknowledge to be inevitable—trying, as he does, to end-run an "auto-immune" slide he himself had triggered, and could only accelerate by out-miming. He would perform like the Angel of History (a mocked puppet in Benjamin's text) who hesitates, looking back at his readers, at the masses of the un-dead, whose eyes would plead for a redemptive angel (Benjamin 1968). The Angel, luckily, gets obliterated by a "storm" before he can display more complicity; Derrida's angelicism in his late phase would be his response, compromised, to the misreadings of his own insulating and servicing missionaries. As this Derrida-angel hesitated, strategically, his generation was simply overtaken by the unfolding of twenty-first century accelerations, the "storm," such as climate change, that flipped the point of identification against the "human," and against the passive complicity of its hermeneutic and neural rituals in a self-consuming arc of hyper-capitalist accelerations ("exponential growth," exponential waste, diminished resource, mutated biosphere, and so on).

Derrida's dark American-Belgian double and nemesis, Paul de Man, following Benjamin's "one-way street," passed over this border, and found it irreversible once done, since the translation event, deconstruction, or transformation at risk would be cognitive, mnemonic, "materialist," sacrificing any persona and with that, a certain capitalisation. So this capacity of de Man to generate endless text of the most intriguing and consequent burrowing – putting on display the performative, prelinguistic, and critical structures of the interface of archive and the production of histories – left a structural blank spot and black hole that re-reads the script now that the irreversible ("climate change") has emerged on the other side of an imperilled "anthropo-narcisst" parenthesis—a parenthesis which also leaves the imprint of the Euro-centred catacombs and labyrinths that Derrida would identify from within. But what happens when that Derridean rhetorical move, that of a certain *folding back* to mime the "community," counter-miming its turns, is suspended as being too twentieth century, as a detour within Derrida's calculations of survival for something whose erasure his writing (and body) would necessitate? Never has a strategy of canonical self-preservation succeeded less well, judging from "deconstruction's" irrelevance, in its various costumes, to early twenty-first-century horizons, even when these have exceeded the formulaic and ethically hubristic premise of giving justice by recognition of the other's otherness, and so on. It is not accidental that Derrida's incomparable inventiveness—by far the greatest rhetorical thinker in the "tradition" – should nonetheless not spawn organizing fields. Where is our *hauntology* today, as other than a jibe? Moreover, it would seem by and large that the orthodoxy of carriers, wanting dutifully to advance this "legacy," chose to fetishize the persona, or turn critical moves into regressive crypto-humanist catalogues (from "animal studies" to the "cognitive turn"), rather than take the wager, which *he* posed explicitly, of dispersing into the power systems of today's totalising mediacracies—where the global bets are played, or fixed. Never have so many intellectual wives cast themselves on the pyre to less avail.

14. Media

The Derrida that future readers may seek to clarify is that of the initial intervention, a Derrida of far greater relevance to a future present at a more advanced stage of resource and climate depradations. By the time this future arrives (hint: it is already past) the category of the species threat, and the threat to itself, would have to exceed and re-name the auto-immune power formations that Derrida toured gracefully. It would have stepped outside the Enlightenment rhetorics that serve as props still today, and depart from the black enlightenment, in which the metaphorics of "light" itself lies at an irreducible grand mal d'archive (we can place, here, the "stored sunlight" of oil, but as a place-holder). There would have been a complicity all along between that most daring side of Derrida's weaponised writing machine, and the non-anthropic perspectives that twenty-first century post-anthropocene thought compels. One could say that whatever *metaphysics* meant as a target of late twentieth-century attacks (and if that did not merely change shapes), the passive socio-mediatric spells of post-democratic states, today, *and* the occlusion of climate change as possible to respond or re-orient toward, suggests if anything a more ripe target, a more necessary (and different) reboot of the deconstructive meme or viral, one which would be absolutely ruthless against its own framing premises and cognitive programs. Why, after all, was all of this weaponry not applied to the core of human self-presence—as Derrida professed to want, to advance towards a transformation that could be reread from "after," rather than be yoked to repeat performances of self-explicatory embedding? This human myopia would become apparent in decades, it is already, but remained the blind of blinds of twentieth-century archival demolitions, "social" encodings, in which an onto-theological-Marxian materialism would find itself captured, smoothly, by the spells and infantilizations of twenty-first-century neo-feudal klepto-mediacracies. Today, the justice Derrida trawled and sometimes manipulated might lie not between some resurrected subject effect and its cat, or any invoked "otherness of the (human) other," but of "life" turning against "anthropo-narcissism" as an adventure and parenthesis.

15. Inhuman

If there are gestures that drop in relevance to this increasingly inhuman future, that even seem embarrassing misfires, others surface. What is on the other side of this turning back, which Derrida's writing, in a gamble for readership misdirected, and increasingly practiced? Why continue to trot out any "messianism" whatsoever—"weak" or otherwise? Why not simply re-cipher a canard like *il n'y a pas hors texte*, and rather than do some clever unpacking, or defense, simply expand it hyperbolically and hypobolically? That is, one might supplement its sense with a more bottomless claim that defines the structure of writing, or mnemotechnics more generally, as a conflicted (human) variant of a biosemiosis and a-biosemiosis—that traverses genetic engineering, photosynthesis, and arcs of auto-extinction? Why not generate an "ethics" out of the irreversibility of accelerated extinction now come "to light"? I have suggested, elsewhere, that Derrida's last interview, in which his remark that "I am at war with myself" would be highlighted (title of the French publication), recognises this split, in which *another* Derrida within the corpus, performing the "others," would turn against those, cut them off with the ganglia of contemporary readers who, he claimed, have not yet "begun" to read him (Cohen 2012). That beginning would take place from a position in which all the veils of corruption, hermeneutic machinality, hyper-consumption, and the proprietary cons of twentieth-century humanisms and subjectalities had no immediate relevance.

16. End

In *Annie Hall*, Woody Allen's character is offered a pile of cocaine at a party and sneezes, producing a cloud of white haze (and a substantial loss of investment). To some extent, this is what the state of attention will have done to the *ashes* of Derrida, in multiple senses. At which point, precisely, a genuine thought party might begin—arriving, as it was always going to, too late.

Bibliography

Works by Jacques Derrida

Derrida, J. 1973. *Speech and Phenomena, and Other Essays on Husserl's Theory of Signs*. D. B. Allison. (ed. and trans.) N. Garver (pref.). Evanston: Northwestern University Press.

——1976. *Of Grammatology*. G. Spivak (trans.). Baltimore: Johns Hopkins University Press. Originally published in French as *De la Grammatologie* (Paris: Les Editions de Minuit, 1967).

——1978a. *Writing and Difference*. Alan Bass (trans.). Chicago: University of Chicago Press.

——1978b. *Edmund Husserl's "Origin of Geometry": An Introduction*. J. P. Leavey (trans. and ed.), D. B. Allison (ed.) Stony Brook, NY: Nicolas Hays.

——1979. "Living On/Border Lines." J. Hulbert (trans.). *Deconstruction and Criticism*. London: Continuum, 2004, 62–142.

——1980. *The Archeology of the Frivolous: Reading Condillac*. J. P. Leavey (trans.), Pittsburgh: Duquesne University Press.

——1981. *Dissemination*. B. Johnson (trans.). Chicago: University of Chicago Press.

——1982. *Margins of Philosophy*. A. Bass (trans.). Chicago: University of Chicago Press.

——1983a. "Dialangues: Une conversation avec Jacques Derrida," with A. Berger, *Fruits*, 1. December.

——1983b. "The Time of A Thesis: Punctuations", *Philosophy in France Today*, A. Montefiore (ed.) Cambridge: Cambridge University Press.

——1984. "No Apocalypse, Not Now (full speed ahead, seven missiles, seven missives)." C. Porter and P. Lewis (trans.). *Diacritics* (Summer 1984): 20–31.

——1985. "Racism's Last Word." P. Kamuf. (trans.). *Critical Inquiry* 12.1 (1985): 290–99.

——1986a. "But, beyond ... (Open Letter to Anne McClintock and Rob Nixon)" P. Kamuf (trans.). *Critical Inquiry* 13 (Autumn 1986): 155–70.

——1986b. "Fors: The Anglish Words of Nicolas Abraham and Maria Torok." B. Johnson (trans.), preface to *The Wolf Man's Magic Word: A Cryptonymy*, by N. Abraham and M. Torok. N. Rand (trans.). Minneapolis: University of Minnesota.

——1986c. "Letter to a Japanese Friend", in D. Wood and R. Bernasconi (eds), D. Wood and A. Benjamin (trans.), *Derrida and Différance*. Evanston, IL: Northwestern University Press, 3–6.

——1988a. *Limited Inc*, G. Graff (ed.) S. Weber (trans.). Evanston: Northwestern University Press.

——1988b. *The Ear of the Other: Otobiography, Transference, Translation*. C. McDonald (ed.), P. Kamuf (trans.). Lincoln: University of Nebraska Press.

——1988c. "An Interview with Derrida." *Derrida and Différance*. D. Wood and R. Bernasconi (eds). Evanston: Northwestern University Press, 71–82.

——1989. *Memoires for Paul de Man*. revised edition. C. Lindsay, J. Culler, E. Cadava, and P. Kamuf. New York: Columbia University Press.

——1990. "Jacques Derrida on Rhetoric and Composition: A Conversation." With G. A. Olson. *Journal of Advanced Composition* 10.1 (1990), 1–21.

——1992a. "Force of Law: The 'Mystical Foundation of Authority'", M. Quaintance (trans.), in *Deconstruction and the Possibility of Justice*. D. Cornell, M. Rosenfeld and D. Gray Carlson (eds). New York: Routledge, 3–67.

——1992b. *Given Time 1: Counterfeit Money*. P. Kamuf (trans.). Chicago: University of Chicago Press.

——1992c. *Acts of Literature*. D. Attridge (ed.) New York: Routledge.

——1993a. *Aporias: Dying – Awaiting (One Another At) the "Limits of Truth"* (*mourir-s'attendre aux "limites de la verite"*) T. Dutoit. (trans.). Stanford: Stanford University Press.

——1993b. "Heidegger's Ear: Philopolemology (*Geschlecht* IV)" J. P. Leavey Jr. in J. Sallis (ed.), *Reading Heidegger: Commemorations*. Bloomington: Indiana University Press, 163–218.

——1993c. *Circumfession, Jacques Derrida*, with G. Bennington (trans.). Chicago: University of Chicago Press.

——1994a. *Specters of Marx: The State of the Debt, the Work of Mourning, and the New International*. P. Kamuf (trans.) New York: Routledge. Originally published in French as *Spectres de Marx* (Paris: Galilee, 1993).

——1994. *Points ... Interviews 1974–1994*. E. Weber (ed.). Stanford: Stanford University Press.

——1995. *On the Name*. D. Wood and J. P. Leavey, Jr, I. McLeod, and T. Dutoit (trans.). Stanford, CA: Stanford University Press.

——1997. *Politics of Friendship*. G. Collins (trans.). London: Verso. Originally published in French as *Politiques de l'Amitie* (Paris: Galilee, 1994).

——1999. *Adieu: To Emmanuel Levinas*. W. Hamacher and D. E. Wellbery (eds). P.-A. Brault and M. Naas (trans.). Stanford: Stanford University Press.

——2000a. *Of Hospitality*. M. Bal and H. de Vries (eds). R. Bowlby (trans.). Stanford: Stanford University Press.

——2000b. "Hostipitality," B. Stocker with F. Matlock (trans.). *Angelaki* 5.3 (December, 2000), 3–18.

——2001a. *The Work of Mourning.* P.-A. Brault and M. Naas. Chicago: University of Chicago Press. [Published in French as: *Chaque fois unique, la fin du monde.* P.-A. Brault and M. Naas (eds) (Paris: Éditions Galilée, 2003).]

——2001b. *Deconstruction Engaged: The Sydney Seminars.* P. Patton and T. Smith (eds). Sydney: Power Publications.

——2001c. "On Forgiveness." M. Hughes (trans.). *On Cosmopolitanism and Forgiveness.* London: Routledge, 27–60.

——2002a. *Without Alibi.* P. Kamuf (trans.). Stanford: Stanford University Press.

——2002b. "Force of Law: The 'Mystical Foundation of Authority.'" M. Quaintance (trans.), in *Acts of Religion.* G. Anidjar (ed.). London and New York: Routledge, pp. 230–98.

——2002c. *On Cosmopolitanism and Forgiveness.* M. Dooley (trans.). London: Routledge.

——2002d. "Privilege: Justificatory Title and Opening Remarks," in *Who's Afraid of Philosophy: The Right to Philosophy vol. I*, J. Plug (trans.). Stanford: Stanford University Press. Partial translation of *Du Droit a La Philosophie* (Paris: Galilee)

——2002e. "Politics and Friendship", interview with M. Sprinker, in *Negotiations: Interventions and Interviews, 1971–2001.* Stanford: Stanford University Press.

——2004. "Living On/Border Lines." Trans. James Hulbert. *Deconstruction and Criticism.* 1979. London: Continuum, 2004. 62–142.

——2005a. *Rogues.* P.-A. Brault and M. Naas (trans.). Stanford: Stanford University Press. Originally published in French as *Voyous: Deux Essais sur Raison* (Paris: Gallilee, 2004).

——2005b. *Sovereignties in Question: The Poetics of Paul Celan*, T. Dutoit and O. Pasanen (eds). New York: Fordham University Press.

——2005c. *Paper Machine.* R. Bowlby (trans.) Stanford: Stanford University Press.

——2005d. *Screenplay and Essays on the Film.* K. Dick and A. Ziering Kofman (dir.) New York: Routledge.

——2005e. *On Touching, Jean-Luc Nancy.* C. Irizarry (trans.). Stanford: Stanford University Press.

——2006. "Dialogue entre Jacques Derrida, Philippe Lacoue-Labarthe et Jean-Luc Nancy," in *Rue Descartes* 52, 86–93.

——2007a. *The Gift of Death* (2nd edn) D. Wills (trans.). Chicago: University of Chicago Press.

——2007b. *Learning to Live Finally: The Last Interview.* P.-A. Brault and M. Naas (trans.) Hoboken, NJ: Melville House Publishing.

——2007c. "Psyche: Invention of the Other." C. Porter (trans.). *Psyche: Inventions of the Other.* Vol. 1. P. Kamuf and E. Rottenberg (eds). Stanford: Stanford University Press, 1–47.

——2009. *The Beast & the Sovereign*, Vol. I, G. Bennington (trans.). Chicago: University of Chicago Press.

——2011a. *The Beast & the Sovereign*, Vol. II, G. Bennington (trans.). Chicago: University of Chicago Press.

——2011b. *Voice and Phenomenon*. L. Lawlor (trans.). Evanston: Northwestern University Press.

Derrida, J. and Dufourmantelle, A. 2000. *Of Hospitality*. R. Bowlby (trans.). Stanford, CA: Stanford University Press.

Derrida, J. and Ferraris, M. 2002. *A Taste for the Secret*. Donis (trans.). Cambridge: Polity.

Derrida, J. with McKenna, K. 2002. Interview, *LA Weekly*, Nov 2002. Reprinted in Kirby Dick, Amy Ziering Kofman, 2005. *Screenplay and essays on the film Derrida; foreword by Geoffrey Hartman; [essays by Nicholas Royle, Kirby Dick and Amy Ziering Kofman; interviews with Jacques Derrida; film to text adaptation by Gil Kofman Copyright 2005 jane doe films]*, 118–26. New York: Routledge, 2005.

Derrida, J. and Stiegler, B. 2002. *Echographies of Television*. J. Bajorek (trans.). Cambridge: Polity.

Derrida, J. and Borradori, G. 2003. "Autoimmunity: Real and Symbolic Suicides: A Dialogue with Jacques Derrida", G. Borradori, *Philosophy in a Time of Terror*. Chicago: University of Chicago Press, 85–136.

Derrida, J. with Roudinesco, Elisabeth. 2004. *For What Tomorrow ... A Dialogue*, J. Fort (trans.). Stanford, CA: Stanford University Press.

Derrida, J., P. Lacoue-Labarthe and J.-L. Nancy. 2006. "Dialogue entre Jacques Derrida, Philippe Lacoue-Labarthe et Jean-Luc Nancy." *Rue Descartes* 52.2, 86–99.

Other Works

Allison, D. B. 1973. "Translator's Introduction," in J. Derrida, *Speech and Phenomena, and Other Essays on Husserl's Theory of Signs*. Evanston: Northwestern University Press.

Anderson, N. 2012. *Derrida: Ethics Under Erasure*. London and New York: Continuum.

Aristotle. 1985. *The Politics*. C. Lord (trans.). Chicago: University of Chicago Press.

——1998. *The Metaphysics*. H. Lawson-Tancred (trans.). Harmondsworth: Penguin.

Baring, E. 2011. *The Young Derrida and French Philosophy, 1945–1968*. Cambridge: Cambridge University Press.

Bennington, G. 2000. *Interrupting Derrida*. London and New York: Routledge Press.

Bennington, G. and J. Derrida. 1991. *Jacques Derrida*, translated by Geoffrey Bennington, 1993. Chicago: University of Chicago Press.

Bennington, G. and J. Derrida. 1993. *Jacques Derrida*. G. Bennington (trans.). Chicago: University of Chicago Press.

Bernasconi, R. 1989. "Seeing Double," in *Dialogue and Deconstruction. The Gadamer-Derrida Encounter*. D. P. Michelfelder and R. E. Palmer (eds). Albany: SUNY Press, 233–50.

Bernasconi, Robert. 1992. "No More Stories, Good or Bad: de Man's Criticisms of Derrida on Rousseau," in *Derrida: A Critical Reader*. D. Wood (ed.), Oxford: Blackwell, 137–66.

Borradori, G. 2003. *Philosophy in a Time of Terror: Dialogues with Jürgen Habermas and Jacques Derrida*. Chicago: University of Chicago Press.

Canguilhem, G. 1991. *The Normal and the Pathological*. C. R. Fawcett with R. S. Cohen (trans.). New York: Zone Books, 1991.

Cohen, T. 2012. "*Polemos*: 'I am at war with myself' or, Deconstruction™ in the Anthropocene?" *Oxford Literary Review* 34 (December 2012), 239–57.

Coleridge, S. T. 1983. *Biographia Literaria*. 2 vols. J. Engell and W. Jackson Bate (eds). Princeton: Princeton University Press.

Condillac, A. 1795. *Le commerce et le gouvernement* in *Oeuvres philosophiques* vol. 17, Paris: Letellier.

Cornell, D., Rosenfeld, M. and D. Gray Carlson (eds) 1992. *Deconstruction and the Possibility of Justice*. New York and London: Routledge.

Creech, J. *et al.*, 1985. "Deconstruction in America: An Interview with Jacques Derrida," *Critical Exchange* 17 (Winter 1985), 1–33.

Critchley, S. 1999. *The Ethics of Deconstruction*. Edinburgh: Edinburgh University Press.

Culler, J. 2008. "'The Most Interesting Thing in the World.'" *Diacritics* 38:1–2 (Spring–Summer 2008): 7–16.

Deleuze, G. and F. Guattari. 1987. *A Thousand Plateaus*. Brian Massumi (trans.). Minneapolis: University of Minnesota Press.

Diogenes Laertius. 1925. *Lives of Eminent Philosophers, Vol. 1*. R. Hicks (trans). Loeb Classical Library. Cambridge, MA: Harvard University Press.

Diprose, R. 1994. *The Bodies of Women: Ethics, Embodiment and Sexual Difference*. London and New York: Routledge.

Dooley, M. 2001. "The Civic Religion of Social Hope: A Response to Simon Critchley." *Philosophy and Social Criticism* 27.5, 35–58.

Dunn, J. 2005. *Setting the People Free: The Story of Democracy*. London: Atlantic.

Equiano, O. 2003. *The Interesting Narrative and Other Writings: Revised Edition*. V. Carretta (ed.). Harmondsworth: Penguin.

Esposito, R. 2012. *Terms of the Political: Community, Immunity, Biopolitics*. R.N. Welch (trans.). New York: Fordham University Press.

Freud, S. 2005. *On Murder, Mourning and Melancholia*. Trans. S. Whiteside (trans). Harmondsworth: Penguin.

Grebowicz, M. 2005. "'Between Betrayal and Betrayal': Epistemology and Ethics in Derrida's Debt to Levinas" in E. Nelson, A. Kapust, and K. Still (eds), *Addressing Levinas*. Evanston: Northwestern University Press.

Habermas, J. 1987. *The Philosophical Discourse of Modernity: Twelve Lectures*. F. Lawrence (trans.) Cambridge, MA: MIT Press.

Habermas, J. and Derrida, J. 2003. "February 15, or What Binds Europeans Together: A Plea for a Common Foreign Policy, Beginning in the Core of

Europe." *Constellations: An International Journal of Critical and Democratic Theory* 10(3), 291–97.

Hägglund, M. 2008. *Radical Atheism: Derrida and the Time of Life*. Stanford: Stanford University Press.

Heidegger, M. 1962. *Being and Time*. J. Macquarrie and E. Robinson (trans). New York: Harper & Row.

Heidegger, M. 1977. *The Question Concerning Technology, and Other Essays*. W. Lovitt (intr. & trans.). New York and London: Garland Publishing.

Heidegger, M. 1993. *Basic Writings*, D. Farrell Krell (ed.). London and New York: Routledge.

Heidegger, M. 2010. *Logic: The Question of Truth*. T. Sheehan (trans.). Bloomington: Indiana University Press.

Hobbes, T. 1998. *On the Citizen*. M. Silverthorne and R. Tuck (ed. and trans.). Cambridge, Cambridge University Press.

Hofstadter, D. 1999. *Gödel, Escher, Bach: An Eternal Golden Braid*. New York: Basic Books.

Husserl, E. 1928. *Vorlesungen zur Phänomenologie des inneren Zeitbewusstsein*. M. Heidegger (ed.) Halle: Max Niemeyer. [English translation by J. Churchill as *The Phenomenology of Internal Time-Consciousness* (The Hague: Martinus Nijhoff, 1964); French translation by H. Dussort as *Leçons pour une phenomenology de la conscience intime du temps* (Paris: Presses Universitaires de France, 1964).]

Husserl, E. 1963. *Cartesianische Meditationen und Pariser Vortrage, Husserliana Volume I*. S. Strasser (ed.). The Hague: Martinus Nijhoff, 1963, 2nd edition. [English translation by D. Cairns as *Cartesian Meditations* (The Hague: Martinus Nijhoff, 1960); French translation by G. Pfeiffer and E. Lévinas as *Méditations Cartésiennes* (Paris: Vrin, 1992).]

Husserl, E. 1966. *Zur Phänomenologie des inneren Zeitbewusstseins (1893–1917)*, Husserliana Volume 10, R. Boehm (ed.). The Hague: Martinus Nijhoff.

Husserl, E. 1980. *Logische Unterschungen*. Two volumes, with volume two having two parts. Tubingen: Niemeyer. [English translation by J. N. Findlay as *Logical Investigations*. With a new preface by M. Dummett and edited with a new introduction by D. Moran (London: Routledge, 2001); French translation by H. Elie, L. Kelkel, and R. Schérer as *Recherches logiques*, in three volumes (Paris: Presses Universitaires de France, 1959–63).]

Husserl, E. 1991. *On the Phenomenology of the Consciousness of Internal Time (1893–1917)*. J. Barnett Brough (trans.). Dordrecht: Kluwer Academic Publishers.

Kamuf, P. 1994. "Foreword to the English Translation." *Points ... Interviews 1974–1994*. By J. Derrida. E. Weber (ed.). Stanford: Stanford University Press. vii–ix.

Kant, I. 1934. *Critique of Pure Reason*. J. M. D. Meiklejohn (trans.). London: J. M. Dent & Sons.

Kant, I. 2001. *Religion and Rational Theology*. A. W. Wood and G. di Giovanni (trans.). Cambridge: Cambridge University Press.

Kierkegaard, S. 2013. *Fear and Trembling; and, The Sickness Unto Death*. W. Lowrie (trans.) Princeton: Princeton University Press.

Kirk, Al. 2011. 'High Court Blocks Government Malaysia Solution'. *ABC News: PM*, 31 August: < http://www.abc.net.au/pm/content/2011/s3306870.htm>.

Levinas, E. 1996. *Totality and Infinity*. A. Lingis (trans.). Pittsburgh: Duquesne University Press.

Llewellyn, J. 2002. *Appositions of Jacques Derrida and Emmanuel Levinas*. Bloomington and Indianapolis: Indiana University Press.

Lowe, E. J. 2002. *A Survey of Metaphysics*. Oxford: Oxford University Press.

Lucy, N. 2004. *A Derrida Dictionary*. Oxford: Blackwell.

Lucy, N. 2011. "From Text to Media." *Vlak: Contemporary Poetics and the Arts* 2: 16–19.

Lynch, D. et al., Dir. 1990. *Twin Peaks*. ABC Network Television.

McClintock, A. and R. Nixon. 1986. "No Names Apart: The Separation of Word and History in Derrida's 'Le Dernier Mot du Racisme.'" *Critical Inquiry* 13.1 (Autumn, 1986), 140–54.

Meillassoux, Q. 2008. *After Finitude: An Essay on the Necessity of Contingency*. R. Brassier (trans.). London: Continuum.

Miller, J. H. 2009. *For Derrida*. New York: Fordham University Press.

Montaigne, M. 1991. "On Affectionate Relationships." in *The Complete Essays*. M. A. Screech (trans.). London: Allen Lane, Penguin Press, 205–19.

Morton, T. 2010. *The Ecological Thought*. Cambridge, MA: Harvard University Press.

Naas, Michael. 2008. *Derrida From Now On*. New York: Fordham University Press.

Nietzsche, F. 1981. *Beyond Good and Evil*. R. Hollingdale (trans.). London: Penguin.

Nietzsche, F. 1986. *Human, All Too Human*, R. Hollingdale (trans.). Cambridge: Cambridge University Press.

Papadakis, A., Cook, C. and Benjamin, A. (eds) 1989. *Deconstruction: Omnibus Volume*. New York: Rizzoli Publications.

Peteers, B. 2013. *Derrida. A Biography*. A. Brown (trans.). Cambridge: Polity.

Plant, B. 2003. "Doing Justice to the Derrida-Levinas Connection: A Response to Mark Dooley." *Philosophy and Social Criticism* 29(4), 427–50.

Rousseau, J.-J. 1992. *Discourse on the Origins of Inequality*. J. R. Bush, R. D. Masters, et al. (trans.). Hanover: University Press of New England.

Rousseau, J.-J. 1998. *Essay on the Origin of Languages and Writings Related to Music*. J. T. Scott (trans.). Hanover: University Press of New England.

Royle, N. 2012. *Veering: A Theory of Literature*. Edinburgh: Edinburgh University Press.

Schmitt, C. 2004. *Political Theology: Four Chapters on the Concept of Sovereignty*. G. D. Schwab (trans.). Chicago: University of Chicago Press.

Schmitt, C. 2006. *The Concept of the Political*. G. D. Schwab (trans.). Chicago: University of Chicago Press.

Schnapp, J. T. (ed.) 2000. *A Primer of Italian Fascism*. Lincoln, Nebraska: University of Nebraska Press.

Searle, J. R. 1977. "Reiterating the Differences: A Reply to Derrida." *Glyph* 1: 198–208.

Spivak, G. C. 2004. "Terror: An Essay After 9/11." *boundary* 2, 31.2 (Summer 2004): 81–111.

Tillich, P. 1951. *Systematic Theology 1*. Chicago: University of Chicago Press.

Turing, A. 1990. "Computing Machinery and Intelligence," in M. A. Boden (ed.). *The Philosophy of Artificial Intelligence*. Oxford and New York: Oxford University Press, 40–66.

de Vries, H. 2001. "Derrida and Ethics: Hospitable Thought," in T. Cohen (ed.), *Jacques Derrida and the Humanities: A Critical Reader*. Cambridge: Cambridge University Press, 172–92.

Weber, E. 2007. "Suspended From the Other's Heartbeat." *South Atlantic Quarterly* 106.2 (Spring 2007), 325–43.

Wollstonecraft, M. 1794. *An Historical and Moral View of the Origin and Progress of the French Revolution: and the Effect it has Produced in Europe*. London: J. Johnson, 1794.

Wollstonecraft, M. 1995. *A Vindication of the Rights of Men and a Vindication of the Rights of Woman and Hints*. Cambridge Texts in the History of Political Thought. S. Tomaselli (ed.). Cambridge: Cambridge University Press.

Index